Contents

Contents

BULLYING SOLUTIONS

LEARN TO OVERCOME FROM REAL CASE STUDIES

BULLYING
SOLUTIONS

LEARN TO OVERCOME FROM REAL CASE STUDIES

Michael Carpenter, Ph.D., and Robin D'Antona, Ed.D.

BARRON'S

Dedication

Dedicated to Ariah, Catherine, Jacob, Jessica, Julia, Justin, Matthew, Reece, and Sara, that they may know a world where the culture is one of respect, tolerance, and compassion.

Thank you to those who gave us their stories with the hope that these stories and memories of hurt, pain, and courage will make a difference in the lives of others and to the memory of Arthur Harden Pratt for his unselfish support for bullying prevention.

All inquiries should be addressed to:
Barron's Educational Series, Inc.
250 Wireless Boulevard
Hauppauge, New York 11788
www.barronseduc.com

ISBN: 978-1-4380-0407-5

Library of Congress Control Number: 2014936400

Printed in the United States of America

9 8 7 6 5 4 3 2 1

Contents

Introduction

The following case studies are written from the perspective of the aggressor, bystander, target, victim, parent, school administrator or teacher's point of view. They are from all over the country and abroad and are individuals of various ages who have been bullied, are presently experiencing bullying, or are involved in being a target, bystander, or aggressor. They represent special populations, such as bullying related to gender, race, disability, autism, Asperger's, attention deficit, weight, and being different. The stories include topics such as sibling aggression, cyberbullying, relational aggression, hazing, harassment, physical bullying, and more.

Each section will have points for parents and suggestions for actions for each case study. This awareness will provide insight for the reader to better understand and prevent similar incidents in the future.

In addressing power-based behaviors such as bullying, coercion, aggression, and intimidation, the writer's goal is to help parents recognize that knowledge of and understanding about bullying behavior can be powerful forces in raising children. Such knowledge may empower a child being bullied or may help a parent or bystander to intervene successfully if a child is targeted for bullying. Such awareness may give the parent courage to navigate a different course and to be able to identify specific warning signs related to interfering with learning, when and where the bullying is occurring, and who's involved.

The stories in the book have been gathered from people who have personally had these experiences. They are all true and have been given to us with the hope that sharing these experiences can make a difference in someone else's life. Therefore, we have re-spectfully retold these stories and included our own insights as well as those of other experts and professionals in the field of bul-lying prevention.

While there has been a great deal of discussion about bullying behavior, there is still much confusion about how bullying can best be handled to protect the target and prevent the bullying from happening again. The "end in mind" is to develop a safety plan to prevent any future occurrences, thereby creating a safe and caring environment for all children. It is our hope that when confronted with a situation, parents can use this book as a resource in making the best choices to protect their child and to prevent the bullying from happening again. We want all parents to be empowered by helping them to overcome bullying and protect their children!

1. Bullying Overview

PURPOSE

The purpose of this book is to prevent bullying behavior by offering hope and optimism for distressed parents who are desperately seeking answers and who are feeling that they are being judged and blamed for their child who is being victimized. These parents seem to be up against insurmountable stumbling blocks, including navigating through educational and judicial systems that seem unattainable. Conversely, to compound the problem, there are some parents who don't care or don't know how to advocate for their children.

In addition, parents may not have been taught the skills of reflective listening and open communication. There are ways to connect with a child. Unfortunately, we have encountered the following scenarios way too often: a parent questions a child by using close-ended questions instead of open-ended questions; a parent communicates with a child by telling him or her what actions to take and not take; a parent tells a child it is his or her way or the highway; a parent does not discuss the obvious because the parent wants to teach the child to handle it; a parent sees the problem as not important and not worth discussing; a parent does not recognize the signs that a child is being targeted; or the parent overreacts and goes on attack, creating havoc against everyone in his or her path.

Since knowledge is power for both educators and parents, it is our hope that this book will educate parents with practical and proven methods on the best and most expedient ways to intervene and resolve these repeated, intentional, and power-based behaviors against all odds. Even though bullying has been sensationalized in the media, new evidence suggests that violence and aggressive behavior is decreasing. However, it seems that, with the number of incidents reported, similar targets and victims continue to be highlighted in the media: bullying related to social media, gender (lesbian, gay, bisexual, and transgender questioning), disabilities, race, and depression seem to be at the forefront.

Those statistics are of little comfort to the child, student, or adult, for that matter, who are victimized by the bullying of others. It is not only devastating, but it also can have serious long-term effects on both the aggressors and bystanders.

INTRODUCTION TO BULLYING: A CODE OF SILENCE

There is a hidden culture of aggression that has become common-place in our schools. Boys demonstrate bullying through direct, overt, open attacks and in-front-of-your-face behaviors, while girls bully more often by indirect, covert, subversive, and behind-the-back encounters. Bullying, derived from the word "mobbing," has always been with us. It is an old phenomenon. With parents spending ten to twelve hours less per week supervising their children, as compared with the 1970s, and with the influence of screen time (television, video games, smartphones, tablets, texting, and social media such as Internet, Facebook, Twitter, etc.), bullying or peer abuse is dominating the attention of our teachers, administrators, parents, and overall culture in our schools. Whether it is relational bullying, social ostracism, name calling, threatening, or gossiping behaviors, bullying is found in all sectors and age groups of our society.

Interest in the study of bullying behavior became heightened in Norway in 1982 when three school children killed themselves after being bullied. This same interest has picked up momentum in the United States with the number of shootings and high-profile cases publicized of young people who have committed suicide, linking the incidents to malicious teasing, taunting, and social media.

In conclusion, every student has a right to come to school and not be called names, threatened, or ostracized. School should be a safe haven for all, with a welcoming social climate and a respectful learning environment.

BULLYING DEFINITIONS

Most authors of bullying books label participants into groups. They may classify individuals who are involved in bullying situations as the bullies, the victims, and the bystanders. They may describe bullying but do not clearly tell what specific behaviors qualify as bullying. Furthermore, these definitions do not explain how bullying compares and contrasts with harassment, intimidation, conflict resolution, anger management, and/or mediation. There is much confusion about just exactly what bullying looks like. Thus, it is not unusual for educators and people in general to confuse bullying with a number of other behaviors. It is often confused with one-time physical actions (such as assault and battery), teasing, taunting, horseplay, or even fighting.

Every state in the United States (with the exception of Montana) has passed a bullying law, and those laws have differing definitions for bullying. Most definitions use the word "bullying" collectively with harassment and intimidation, while others mention conflict resolution, mediation, and anger management. Conflict resolution, mediation, and anger management are common strategies to deal with conflict among students in which the parties are partly right and partly wrong. Bullying, on the other hand, is not a conflict but is a form of victimization or peer abuse. Both the influence of power and repeated incidents are important aspects of bullying, and neither of these is mentioned consistently in the various state definitions.

Furthermore, we have seen relentless signs and symptoms of aggressors and targets while labeling these individuals as bullies and victims. Since many of these lists don't differentiate between the intentions of students who bully, most readers assume that the intentions of aggressors are the same even though some aggressors are remorseful; some act without a conscience; and a few act out of fear, anger, or frustration. Parents need concrete, research-based, practical ways to address bullying. However, parents often feel overwhelmed, isolated, and trapped. These bullying occurrences can be very stressful and exasperating, and possibly a life-threatening situation.

Parents can and will react to bullying behaviors if the definition is made clearer and concise. The research community describes bullying as having three characteristics: *repeated* behaviors over time and against the same individual, behaviors that are *intended* to cause harm, and behaviors that are *power-oriented*. The acronym "RIP" (Repeated, Intentional, Power-based) can be helpful to remember the definition.

The Centers for Disease Control has just published their definition for bullying (2014).

"Bullying is one type of youth violence that threatens young people's well-being. Bullying can result in physical injuries, social and emotional difficulties, and academic problems. The harmful effects of bullying are frequently felt by others, including friends and families, and can hurt the overall health and safety of schools, neighborhoods, and society.

Bullying is any unwanted aggressive behavior(s) by another youth or group of youths who are not siblings or current dating partners that involves an observed or perceived power imbalance and is repeated multiple times or is highly likely to be repeated. Bullying may inflict harm or distress on the targeted youth including physical, psychological, social, or educational harm. A young person can be a perpetrator, a victim, or both, called bully/victim.

Bullying can occur in-person and through technology. Electronic aggression or cyberbullying is bullying that happens through e-mail, chat rooms, instant message, a website, text message, or social media. Research is still developing and helps us to better understand and prevent bullying. School-based bullying prevention programs are widely implemented but not always evaluated."

Bullying is on a continuum of aggressive, violent behavior that includes assault and battery, child abuse, dating violence, domestic violence, hazing, peer abuse, gang behavior, sexual violence, elderly abuse, and so on. All are bad, but not all are bullying. Parents should be equipped to distinguish among commonly used terms such as bullying, picking on, teasing, horseplay, intimidation, peer abuse, assault and battery, and harassment.

Bullying is behavior that occurs repeatedly and over time. The act is intentionally done to cause harm. And, more importantly, there is a perceived power difference between the two parties. The perpetrator(s) targets a less powerful or weaker individual who feels overwhelmed by the individual or group of individuals, as well as the size, the popularity, or perceived strength of the perpetrator(s).

Questions come up immediately about how many times the behavior should happen before it is considered repeated. The answer to that is complex. Of course, we do not want any child to suffer public humiliation, be threatened, or be hurt physically even one time. Therefore, we would stop the behavior immediately and step up our observations of these children to prevent reoccurrences. In the same manner, those mean behaviors that are under the radar, such as cruel jokes or eye rolling, need to be addressed. Those behaviors are the gateway to bullying. They are part of a climate of disrespect and intolerance. They actually set a hostile tone that allows and encourages bullying behavior.

There may also be students who target different peers. This is serial bullying behavior. For example, the bully one day will not allow a particular student to sit on the bus; on another day, the bully will take someone's lunch or make fun of another student's style of dress. While there are three different targets, it is still bullying behavior because of the pattern of aggression.

If an aggressor chooses the same student, that target can be perceived as "weak." There is potential for psychological damage if the target is unable to stand up to the aggressor's attacks or demands.

An imbalance of power can involve a larger individual, an aggressor supported by a number of bystanders, or someone who is perceived to be more popular or affluent. There are many factors that can create an imbalance of power, some of which may not be obvious. The key is to not make assumptions about where that imbalance might be.

TYPES OF AGGRESSORS

Bullying is a social, cultural issue more than it is an issue about an individual, but it is individuals who initiate and carry out this behavior. In other words, we know that bullying happens in a climate that supports the behavior—because everyone participates in some way—or a climate in which others ignore it, giving tacit approval to that behavior. There is no one particular profile of a student who bullies others; however, there are some common characteristics of students who are more likely to be aggressive toward others.

These students tend to have more positive attitudes toward violence than peers. They are more quick-tempered and are easily frustrated. They don't take rules seriously and can be aggressive toward adults. They have little concern or empathy for their peers. It is all about them and their social dominance. They vary in popularity and have average or above-average self-esteem. In addition, they tend to be very good at talking themselves out of situations.

There are some aggressors who are marginalized and can act as both the aggressor and then the target. They are often marginalized students who have developmental deficits, have difficulty fitting in, and lack social emotional skills such as getting along with others.

Another group of aggressors tend to be socially connected and are popular with peers and adults, have excellent social skills, and often are seen as school leaders. When these students are accused of bullying others, the accusation is met with resistance, as it does not seem possible that they could be guilty of bullying and social aggression.

However, it is important to understand that ANY child can become a target for bullying. It can take any little occurrence or shift in the social strata of their peers to leave a child vulnerable to aggression and victimization.

CHARACTERISTICS OF TARGETS

Students who tend to internalize their feelings and may appear to be passive, sensitive, quiet, different, weak, or insecure are more vulnerable to becoming a target of bullying. Students who have little confidence and tend to be anxious or depressed also tend to be at risk. However, the most important characteristic to look for are those students who have no friends—that support system to insulate them from aggression—are particularly vulnerable. We are also concerned about students who may be academically challenged and who are in what is called protected groups (e.g., a child who has special needs, a GLBTQ (Gay/Lesbian/Bisexual/Transgender/Questioning) child, a child with same-sex or interracial parents).

TERMS USED SYNONYMOUSLY WITH BULLYING

Even though the focus of this book is bullying, other terms that may be more appropriate to use are coercion, aggression, harassment, intimidation, hazing, relational aggression, and cyberbullying. These power-based behaviors have similarities and differences that originate from different frameworks while overlapping and making appearances in similar settings. For example, harassment has a federal definition and is linked to legalities related to gender, disabilities, and race.

Relational aggression focuses on destroying relationships using covert methods such as gossip, rumors, and lies.

Hazing, unlike bullying, does not involve selecting a "weaker" individual. It refers to a ritual required to join or maintain a position in a club, team, or social group that requires participation in a humiliating and physically or emotionally dangerous activity.

Cyberbullying is a type of bullying that uses social media and other technologies to harass others in a hostile manner.

This book is not limited to identifying bullying behaviors that are found at school and only among peers. Bullying can also transpire among siblings, which is called sibling aggression. Sibling aggression occurs primarily in the home, but also in the car, the neighborhood, churches, recreation centers, after-school centers, or on the Internet. It may be difficult for parents to distinguish between bullying and fighting and horseplay among children. Brothers and sisters arguing over the remote control and what shows to watch on television are less problematic than intentionally and repeatedly hurting a sibling physically or psychologically. Again, to assess bullying, it is important to determine if the behavior is repeated, the intent of the action done by siblings is to cause harm, and there is a power imbalance between the aggressor and the target. Research has found that sibling aggression is a type of peer abuse and is connected to mental health problems among youth.

Society is concerned with the national statistics cited by the Centers for Disease Control that nearly 30 percent of adolescents in the United States have been an aggressor or target, or exhibit both bully/victim behavior. We know that adolescents who are bullied are at greater risk for sleep deprivation, depression, and anxiety that may last into adulthood, as well as lower academic grades. Being an aggressor also carries health risks such as engaging in early sexual activity, abusing partners or children, or being involved in criminal behavior. Both the target and aggressor are also more likely to use alcohol and other drugs.

CURRENT BULLYING AND CYBERBULLYING MYTHS

While research has been conducted and analyzed over the last 40 years, many of those who are unfamiliar with bullying prevention may not have been informed of the current facts and myths. Television, social media, and education have facts and methods that have proved to be ineffective and outdated. Teachers often take this inaccurate information and share and model it with their students and parents, and this cycle continues to exacerbate the problem.

Bullying Myths

- *Bullying is a part of growing up.* Bullying is not a normal stage of child development. It can cause emotional scars, with the effects lasting a lifetime. Adolescents being bullied may suffer from depression, anxiety, and/or sleep deprivation.
- *Ignore the bullying and it will go away.* If your child is being bullied, keep a journal and share it with the school. Don't confront the student bullying or the parents. Don't blame your child. Don't keep it a secret. Stand up, speak up, and be your child's advocate.
- *Children who bully tend to grow out of it.* Adolescents who bully may experience a higher probability of legal troubles as adults.
- *Bullying behaviors begin as early as middle school.* While bullying peaks during the elementary school years and then starts decreasing in the middle/high school years, children often show signs of bullying behavior before preschool.
- *Bullying is mostly physical: hitting, kicking, and pushing.* Bullying has psychological as well as physical manifestations. While bullying can be physical, the most common forms of

9

bullying are name calling, exclusion, gossip, rumors, and lies. Boys are more likely to engage in overt tactics (i.e., physical), while girls use covert tactics.

- *Adolescents who bully are typically loners.* Adolescents who bully tend to be rather popular in the early school years and have both friends and followers. Furthermore, adolescents who bully have an average to above-average self-esteem.

- *It is usually the parent's fault that their child is being bullied.* Thirty percent of children are bullied on a regular basis. Perpetrators choose individuals who are weak or perceived as weak. Take the initiative to talk with your child and ask for specifics. Believe your child; monitor; and log what, who, where, when, and any witnesses during a bullying situation.

- *The responsibility for preventing bullying belongs to the child being bullied.* The majority of adolescents neither bully others nor are bullied and fall into the category of bystanders. The goal of effective bullying prevention is to encourage bystanders to stand up, step up, and speak up. Adults who are aware of bullying situations must also intervene.

- *If your child is being bullied, tell your child to fight back.* Fighting back is likely to escalate a bullying situation and may lead to further aggression and serious injury. The person bullying selects a target that is (or is perceived to be) psychologically and/or physically weaker.

- *Most bullying occurs in isolated areas.* Bullying occurs in and around school where there is little or no adult supervision. In elementary school the hot spots are typically the playground, lunchroom, and buses, while in secondary settings bullying is found in the hallway, lunchroom, and classroom. Increasing active supervision can decrease bullying.

- *Keep the bullying a secret and hope that it will go away.* If your child is being bullied, keep a journal and share it with the school. Don't confront the student bullying or the parents.

Don't blame your child. Don't keep it a secret. Stand up, speak up, and be your child's advocate.

- *Children who bully are older, larger, and/or stronger than their peers.* A child who bullies is typically physically stronger, impulsive, hot-tempered, confident, and lacking in empathy. These children read hostile intent in the actions of others when none exists.

Cyberbullying Myths

- *Boys and girls are involved equally in online social cruelty.* Girls are twice as likely as boys to cyberbully and be cyberbully victims.
- *Parents should trust their children to monitor and actively supervise their own online computer use.* Parents have a responsibility to actively supervise their child's computer, smartphone, and tablet use. Become familiar with tracking resources. Consider pros and cons for parental control downloads and other tracking products.
- *When reporting cyberbullying, contact law enforcement after using every exhaustive effort.* Contact police immediately if cyberbullying involves threatening violence, extortion, obscene calls, texting, harassment, stalking, hate crimes, or pornography.
- *Cyberbullying rules and procedures occurring off-campus are primarily the parent's and not the school's responsibility.* Schools are becoming more proactive in dealing with on- and off-campus cyberbullying incidents. Many are developing consistent actions if a student is involved in cyberbullying, in addition to posting the rules and placing them in the student handbook.
- *Most adolescents don't tell if they are being cyberbullied.* Preteens, as compared with teens, are more likely to tell a parent if they are being cyberbullied. Both are less likely to tell a teach-

er at school but have been reported to tell a friend or sibling. More than 15 percent don't tell anyone. Monitor your child's online activity. It is not about their privacy—it is about your responsibility as a parent to keep them safe and keep them from hurting someone else.

- *If your child is being cyberbullied, save all e-mails, texts, or pictures as evidence and report the incident to the school.* If your child is cyberbullied, ask him or her not to respond and change his or her phone number, e-mail, and social media accounts. In addition, know all your child's passwords. Report the incident to both the school and law enforcement.

- *If your child is involved with cyberbullying, begin by taking away his or her computer privileges until you understand the full effect of his or her actions.* Remember that a cell phone, tablet, e-reader, and electronic game console can also be used to access the Internet. Discuss and outline your expectations for responsible online behavior and discuss with your child in advance, if and when the agreement is broken, what the consequences are.

- *Place computers throughout the home so that younger children can learn to be computer savvy at earlier ages.* Keep your home computers in places where you can easily monitor your child's use, such as in the kitchen or family room, and away from the bedroom and isolated areas. Don't forget about those other electronic devices that can access the Internet. It is not unusual for a student to be checking social media at night when they should be sleeping. It is a good idea not to allow electronic devices in the bedroom.

- *Sexting (sending explicit/nude pictures) is one of the most common forms of cyberbullying.* Common methods of cyberbullying are through instant messaging, texting, e-mailing, or placing comments on a website or chat room. Other ways are sending text messages and blogging. These vehicles are changing so fast that it is nearly impossible to keep up with all the different apps and websites that are being created almost on a daily basis. Teaching children to be respectful of themselves and others begins long before they are handed a cell phone. However, when you do, make your rules and expectations very clear when you give them a cell phone. It is, after all, a privilege that you are granting them – not a right!

IMPORTANT FACTS LEARNED FROM THE BULLYING PREVENTION FIELD

- *Teasing and bullying have distinct differences and should not be treated the same.* Teasing is not repeated or intentional and does not involve a power imbalance. Teasing usually happens between friends who remain friendly. It is a pleasant, joking exchange between two people. In order to be able to tease another person, one must understand how to read both facial expressions and body language, know the difference between fun and hurtful words, and be able to understand humor. It is a very complex social function, and many adults do not know how to handle teasing, so it makes sense to discourage children from teasing each other until they really understand what it means. Also, don't make the mistake to assume that laughter means horseplay and/or teasing. Many students who are bullied try to "save face" and laugh with the group, but inside they feel embarrassment or hurt.
- *Bullying, horseplay, and fighting differ distinctly from one another.* Bullying involves power.

  — General misbehavior happens between students of equal power (physically, socially, and intellectually) and is not repeated over time. It can happen in the heat of the moment, but there is no intention to do any long-term harm. It is often an aggressive situation that has originated from a minor infraction.

— Roughhousing is a playful physical interaction between children. It is mutually acceptable and is done in a good-humored manner. The children are playful and usually laughing. It often occurs between children of equal size and power. Children make up and agree on the safety rules. They are friends when they begin, and they continue to be friendly afterwards.

— Teasing is mutual joking or fooling around between students of equal power. Agreeable teasing is a mutual exchange between peers, which involves wit and fun. Unpleasant teasing can be edgy and often involves sarcasm. It is insulting and/or hurtful, and when it is, it can cross the line and be considered bullying. Teasing can involve a group of children.

- *If your child is being bullied, do not assume that your child is provoking the bullying.* There are many reasons why a child can be targeted, some of which are well out of their control. The best thing to do is get the facts and look for a pattern. For instance, if it is usually happening in the same place, then one solution may be increased supervision.

- *Bullying is not a conflict and cannot be resolved by conflict resolution, anger management, or mediation.* Bullying is about victimization and needs to be dealt with in that context. Conflict resolution works when it is an issue between persons of equal power. A conflict implies that either party can defend themselves, and the mediation is a way for them to resolve the issue. Anger management is for someone with emotional control issues who needs counseling or therapy. Most times the person bullying is not angry but thinks he or she has the right to treat others with cruelty, or, the person bullying continues because he or she has never been told to stop.

- *Teaching children not to tattle can discourage children not to report bullying.* Think about this from the child's perspective.

14

They are coming to you to help them resolve an issue. If the adult responds by giving them a lecture about tattling, all they are experiencing is that the adult cannot or will not help them. They are then less likely to come forward again for assistance. The key is to listen carefully to the child and then help them resolve the issue, either by giving them directions or through your direct involvement. If it is truly a superfluous report, simply say, "Thank you for bringing this to my attention."

- *Reporting bullying can make things better but equally may make things worse.* Retaliation is the number-one reason why students do not report being victimized by bullying. It is about a power imbalance, and the target is vulnerable not only to the aggressor but to others as well. In the age of cyberbullying, retaliation is of particular concern because it can be so widespread. Therefore, a basic issue of bullying, once reported to an adult, can quickly escalate to involve untold numbers because of instant cyber communication.

- *A parent should think twice before contacting the parent or a child suspected of bullying his or her child.* This is not a good idea, even when you know the parents of the child involved. The school is in a better position to handle the situation. Usually, anything that happens in a neighborhood or on an athletic field will also happen in school. Therefore, not only can the school intervene, but they can be put on notice to increase supervision of those students.

- *Boys bully more than girls; however, boys are more physical, while girls use more exclusion and gossip.* It's all about style; however, in any case, bullying behavior must be stopped and students need to learn to understand the impact of their actions on others.

- *Students who bully have an average to above-average self-esteem and feel good about bullying others.* The myth is that bullies do so because they want to feel better about themselves.

The exact opposite is true—those who bully others have strong self-esteem. Remember, for the most part, bullying is a social climate issue. It happens because rude and disrespectful behavior is sometimes seen as the norm or as the regular way people treat each other.

- *Most students who bully others use hard-to-detect methods such as name calling, exclusion, gossip, rumors, or lies.* The average instance of bullying takes a split second. It can be that eye roll or that mean look that is part of a pattern of mean behavior. It can be devastating to a student, and most adults never see a thing. This is why bystander involvement is so important. They do see what is going on, and a simple word from a bystander can stop the bullying.

- *Because bullying involves a more powerful aggressor, it is not recommended for the target to use physical tactics as a method of solving the issue.* Fighting back is never a solution to bullying victimization. To begin with, if a student is capable of fighting back when he or she is being attacked either verbally or physically, it is more likely that this is a conflict. In any case, a physical response almost always escalates the conflict, and in today's world, that can be a very dangerous thing. When a student is being victimized, it is better to problem solve in order to find a way to get the behavior to stop. It is very important that we give children the tools so that when they are confronted with an abusive situation as adults, they will be able to handle it. In the adult world, fighting back is called battery and can be a criminal offense. Given that fact, why would we teach a response that would be illegal if they were an adult? We are not suggesting that a person should not stand up for himself—on the contrary, everyone should have the self-confidence and peer support to be able to do just that. We are talking about teaching children life-long skills.

- *Most targets are passive (80 percent) and do not respond after being bullied.* If your child does not respond to being targeted, know they are in the majority. This is because bullying is, by definition, about victimization. If the child does respond and is able to defend himself, it would be a conflict.

- *One in five targets (20 percent) provoke their aggressor and are involved with both bully and victim behavior.* These children are known as bully-victims. At times peers victimize them, while at other times they are the aggressors. This can be a very complex issue. If you are hearing of your child in both these roles, it is important to work with the school and ask about some form of support or counseling for the child. In the meantime, when the child is being victimized, it is important—regardless of their history—to treat them as you would any child who has been targeted by others.

IMPORTANCE OF PREVENTION

How do we protect our children from bullying? Build on their strengths and emotional intelligence, strengthen their assets, and—at the same time—empower them to be more resilient. Both prevention and intervention should be addressed. For every dollar we spend on prevention, we save on intervention costs for health care and hospitalization. Protecting our youth from peer abuse is not accomplished with a checklist; however, it is achieved by sharing powerful knowledge such as a commitment of parents to establish family agreements and advocacy for children. For parents, the overall goal is to work collaboratively with the school community to empower students to stand up, step up, and speak up against bullying, intimidation, coercion, harassment, and other power-based behaviors.

2. Relational Aggression/ Bullying

NOTE: While the following cases all involve girls, relational bullying can and does happen between boys. Examples of this can be found in the chapters on cyberbullying and physical bullying, as well as elsewhere.

Case Study: Excluded by Peers Because Not as Attractive or Well Dressed

Type of Bullying: Exclusion
Age of Onset/Gender of Target: Kindergarten, female
How Long Did the Bullying Last? Weeks
Hot Spots: Classroom, lunch, recess
Did You Tell? If So, Whom? Teacher, parents

One morning, a kindergarten teacher visited my office and expressed her concern about how one of her kindergarteners was treating two other girls in class. We believe that Megan was excluding two of her classmates because they were less attractive and not as well dressed as she was. Megan would put her nose up in the air when they walked by and make sounds. She would noticeably roll her eyes and ignore them when they came over to play or to work on an activity. The teacher asked if I would talk with her.

As the counselor, I went to observe Megan in the classroom before I called her to my office. It was the beginning of the school year, and I was not familiar with the five-year-olds. I observed the way she was dressed and how she interacted with others, especially the two girls in question whom she excluded.

I would describe her as petite, a perfectionist in her dress, having every hair in place, and wearing a pink tiara. I had to hold

18

back a usual comment that I would make, which was, "You are the cutest kindergartener that I have ever seen." Instead, I asked Megan to sit in a chair in my office.

As we talked about her behavior in class, I asked her about the others. I had observed the other two girls she was excluding. Both were a different race than she, and both were different from each other. One was not as well dressed, and the other seemed to be very introverted and shy. During our talk, Megan acted very proud and was not apologetic for how she acted. We did discuss how it felt to be excluded.

After school I discussed with the teacher my meeting with Megan, and we brainstormed some inclusion activities that the teacher and I could share with the other students.

POINTS FOR PARENTS

The teacher in this story was very observant. In fact, she recognized a problem long before it erupted into a bullying situation. Teachers and parents need to be aware of how early children form their groups. When one child is not participating, a closer look at what is going on is needed. While some children are shy and natural observers, not joiners, it is important that all children have the opportunity to join in social activities. Although deliberate exclusionary behavior can be very common in young children, it is hurtful to the child being left out. In this case, by involving the guidance counselor early on, a serious bullying incident had been avoided that could potentially have left the targets devastated and isolated from their peers. Even though the teacher was experienced, she did not think she had the skill set to intervene with the children or address this situation with the parents.

SUGGESTIONS FOR ACTION

- The key here for parents is that it is important to regularly talk with their children about their day at school. The best times might be when you are in the car or sitting down for a snack. This should be done with open-ended questions that allow for more than a "yes" or "no" answer. For example: "Who are your friends at school?" "What are your favorite play areas in the classroom?" These simple questions can give you essential information about who the child's friends are and how he or she feels about school.

- Once the issue has been addressed, it is valuable to remember that bullying is a repeated behavior. Therefore, follow-up is necessary with the school. Be certain to check in with the teacher to see if the child has made new friends and if there is any more of the exclusionary behavior. If your child is the one using exclusionary behavior, you might ask him or her how it might feel if another student did not select him or her on his or her team.

- Some inclusion activities would be: the teacher assigning the children to groups for a project in order to give Megan the opportunity to be with the girls in a controlled setting; the teacher giving every child the responsibility to be the class leader, with a responsibility to include students who are easily left out; the teacher having discussions with all the children about what makes them similar rather than focusing on differences.

Case Study: Our Class Does Not Accept New Students!

Type of Bullying: Exclusion, name calling
Age of Onset/Gender of Target: Second grade, female
How Long Did the Bullying Last? Six months
Hot Spots: Classroom, lunch, recess
Did You Tell? If So, Whom? Teacher, parent

In December, when I was in second grade, my family moved from Texas to Oklahoma. I started a new public school in a suburban area, and my second grade class probably had 20 students. This school was one of the only elementary schools in that district; in contrast, my last school system had many elementary schools that were frequently in collaboration with each other.

As I entered my class for the first time, unbeknownst to me, the second grade students in the class had agreed that they would not accept any new students in their class during the year. One popular girl who could easily manipulate and intimidate the rest of the students led the class.

I was the first person to move into the class, and two weeks later a boy followed me. No one else came in new to our class. As you might imagine, the others never accepted us. Instead, we were ostracized and excluded from playing with others during playtime. We were also not invited to any sleepovers or birthday parties outside class. We definitely felt like outsiders.

Students in general were not allowed to talk during class time, with the exception of our phonics lessons during independent study time. Stations were set up where students would pick up their words, etc., and then gather for group work. The teacher's desk was on the other side of the room, and the teacher was focusing on helping different groups of students. While the teacher's attention was elsewhere, the popular girl selected me to taunt. Because of the configuration of the chairs, the popular girl was able to get away with whispering her insults without anyone hearing her taunting messages. Almost daily, as I walked by her desk, she would make statements such as "I hope you know how ugly you are" or "You're really stupid" or "Your clothes stink." Because I was shy and didn't have any friends in the class, I questioned myself and wondered if something was wrong with me. During lunchtime, I would eat by myself, and during playtime, I had only the new boy with whom to play.

This behavior of excluding this new boy and me continued for about a month. I didn't tell anyone at first; instead, I just tried to ignore it. I wanted to tell my dad, but since he was traveling, I decided to tell my mom. She readily admitted that she didn't know what to do but said their mean statements about me were not true.

Finally, I decided to report the incidents to the teacher. After questioning the students, she concluded that I must have been misreading their intentions. As an eight-year-old, I didn't know how to react to her statement and was confused with what I was feeling and what the teacher said wasn't happening. For the remainder of the school year, I continued to be alone, with only the other new student as a friend. This left me feeling miserable until school ended in May.

During the summer, I was anxious about starting the new school year and wondered who would be in my class and if I would continue to be excluded by the same students. When I started third grade, I was surprised that the same students who excluded me were now friendly to me. The popular girl was in another teacher's class. The students who had excluded me informed me that they were fearful of how the popular girl would treat them. She controlled the classroom.

In my elementary grades, I moved again in third and seventh grades. The problem of students accepting me never arose again. However, looking back, I still carry with me the insecurities of walking into a group and being excluded. I have a hard time making friends and feeling safe in new group situations.

Presently, I am 26 and completing a master's degree in divinity. I am preparing to go into full-time ministry. I now work with young children, children's chorus, and administration. Until now, looking back and telling my story, I never thought of what happened to me as bullying.

POINTS FOR PARENTS

Generally speaking, when a child is new to a school, it is a good idea to closely follow the child's adjustment. Connecting with the teacher when the child enrolls and then periodically following up by checking in to see how the child is progressing is important.

SUGGESTIONS FOR ACTION

- Be aware. A child who is isolated or socially excluded may not be included in activities outside of school. Please know that we are not suggesting that every child be invited to every event; however, if a child is continually left out of activities, it could be a "red flag" that there may be greater problems.
- Ask general and then more specific, open-ended questions that give you a sense of how the child feels about school. This can be an indicator of the child's experience and will give you a view of how the child is doing in school. If your family is re-locating to a different area during the school year, ask the administration at the new location if they have developed a plan to integrate new students into the school setting. If the answer is no, share your expectations.
- Talk to the school. Ask whom the child is interacting with during lunch, at recess, and at other social times during the school day.
- When you have ascertained that your child does have friends, invite them over and have them set up a playdate or, for older children, an opportunity for them to "hang out" together. This will give you the chance to observe how they interact as a group.

This is an illustration of the long-term impact of bullying on a target who has emotional scarring from the treatment she received about 20 years ago. She says, "I still carry with me the insecurities of walking into a group and being excluded. I have a hard time making friends and feeling safe in new group situations." It is helpful for her to recognize this and understand why she has those feelings. But this is a message to all of us regarding the im-

23

portance of prevention, so hopefully every child can grow to his or her potential without these hurtful experiences.

Case Study: Small Community Influence

Type of Bullying: Exclusion, relational aggression
Age of Onset/Gender of Target: Second grade, female
How Long Did the Bullying Last? Through elementary school
Hot Spots: Classroom, lunchroom, sleepovers
Did You Tell? If So, Whom? Parents

I attended parochial school, and I distinctly remember an event that happened in second grade. There was a girl who followed the trends and took over the leadership position in the class. She gave herself the proverbial title of "queen bee." The other girls followed whatever she said. The school was rather small, and she ruled the roost. Some girls who were part of the "in" group typically did not understand the power that this girl had over them; however, some days they included me at the popular table, and other days I was excluded and had to sit with the boys. The sad thing was the adults seemed to not grasp how others—including myself—were being treated. I was teased about the food that I brought from home and the clothes that I wore. Every day was complex and confusing; I never knew if I would be included or excluded or accepted or rejected that day. I don't know if I was the only one, but it sure felt like it.

My mom would see me coming home from school four out of five days crying. I would beg my mom to send me to public school. However, my family was very involved with the church, and with my father being a fourth-generation German settler and one of the church's founding fathers, my family had the perception that it was safe attending parochial school but scary attending public school. During second, third, and fourth grades I was constantly

24

tormented as I was shunned and emotionally rejected by my peers. It was my perception that it was only happening to me.

I remember being invited to a sleepover birthday party, and the "queen bee" and I were paired together for an activity. We played a game named "mirror" in which I had to follow what she did. At one time I had to rub underneath my plate and then rub my face. Because there was soot on the bottom of my plate, I had soot all over me. I was embarrassed and hurt as my peers laughed and made fun of me. I felt so horrified that I swallowed the pain for the entire evening. I didn't have the courage to call my mom to come get me. Looking back, I am not sure that the others acknowledged the power that this individual possessed. I was also befuddled that the girl's mom would allow this to happen and would let her daughter treat the others this way. The adults did condone this behavior.

Looking back, during the third and fourth grades it was acceptable culture to treat others this way. Remember: the students, families, and teachers were all part of the same school, church, and community. It was difficult to call out someone in our community who was creating drama when these members of the community were so enmeshed within our families. I had reported this destructive behavior repeatedly to my parents. It finally got my parents' attention when the "queen bee" ran away from home and was transferred to public school. Finally, the behaviors that corroborated what I had been reporting to my parents this entire time finally were recognized.

Things got better at this point. However, the mother of the "queen bee," still part of the church, had a high-risk medical condition. Therefore, my parents—who are very caring and inclusive individuals—opened up our home for the mother to stay in while she was on bed rest. My parents were always sacrificing and sharing what we had with others. However, the other family never acknowledged the hurt and pain that had ensued because of the actions of their daughter.

Fast forward to after high school, when the aggressor became involved in the health field and was hired to work in the same district in which I had been working for more than twenty years. As an adult, my classmate no longer intimidated me. But this thread has been a part of my entire life.

POINTS FOR PARENTS

Many questions come up in the story, but the main question is this: How could the parents not be aware of what was happening to their child? This is a common occurrence for a number of reasons. Often, when youths talk about their experiences, parents may not know how to respond. Parents typically refer back to their own experiences and feel that they went through bullying or know someone who did and who "survived," implying that there were no scars—at least ones that are visible. They then dismiss their child's complaint as part of growing up. Parents who dismiss bullying behavior as trivial simply do not hear what the child is saying and feeling, and parents who have a different perception than their child—the target—may contribute to the trauma the child is experiencing.

When the student's concerns are ignored, dismissed, or otherwise not taken seriously, the student is deeply impacted. In some instances, the parent's perception can influence the student's perception of the seriousness of the bullying behavior (Waasdorp et al. 2011). The parents' response can influence how a child interprets and reacts to bullying behavior.

In this case, the victim—now an adult—describes how she came home repeatedly in tears and told her parents about the bullying she was experiencing. She describes how she was compelled to return to school and was continually impacted by the repeated bullying from her peers.

When parents respond and support the child, both the parents and child feel a sense of connection. The child feels less anxious and develops a sense of confidence. Therefore, it is important to listen to your child no matter how close the relationship of the family is with the parents of the aggressor. Also, log the incidents and, when appropriate, share your list with an adult at school with whom you have a connection. There is no one point at which bullying becomes a traumatic event, so the recommendation is that adults not wait for a pattern of abuse before they intervene (Shemesh et al. 2012). This includes cases in which the bullying appears to be relatively minor but cumulative, and the repetition becomes very traumatic for the victim, causing emotional scarring.

SUGGESTIONS FOR ACTION

- If a child is repeatedly coming home from school upset and emotional, this may indicate issues at school. The key is to listen to your child. Even if you perceive the issue to be minimal, it is essential that you show your child that you care and will help them to resolve the problem. Ask about the details of their problem. If they cannot talk about the problem, simply ask them to describe their feelings and why they feel so upset.

- If you cannot get a sufficient answer, then it is wise to talk to the child's teacher, counselor, and/or the school nurse to see if they have any information about the bullying. You need to put the pieces together to get a solid sense of what is going on. Look to the school as a partner in helping you find out what is disturbing your child. Remember, parents may only see the tip of the iceberg.

- In this case, the student who bullied was a child of the parents' close friends. Even if you know the family well, it is not recommended you confront the other parents. Too often, these situations escalate to a point at which relationships are seriously jeopardized. To preserve a friendship, increase your supervision of the children when they are together. That may mean that the get-togethers may be at your home.

Case Study: Friendships Gone Wrong

Type of Bullying: Exclusion, relational aggression
Age of Onset/Gender of Target: Seventh grade, female
How Long Did the Bullying Last? Through eighth grade
Hot Spots: Texting, phone, in and out of school
Did You Tell? If So, Whom? Parents, peers

When I was in seventh grade, our family moved across the United States, from the north to a southernmost state. It was incredibly difficult coming from an area where there was little emphasis on what you wore or what kind of car your parents drove to a middle school whose culture focused on material possessions. I didn't fit in well, being a new student in this setting. The mind-set of many of my classmates was different. I was placed in regular classes instead of an advanced curriculum like at my old school. I continued to struggle to connect with the other students, but I was finally placed in the appropriate upper-level classes toward the end of seventh grade.

I did not have many friends and was desperate to connect with students with similar interests. I was yearning to have a close friend like I had in my last school. Entering the eighth grade, I become focused on this one girl who I thought at the time was the coolest person in the world. At the time, it seemed that we had a lot in common. We could easily talk about things; however, she never seemed to be as infatuated with me as I was with her or care about me as much as I did her. Over the course of the year, we became close. I struggled with the fact that our relationship never seemed reciprocal. Problems started to arise, and we developed a hurtful way of communicating with each other. The jokes were never funny but were made to get a reaction out of one another. This was not only her being rude to me but was also a poisonous relationship. It got worse as the year progressed, as one of us tried to have some leverage over the other.

All of this led up to one weekend when there was a band trip and I was home alone. As I had stated, we had a tumultuous relationship and had been fighting back and forth. I felt horrible about how things had progressed and the things that were being said; however, I was trying to stay true to myself and didn't know how to act differently in this situation. The phone rang, and my friend was calling me after she arrived back from the band trip. She continued to tell me that she did not want to be friends or talk with me ever again and that her friends wanted to have nothing to do with me. I was so heartbroken to hear the rejection from these so-called friends, that years later this incident has made me very cautious when meeting others and reluctant to develop new friendships.

This was confusing for me, and it took me a step back because I did not know that other individuals were involved with our friendship. Because girls tend to rally other girls, I took on the victim role and stepped into the drama. In my opinion, in middle school, we take what we see on television and act it out in our lives in school. That day I cried a lot and called my friends because I was confused and shocked about what had happened to me. I was so embarrassed because my friend and her supporters dumped me. I didn't want to go to school. It felt like heartbreak and something that I had never experienced before.

I did go to school, and things were awkward. It was very apparent that students had taken sides. I have this clear mental image of being in a friend's class, sitting down with three friends, and talking about the situation, and on the other side of the room my former friend and her supporters were staring and shooting mean looks back and forth like a scene out of the movie Mean Girls. *I did not handle it well, and most of the parties involved continued to talk it up.*

My former friend would tell others that I was a crybaby and a terrible friend, and that I had created the drama. In response, I had a similar reaction, and things continued to be nasty. It was a tug-of-war—who could make the other one look meaner? It got to the point that any comment I made became a source of ridicule. Looking back, both of us were being inconsiderate and rude.

The most hurtful part for me occurred about two weeks after the phone incident, when I was texting another friend. I was finally conceding that I was glad this incident was over, that it was probably for the best, and that we could both continue to find happiness in our other relationships. The friend I was texting was consoling me, agreeing with my suppositions, and comforting me. I was finally in a content state of mind knowing that I had other friends who supported me. Five minutes later, I received a text message that I read and could tell wasn't meant for me. It stated that this girl, referring to me, could seriously write a novel, that her whining was pathetic, and that the remainder of her text messages would be sent "for your entertainment."

I immediately called my texting friend and confronted her with what she had accidentally texted me. She continued to deny that she had been sharing our private conversations with the other parties and forwarding our text messages. I was heartbroken again because I trusted this friend and thought she trusted me. I was so distraught that I knew I could not continue in this same path—being both a victim and part of the problem.

I decided to take a hard look within myself for a solution. I convinced myself to stand up for what was right and take the consequences for my behavior. I did not talk or associate with any of these individuals for three years. When I heard rumors about what someone had said or about who had been excluded from being invited to a party, I ignored the rumors, did not pass them on, and kept myself active in other social gatherings.

Incidentally, my texting friend and I started conversing again in tenth grade and continue to be best friends attending the same university. She never admitted sending the text but did admit it to others. We never talked about it. I have never spoken to the others since the incident in middle school. However, the initial aggressor attends my same university, but we have no contact.

POINTS FOR PARENTS

We are currently having a national discussion about the impact of bullying behavior in schools. We have learned that having a strong social bond in school is essential for developing a positive attitude toward learning. The experiences of school-based victimization can have a negative impact on a child's academic success (Popp and Peguero 2012). It is difficult for a student such as the one in this story to succeed in school in this hostile environment.

Bullying often begins as fun. There may not be clear intent to hurt someone else. Since bullying occurs most often in groups, it can begin as teasing. The student who is attempting to be part of the group will accept this behavior as an opportunity to belong to the group that is perceived as popular. In this case, he or she tells us, "The jokes were never funny but were made to get a reaction out of the other." Even though the "jokes" began as give-and-take, they became toxic because, for the victim, they were attempts to be connected to a friend.

Fitting in with peers is very important to students at this age. Students who are perceived as popular are often the same students who are bullying others (Espelage 2002). They use bullying behavior to gain social influence. On the other hand, if those students who are looking to fit in or belong reciprocate the back-and-forth banter that is described in this case, there is not a balance of power. The student who is bullying has social power, and she used the power in a malicious way by deliberately involving other students to exclude the victim. Under these circumstances, it is difficult for the victimized student to form positive social bonds in school.

SUGGESTIONS FOR ACTION

- Whenever there is a change in schools—particularly in middle school—connect with the staff to see what provisions they are making to welcome the new student. For instance, some schools have a "buddy program" in which they match the new student with another student to help them find their classrooms and to introduce them to other students.

- As a parent you can set up opportunities for the child to include others. For example, encourage the student to invite friends over to do homework or to participate in other social activities.

- Look closely at the needs of the student acting out by observing how the children act in a group. Notice how your child fits in—does he or she interact directly with the others, or does he or she play a more peripheral role?

- Consider the following questions: Are they sharing the leadership, or is it a matter of your child always following others? Is anyone mocking a member of the group? Do the other children respond in a positive way to your child? Does your child appear to be angry or stressed after being with those certain peers? If you are concerned about any of these issues, consult the school. In the meantime, you can talk to your children about independence and praise them when they make a good choice.

Case Study: Overprotective Parents

Type of Bullying: Relational aggression, exclusion, rumors, theft, property damage
Age of Onset/Gender of Target: Thirteen, female
How Long Did the Bullying Last? Four years
Hot Spots: Hallways, classroom, school bus
Did You Tell? If So, Whom? Administration, parents

My daughter, Melissa, was thirteen when she was first bullied. Since we were older parents and she was our only child, her father and I were very protective. We did not encourage her to socialize with others outside of school, and consequently, she didn't have many friends or acquaintances. Melissa had peers who mocked her, probably because she wore less fashionable clothes and had a mullet haircut. They excluded her by calling her names, laughing at her, and referring to her as a boy. Making good grades didn't help her to fit in. We knew she was being mistreated at school because when she came home, she would go into her room and isolate herself from the world. It would take everything to get her to open up and tell us what was happening. She did not react to the bullying; instead, she became passive and blamed herself.

As time passed, my daughter made friends; soon after, these "friends" ignored and excluded her. This group of girls would tell her that she couldn't ride the bus. When she did ride it, they took her phone and threw it to the back of the bus. Another time these same students stole her phone. After I reported the incident and the administration reviewed the tapes, the aggressors were suspended from school for their actions. However, this made Melissa's life even more painful, as they continued to retaliate against her. In band class, this same group hid her instrument from her, and when she found it they had duct taped it in the case. Another time, a student who had spent the night in our home spread a rumor that my husband had molested her. She asked Melissa in front of a group, "Do you think your father will go to jail for trying to molest me?" Nothing ever checked out, so the accusation was found to be untrue. What more could we take? Melissa's morale plummeted, and we were worried for her emotional stability. The aggressors continued their intimidation into high school. When Melissa was in her sophomore year, I walked into the bathroom and discovered she had cut marks all over her arms. She said she was relieving the pain from the repeated and intentional bullying from the same popular group of girls who bullied her in middle school. After she refused to ride the bus and I drove her to and from school each day, the bullying became more intense at school in the hallways and classroom. So, feeling helpless, I immediately made an appointment for her and myself to see a therapist.

During these last two years of high school, it seemed that Melissa had good days and bad days. Because she had a select group of friends she associated with, she seemed to be insulated from these mean girls. Consequently, she developed into an overachiever and became distressed when she did not perform academically at the top of her class.

Presently, Melissa will be graduating from high school soon and has plans to attend a community college and then transfer to a university to major in music education.

POINTS FOR PARENTS

Children need to have the opportunity to make friends and learn how to navigate through social situations. Through play, children learn how to integrate into a group, interact with others, share, and work as a team. When young children do not have the time to learn with their peers or there is stress in the home (e.g., financial problems), they have a difficult time communicating and interacting with their peers. As they get older, it makes them vulnerable to relational aggression, leaving them isolated, lonely, unhappy, and even depressed. However, many students with similar experiences themselves tend to become socially aggressive (Crick and Grotpeter 1995). It is as if they go from from being the target to victimizing someone else.

In this case, Melissa focused her energy on overachieving in school, yet she remained passive and socially isolated. Over time, victimization from bullying causes a decline in self-esteem. The decrease in self-esteem is an indicator of the continuation and perhaps even the increase in bullying behavior. This case also demonstrates the power of the students who bully others. Students describe those who are likely to bully as popular. Those students are using their hurtful behavior to gain social status. For girls in middle school, it is a way of gaining attention from boys, establishing a following of girlfriends, and feeling popular (Guerra et al. 2011).

A school climate that does not address this issue immediately is indirectly sending a message of approval. Melissa's parents did go to the school, and the problem got worse. This is one of the main reasons why bystanders do not speak up to defend the victim. Many times children will confide in their parents about a situation and then end the story by asking the parents not to do anything about it. Our role is to, at the very least, protect our children from being victimized; yet at one time or another, we have been confronted with the dilemma of keeping things to ourselves or speaking up. In this case, the school was not adequately able to prevent retaliation once the bullying had been reported.

SUGGESTIONS FOR ACTION

- When a pattern of abuse is apparent, it is important to talk to the school and report the incidents. Reports should include specific names, including all those present, dates, location(s), and other relevant details.
- The school most likely will want to investigate the issue. Therefore, it is equally important to follow up with the school. When reporting to the school, ask when they will get back to you with their findings. If you do not hear from them, you should pursue them for information.
- Ask the school for a plan of safety. Ask what are they doing to monitor the situation to prevent it from escalating.
- Talk to your child daily about how things are going in school. This can be casual conversation that will give you an idea about how things are going.

35

- While all this is going on, look for ways for your child to have some positive experiences with other friends. This can be in a class outside of school or visits with friends who are not involved in the bullying that the child is experiencing.
- If your child is found cutting or hurting himself or herself in other ways, ask the school social worker or counselor for a professional licensed therapist who feels comfortable working with children who are involved with self-mutilating behaviors.

3. Cyberbullying

> **Case Study: I Never Fit In!**
>
> **Type of Bullying:** Relational aggression, rumors, gossip, exclusion, sexual, name calling, threatening, cyberbullying
> **Age of Onset/Gender of Target:** Seventh grade, female
> **How Long Did the Bullying Last?** Seventh grade through high school
> **Hot Spots:** Lunchroom, hallway, bathroom
> **Did You Tell? If So, Whom?** I told the administration but student retaliated.

I was introduced to bullying in seventh grade in a regional middle school that was composed of students from surrounding towns. I would describe myself as scrawny and flat chested, with severe acne. I was from a middle-class community. Even though they could afford it, my parents did not purchase expensive, fashionable clothes for me but instead bought cheap and even second-hand clothes. I am the oldest of six girls; I have one biological sister and four adopted sisters.

The bullying started the first week of school during lunch when I told a girlfriend, Samantha, who was very popular, that I had a crush on a boy named Logan. I had had a crush on him from as early as kindergarten. Later, a friend of Samantha's, Courtney, came up to me and said she heard I had a crush on Logan. She further stated that he liked me too and that I should ask him out. We then went to Logan's locker and when I told him that I had a crush on him, he looked at me with a surprised look and said that he had no idea what I was talking about. He emphatically stated that he thought I was disgusting and that he didn't understand what I was saying and wanted to have nothing to do with me.

Observing from a distance, Courtney and Samantha had gathered a group of friends together who were watching my interaction with Logan and laughing at my embarrassment. It was a setup. They even used relational aggression by spreading nasty rumors about me with the goal of getting others to dislike me. It occurred mostly in the lunchroom, where I was ostracized, excluded, and isolated by groups telling me that I couldn't sit at their table. They would talk openly about me, and it was so loud that I couldn't help but hear it.

The girls who were bullying me were popular, very pretty, and liked by adults. They were involved in athletics, cheerleading, student council, and clubs. I, on the other hand, did not get involved with extracurricular activities because I did not want to spend time with these same students who were always harassing me at school.

When I was bullied, I did report it to the administration. They would call the girls down to the principal's office, and every girl would deny that she was involved in what I had described. After being called to the office, the girls would retaliate by sending me social media messages and text messages that threatened me with bodily harm. If I reported being bullied, I discovered very quickly that I had to live with the fear of not knowing how I was going to be treated and threatened at school. Dealing with the unknown caused me great anxiety.

I had acquaintances, mostly girls, who at the time I thought were my friends. At school they would join in with the other bystanders and gossip about me and call me names like the others. This would occur in the hallways, bathrooms, the lunchroom, and wherever teachers weren't present. However, when I came home, these so-called friends would treat me differently. They made it clear that at school they had to join in and laugh at what the oth-

ers were doing and saying, but at home they acted friendly and inclusive. They said that they would be targeted if they didn't go along with the popular crowd.

In high school the bullying moved into a different realm—cyberbullying. Also, at that time I grew into myself and was curvy and more attractive. Since social media had just started, students went too far with their comments. When I looked at my Facebook page, students had anonymously written that I should kill myself and that everyone hated me. From the time that I left school and returned to school the next day, I discovered that students had created a fake profile about me. They stated on Facebook that I had slept with both the football and wrestling teams, had oral sex with an English teacher, and had performed sexual acts that I was oblivious to. They went so far as to list my home phone number to encourage students to call and harass me. My name was clearly in the rumor mill, and I was called every name in the book. I wanted to kill myself because the students who were spreading rumors about me tried to convince me that I would be better off dead. I fantasized what it would be like if I were dead. This lasted until I graduated from high school.

Thank goodness that I had kept my grades up because I knew that this was my only way out. After high school, I went to a college far from home to get away from the students who tormented me during my middle and high school years. In college I became president of my junior class; was a resident assistant; and traveled abroad, volunteering to help the less fortunate. My goal was to change the messages in my head. I repeated to myself that I was beautiful and that I could be loved. I was so fortunate that this part of my life was behind me.

My parents were involved in my life at the time this was happening. They both had jobs in the helping profession and were my advocates. However, they didn't know what I was experiencing. I was able to act normal even though I was in so much pain. During those days, that was the best I could do because I didn't have the emotional maturity to share with them what my peers were alleging about me because I was too embarrassed.

POINTS FOR PARENTS

A few words about cell phones: We live in the digital age, and technology has become an integral part of our lives. It has been evolving rapidly and will continue to do so. The history of the Internet began in the 1950s, but it was in the mid-1990s that it became the World Wide Web, and then the technology really impacted our lives with an overabundance of information and instant communication. The world of cyber communication has exploded into our traditional manner of communication. The first mobile phone was used in 1984—over 30 years ago! The equipment has morphed from a "brick" that weighed over two pounds to the smartphones most people use today. In fact, children born in 2006 have never known life without a Blackberry or iPhone.

With all of these rapid changes to technology, people have been able to communicate instantly. Access to cell phones has increased to the point that the question is, "What kind of cell phone do you have?" rather than, "Do you have a cell phone?" A 2010 study found that 23% of students had a cell phone, but by fifth grade the number jumps to 55% (D'Antona et al. 2010). School administrators tell us that the number has increased substantially since then. Clearly, the presence of such large numbers of cell phones in school presents a whole new set of issues to be discussed.

Most schools today have policies for both staff and students about the use of cell phones during the school day. Teachers tell us it is very difficult to keep cell phones out of the classroom, even with a policy that restricts usage during class time.

The rapidly expanding use of technology seems to have far surpassed social expectations. In other words, we have not been able to reconcile the presence of cell phones in our lives. There are many unanswered questions, such as: Is it necessary to have instant and constant contact with others? Where and how can they be used appropriately without infringing on others? How can youth protect themselves from unwanted messages and information? On the other hand, some are asking if cell phone usage can be integrated into curriculum. These questions have yet to be answered, but cell phones are in students' pockets and backpacks, ringing and vibrating while stealing attention away from class lessons. Therefore, the possibility and the probability of victimization increase dramatically.

According to *stopbullying.gov*, cyberbullying is bullying that takes place using electronic technology. Electronic technology includes devices and equipment such as cell phones, computers, and tablets as well as communication tools including social media sites, text messages, chat, and websites. Examples of cyberbullying include mean text messages or e-mails; rumors sent by e-mail or posted on social networking sites; and embarrassing pictures, videos, websites, or fake profiles.

The most disturbing thing is that when third through fifth graders were asked if an adult had talked to them about bullying online, 11.9% said they had (D'Antona et al. 2010). That means that over 88.1% of those children who have cell phones have had no instructions should they be confronted with difficult, hurtful, or inappropriate information. Yet, 20% to 40% of all young people report being cyberbullied at least once (Tokunaga 2010).

For the girl cited in this case study, the abuse began as relational bullying. Often between girls, it becomes a great tangle of who said what to whom and who was there to encourage and support the action. It is very difficult for adults to decipher. In fact, students who are different and not connected are particularly vulnerable, and they tend to be more disliked or rejected by their peers (Zimmer-Gembeck et al. 2013). The girl in this case study describes herself as feeling different and not fitting in. By taking a friend into her confidence, she inadvertently became the target of cruel pranks by her classmates.

Because these students did not receive any consequences for this humiliating prank, the cruel behavior continued. She reports that her friends behaved differently out of school and in fact were able to maintain a sociable relationship. Fear of retaliation is often a main motivation to deter students from standing up for the victim or to choose not to participate. However, in this case, the bullying escalated to cyberbullying by the time the students were in high school.

As much as we would like to believe that we know our children, the parents in this story were close to their child and, according to the girl, were part of the "helping professions" and were her advocates. Yet, they had no idea that their child was being victimized and that it had escalated into cyberbullying. This miscommunication happens more often than we would like to think. In fact, research suggests that 56% of parents whose children had received nasty or mean messages had no idea that was occurring (Livingstone et al. 2011).

The bullying then expanded to include Facebook. Research says that 56% of nine- to sixteen-year-olds have a social media profile (Livingstone et al. 2011). They each have multiple contacts that radiate out from their social circles to reach many, many more people. It becomes almost impossible to guess how many people a post reaches, so it is particularly cruel when a message is posted that is not only false but also seriously damaging to one's reputation.

When it happened to this girl, she felt so distressed that she wanted to die. Under these circumstances, this feeling of helplessness and desperation—while common—is particularly difficult because her parents had no idea that all of this was happening. She felt totally alone.

Yet somehow, she was able to keep up her grades and, in her

own words, told us, "Rumors do not define a person. The past does not define who I am, what I do, and what I think of myself for the rest of my life. I have the choice to be or not to become a victim. I have the power to change my thinking and the way I feel about myself, and to make any necessary changes. I have given myself permission to move on and choose happiness. Everyone has a choice." She is one of the few people who are able to navigate through these incidents and come through with such a courageous philosophy.

While the outcome to this story is positive, the real question to consider is: Should anyone have to be subjected to that type of victimization, even when they are able to grow beyond it? The answer is absolutely not! The aggressors and the adults who let it happen literally stole a piece of her youth and those characteristically carefree school days.

SUGGESTIONS FOR ACTION

- Let your child know that any type of mistreatment is unacceptable. You can talk about things in daily life as well as in the news. The point is that you want them to know how you expect people to be treated. This sets the stage for the child to know that you would support them if he or she needed your assistance to deal with mistreatment.
- Let your child know that you are available. Everyone is busy nowadays, and to a sensitive child, it may be a signal that you are not accessible. Be certain to make time on a regular basis for one-on-one time with your child. He or she may not choose the time to talk about anything that is bothering him or her, but it will give you an opportunity to get to understand your child better.
- Set some basic ground rules for electronic communication. This can be as simple as agreeing to not do or say anything online that you would not say or do in person. Another way to

check this out is to let another trusted individual read what you want to post before you send it. You can be more detailed and limit the usage, but whatever you choose, be certain to include the ethics of online communication in the rules.

- Monitor your child's activity online. The question of privacy applies to the old-fashioned diary with a key that is kept under the bed. When it comes to the Internet, you are in a public domain and therefore have a responsibility to not only protect your child from electronic aggression but to be certain that your child, intentionally or not, is acting inappropriately.

- Talk to other parents and caregivers to see if they are aware of what their children are doing online and to see if there are any problems. Not only can you support one another, but you can also get a sense of whether your child may be involved.

- Keep current with the technology. There are new apps and websites that are launched on a regular basis, and most youth know about them long before adults!

Case Study: Targeted from Elementary Grades Through College

Type of Bullying: Relational aggression, exclusion, name calling, cyberbullying, prank calls, cutting in line
Age of Onset/Gender of Target: First grade, female
How Long Did the Bullying Last? Through college
Hot Spots: Playground, classroom, home, and school
Did You Tell? If So, Whom? Telling never worked for me because I was afraid of retaliation.

I have been bullied since I started school. My younger brother and I were atypical since we went to a private religious school through high school with a small white student population of about 50 to 60 students in each grade. If you were athletic at the school you were popular, and if you were not you were an outcast. We both hated gym class and outdoor activities and would rather be reading and playing video games. Subsequently, we did not fit in with most of the other classmates. I think my brother was able to handle the situation better. I was not feminine enough and just didn't fit in to the different girl cliques. The bullying was exclusionary at the elementary level, with girls excluding me by choosing me or letting me sit by myself in the cafeteria. During recess, the popular students clearly stood out because if you were athletic you were included in the games, whether it was football, soccer, kick ball, etc. Losers were excluded. Again, I would rather sit and read since it was so obvious that I wasn't interested in playing a hot and sweaty game that I had never played before. Even though I had no experience playing sports, I felt slighted because no one would sit and talk to me.

Our private school was very conservative and traditional. Because the student body was static, each year there were fewer and fewer students entering or departing. If you entered the school as a kindergartner, the same group of students would follow you through eighth grade. I entered the school in the middle of first grade, which was an awkward fit because the other children knew each other. I did not have the opportunity to assimilate and always felt that I was catching up. Again, if you were popular and athletic, you were cool and everything worked in your favor.

The bullying seemed to increase in middle school. To my surprise a new student entered seventh grade, and she and I hit it off. This was the first time I thought I had a best friend. In addition, another girl who was also excluded from the popular crowd joined us. The three of us could always be seen walking together and talking. When we were in different classes we decided to journal our thoughts in a notebook. It was common practice with girls our age. Since we saw no harm in writing down our opinions, we wrote about what we loved and hated, and we named friends and teach-

ers. *One day one of my girlfriends convinced my other friend I was the enemy and shared our notebook with the school principal. The girls convinced the principal that the journal was my idea and that I had written all of the entries. Before they turned the journal over to the administration, they deleted certain incriminating pictures and entries. When I was called in, I was given in-school suspension for two days, and my so-called friends received nothing. Suddenly, without warning, I had no friends once again. Because our school was so small, everyone knew that I had been punished and suspended. Since I had never been in trouble in school, this was a big deal with my parents. They were confused and perplexed and acknowledged that it wasn't fair to me. However, they supported the school's decision to give me in-school suspension and stated that life wasn't fair, but I had to deal with it because I was part of the problem and not the solution.*

I continued to be depressed and, while I attended this school, felt very unhappy. We wore uniforms, so the only way I felt that I could stand out and be different was to take on the goth look. It was then that I was labeled a "bad influence." Teachers would single me out when it was obvious to me that I needed help and support. One day I was carrying an art book that had a questionable title, Emily's Strange, *with four black cats on the cover, and a teacher confiscated the book, took it to the counselor, and implied that I needed to receive outside help. I pleaded with my parents not to send me back to the school, but they stuck with their belief that I could fit in; however, it would take time. Thus, not knowing how to handle the stress of the situation, I relented and started cutting myself in order to relieve the pain that I had inside.*

I felt further victimized when peers chose friends to play and eat with during school and didn't select me. The school instituted an incentivized game. Those students who received the most points during the week would be able to choose four friends to eat with in a private area in the lunchroom. Even though I had few friends in school, I did have friends who socialized with me after school. However, these friends never chose me as a friend to eat with them in the private area of the lunchroom. I learned quickly that I felt like an outcast. No one wanted to have anything to do with me during school, and seventh grade was the worst year ever.

Puzzled with my behavior, my parents sent me to a therapist who placed me on antidepressants. As a result of one of the medications, I gained 25 pounds in the first month. At the time I was shorter than five feet, so my height and weight were disproportionate. Peers started calling me fat and making sounds as I passed by them in the halls. Everything continued to pile up, and the bullying increased in frequency. Because my parents didn't realize how difficult my life was and how much I hated school, I got a box cutter and started cutting myself. I was taken to the hospital and received stitches. Only then did my parents realize how much pain I was in. I had kept the cutting a secret from my parents all of this time.

The next day my parents escorted me to school to transfer me to a public school. The reaction of my peers was most interesting. The students who participated in the bullying displayed sorrow and didn't understand why I was leaving. It was confusing. Was this a show for the adults? Did they like to have me around like a punching bag? Anyway, I left the private school after the first quarter of eighth grade and transferred to a school that had a diversified population and more than 200 students in a grade. It was overwhelming and I was scared.

Looking back, my personality was different from that of my peers. I was like an old soul and skipped the things that my friends were interested in. I was introverted and enjoyed coming home to enjoy the peace and quiet and to do my homework. I was a homebody and wasn't into partying or dating; however, I enjoyed thinking about it but not actively participating in it. It was too scary for me at the time.

When I changed schools I knew I was alone again. But, to my surprise, a small group of girls showed me around and initiated me to the school culture. I then realized that the cookie-cutter mold that I was used to—white girls from rich families who were cheerleaders and had parents who were doctors —wasn't the same in other settings. I found a group that I integrated in that was an eclectic group of punk girls my age, which excited me at the time; however, it turned into a nightmare because I was then introduced into cyberbullying.

I had always been interested in being social online, but until this time I did not have the skills nor did I take the time to develop them. I always wanted to instant message, but since that didn't work out I got interested in some of the kid-friendly websites and blogging. We took pictures of what we did on the weekend, posted them, and wrote about our experiences. One day, which had happened similarly in the past, a friend decided that I wasn't her friend anymore and started posting how I was stupid and mean to her. This time, however, it was posted online where the world could view it. I was frustrated because this time what was posted online became a record of sorts. These lies were her words against mine. I had no way of proving that what she said was untrue. I felt helpless. To make the situation worse, an anonymous person took my information and created a website that made me look even more stupid. I was stumped because I did not know how to get the website to delete the information.

I showed the site to my parents, and they didn't know what to do either. My father discussed it with my counselor at school, and the school acknowledged that it was not the school's responsibility to intervene since a school computer was not involved. So, my parents and I made a decision to take everything down and shut down my account online.

The eighth grade school year ended with an end-of-the-year exit party. Looking back, it seemed like a teen movie. My mother and I went shopping and couldn't find what I wanted to wear, so I got a dress made. I was never asked to join a group to attend the dance, so I went on my own. I expected my dress to be a hit, but students made fun of it. So I realized at the dance that whether you're popular or not doesn't really matter; we all have things in common. Maybe I was choosing the wrong crowd to be around and impress. That night I chose to be around the unpopular kids and had a wonderful time.

Summer came and in the fall I entered ninth grade. I was re-districted for a high school where most of my acquaintances from middle school were not attending. I was again ready for a new start. Now I could focus on art and the art community, which was my love. I signed up for as many creative courses that I could. However, thinking about what had happened to me in the past, I stayed away from conversing with peers from school on the Inter-net. I was finally trying to control my environment and not placing myself in a vulnerable position as I had done in the past. Subse-quently, I became more of an Internet dork because people whom I met online never betrayed me. This was a safe way for me to make friends while not sharing with them my past.

During high school I wandered in and out of groups and different cliques, and it still felt like I didn't have friends. It felt awkward and disheartening. At this high school, which was five times larger than the private school, bullying came from individ-uals whom I did not know, as compared to students with whom I knew in the past school settings. For example, there were twin girls whom I had never met before, and they started bullying me for no obvious reason. They would cut in front of me on line, call me whore, ugly, and fatso, and then prank call my home in the middle of the night. My father got involved and tried to contact the families to no avail. Finally, the harassment stopped when we had our number unlisted.

During my sophomore year I signed up for a course called the-ater productions. The experience enhanced my art skills, as I was asked to design sets for the upcoming production. One day during class I caught the eye of an older male student whom I thought was attractive. However, as we got to know each other, I was told that he had a long-term girlfriend. Because I had shown interest and flirted with him, the other girls in the class tormented me. Whatever I did, however small, I was put in my place. It seemed that anything I did was attacked and ridiculed.

Things continued to get better until I entered my senior year. I had not been motivated in any arena until now, except I had always been an avid reader and consequently did well academically. For some time I was fixated with the academic decathlon team because if you were a member you received special parking in front of school. I had not been involved in any club or activity at the school, but if I were selected to be on the academic decathlon team, maybe my peers would think that I was cool, I thought. There were slots on the team, and fortunately I got selected. However, only the top four academically would be granted one of the parking spots. My goal was to have a parking spot in front of the school my senior year.

As usual, there was one obstacle that raised its ugly head. A girl joined the class after me whose mission in life was to be my nemesis. She was not as well-rounded as me academically, but she tried to intimidate, coerce, and bully me at every opportunity. She gave me backhanded compliments, which I usually brushed off and ignored. She then stepped up her attacks even more.

Even though she was a handful, the teacher was supportive of me. Because I was a top performer in the class, the teacher gave me special permission to skip lunch and stay in the classroom to read and study and be by myself. Consequently, when this girl realized that I had isolated myself in this quiet sanctuary, she invited herself and her friends to join me in the room. Their goal was to threaten and intimidate my every move with their subtle and covert aggressive acts. One day I went to turn homework in to another teacher, and this student threatened me. It was so obvious, and since this teacher had observed everything, I thought the best way to proceed was to go to the principal and report the threat. I asked the teacher if she would support me reporting the threat and the teacher said she heard nothing. She turned a blind eye.

I learned quickly that the teachers ignored what they heard and that's what they expected me to do. So at times when I was isolated or alone I would listen to my MP3 player and totally ignore what was going on around me. At other times I responded to any comments directed at me by making jokes out of them.

After striving to be the top performer on my school's academic decathlon team and achieving the highest grade point average, I was selected as the team captain. I assumed that this would make me highly respected and that the others would start listening to my ideas. Wrong. I continued to score the highest in competitions individually, but when I encouraged the others on the team to study, they acted too cool to change their behavior. So, instead of focusing on being friends with my team, I started hanging out and meeting individuals from other schools.

When I was in college the bullying came back. Some students made anonymous threats and hurtful comments on a website about my friends regarding their feminist and/or gay right's position. I posted a rebuttal defending my friends and signed it with my real name. Others responded with disparaging comments, making personal attacks and calling me names such as lesbian. The university shut down the site and supported taking action against those who were cyberbullying me. I even had a professor from one of my classes who offered his support. This was a first.

Being bullied for such a long time and being able to come through it has made me realize that it does get better. When I was bullied, I think I was selected because I was different. When I was singled out, I stayed true to who I am. I could have changed, but I would not have been true to myself.

POINTS FOR PARENTS

There are many issues in this story, but at the heart of it is the fact that this student was bullied for such a long time. There are many reasons for this, and since the one who was targeted tells the story, we only have that perspective. She was, as she described, different and clearly was not able to socially navigate through social situations with her peers.

The cyberbullying in this story occurred through social media. Social media bullying is an additional platform for people to network. At the same time, it brings bullying from school into the home. In fact, nowadays, with smart phones, it is carried in backpacks and pockets, making it available everywhere —24 hours 7 days a week. There is a connection between bullying in school and bullying through social media (Kwan and Skoric 2013).

Keep in mind that children under the age of thirteen are not allowed on Facebook. Some parents allow Facebook accounts for younger children because "everyone is doing it," but that is a mistake. You are actually teaching your child that the rules do not apply to them right from the beginning. If your child is under the age of thirteen and requests to be on Facebook, agree that it sounds like a great idea and sit down with them at the computer. As you assist them to be a subscriber on Facebook, when the screen comes up to confirm that your child is thirteen, it is a perfect moment to discuss that your child is not eligible and what it means to break rules. When your child is old enough and you decide to give permission, be certain that you know the password and are a "friend." At the same time, it is also important to let your child know right from the beginning that you will be monitoring his or her profile.

But, most important, all parents need to talk to their children about feelings—their own feelings and feelings of others. Empathy is key in bullying prevention and should be part of any discussion about what not to do online. We want youth to understand the impact of cyberbullying and choose to avoid participating in this behavior because of the hurt it can cause.

This story suggests that removing a student from a school to attend another does not necessarily solve the bullying problem. When addressing bullying victimization, it is important to consider the target and what can be done to help the victim cope. In addition, it is a good idea to work on a safety plan should the problem arise again. This is a girl who self-describes as different from her peers. She needs support to help her understand how she can handle social situations and to basically feel better about herself. She describes how she does not relate to peers and feels more comfortable with adults. If she has a counselor or therapist, she can work out those feelings and have a safe place to talk about her problems at school.

This should occur long before she has resorted to self-inflicted bodily harm. This girl resorted to cutting—a behavior that is most common among young adults. This type of behavior serves both an intrapersonal function, by removing the person from a difficult situation, and an interpersonal function because the physical pain relieves the emotional pain (Nock 2010). People who self-harm can be very adept at hiding the scars and marks of the act. They can also be very clever at explaining them away. Therefore, the signs may be difficult to detect, so look for long sleeves and other concealing clothing. Sometimes they will avoid social situations where more revealing clothing is required or claim to have frequent complaints of accidental injury (Nock 2010).

It is important to note that by suggesting a counselor, we are not—by any means—saying that the victim is at fault and should change to meet the social expectations of peers. The victim should never be blamed for the bullying. We do believe that a student who is under this level of stress has all the necessary support possible to help him or her cope. The research is clear: students who are targeted by cyberbullying have been found to suffer psychological harm because they feel threatened and out of control because of the potential numbers of bystanders who can view or participate in the bullying (Kwan and Skoric 2013).

SUGGESTIONS FOR ACTION

- Suggestions for Social Networking:
  — Check privacy settings to be certain that the general public cannot see all posts.
  — Use filtering software. You can get software that will limit areas on the Internet, but do not take it for granted—still check for yourself.
  — Monitor Internet usage. There is software that tracks keystrokes so you can check all computer activity. Monitor all pictures and posts.
  — Create ground rules and discuss them periodically so they are not forgotten. Do not forget that many cell phones can access the Internet, so they need to be monitored as well.
  — Don't forget to consistently enforce those rules.
  — Keep the computer in a central location, and keep cell phones out of bedrooms at night to discourage late-night checking of social media accounts.
  — Be a good model. Use social media at appropriate times and in appropriate ways.

- When introducing a child to a new school, meet with the principal and the teacher to help the child integrate smoothly by creating connections to other students.
- When the child seems to be isolated—even when he or she is successful academically—look closer. School is more that academics; it is the place where children learn social skills.
- If the child is showing serious signs of distress, involve the school immediately. If it gets to the level of self-harm, contact a mental health professional immediately for assistance.

Case Study: Parents Blame the School for Their Child's Aggression

Type of Bullying: Name calling, pushing, rumors, cyberbullying, texting
Age of Onset/Gender of Target: Eighth grade, male
How Long Did the Bullying Last? One year
Hot Spots: Hallways, Facebook
Did You Tell? If So, Whom? I told an administrator, and the students attacked me and evened the score. I was embarrassed to tell my parents.

Bullying started in eighth grade, in my upper-class, high socio-economic community school that I attended when a popular boy in my class stood up, pulled down his pants, and mooned the entire class. The substitute teacher, who was oblivious to this incident, saw nothing. Embarrassed by what the student had done and the disrespect he had for the substitute teacher, I decided to report the incident to an administrator in the front office.

Because my identity was not kept confidential and the student found out my name, I was retaliated against and was targeted by the boy and his friends. He had a huge following and was popular in our middle school. During the day in the hallways, he and his cohorts would call me names, laugh at me, whisper when I walked by, send rumors around to get others to dislike me, and push me when I was walking to class.

After school he and his friends would turn to social media and would cyberbully me on Facebook and send texts out about me. He would post lies about me, and they would go out to other kids in school. The texts were the same lies, only they went directly to kids in my class. With a click of a button, these texts were forwarded on to many others. I could not refute the lies nor defend myself in any way. Not knowing how to handle this situation, I started avoiding school because of the intimidation and aggressiveness of this group of boys.

I didn't tell my parents because I was embarrassed. However, when another parent told my mother about the situation, my mother reported it immediately to the principal. The school promptly investigated the bullying and cyberbullying and handled the situation swiftly and appropriately. The boy was not allowed to play in the next basketball game and was required to post a public apology on Facebook. Even though the incident only lasted weeks, the aftereffects carried on throughout most of the school year.

The boy is in my tenth grade class, but we hardly have contact with each other. He seems to still be a handful, and his aggressive behaviors continue to get him in-school suspension in high school. His parents, instead of taking ownership for the problem, blame the school.

POINTS FOR PARENTS

This is a story about a boy who reported an inappropriate behavior to the school administrator and, as a result, became the target of bullying behavior. This is not unusual. A student who is trying to do the right thing is often penalized by his peers and experiences retaliation. In this case, the backlash from reporting the incident in class became the provocation for bullying. It began with mean name calling and humiliation in the classroom and hallways.

When a student reports an incident that involves discipline, it is imperative for the school administration to anticipate a reaction that involves retaliation. Therefore, keeping the name of the student who made the report confidential is critical. School staff can use many different techniques to handle the aggressor without divulging the source of the report.

Of the students who reported being targeted with cyberbullying, 85 percent of those students reported that the bullying began in school as name calling and other insults (Juvonen and Gross

2008). Furthermore, the research shows that two-thirds of those students who had been cyberbullied knew the person who was attacking them on the Internet. Repeated school bullying is a predictor and may be a precursor for cyberbullying. It essentially begins in school and is continued long after the school day ends by way of electronics.

It is also important to note that in most cases—in fact, over 90 percent—students reported that they did not tell a parent. Parents will often tell us that they know everything their child is doing online, but clearly there is a large majority of children, once they have been targeted, who do not say anything to their parent. This is an important fact for parents to consider. Their child may be involved in bullying online as either a target or aggressor without any adult having any indication of the problem.

To say it is important to communicate with your child is simply not enough. This parent found out inadvertently from another parent. Everyone needs to be part of the solution. This is evidenced by the fact that the other parent went to the boy's family to alert them of the problem. This is an excellent example of others caring for the well-being of children by speaking up and recognizing that even though it may not directly involve them, bullying effects everyone.

Once they had the information, the parents immediately went to the school and reported the incident. Apparently, the school responded by dealing with the aggressor and assigning appropriate consequences. The good news is that the cyberbullying stopped. Even though they are in the same school, the aggressor and the victim have limited contact.

SUGGESTIONS FOR ACTION

- Schools need to have a plan for protecting a student who reports an incident that may become a discipline issue. Students need to trust that they will not become a target of retaliation.

One way would be to report that an adult or several students made the report. It is important to impress on the aggressor that the focus is on the inappropriate behavior and how it can be prevented in the future.

- When going to the school to report any incident of bullying or cyberbullying, it is important to discuss how the school plans to protect the target from retaliation (a safety plan). In this incident, it seems that the school was able to do this. However, it is advisable to ask about their procedures. Also check into them on a regular basis as a follow-up.

- Every day it seems we are learning about ways that students are communicating electronically. It is happening twenty-four hours a day, seven days a week. Therefore, at the very least, limit the exposure by allowing electronic use during certain times of the day and eliminating use at bedtime. Many students check Facebook and other social media during the night.

- Know the passwords for all social media and check the site pages regularly. This cannot be overstated—your child needs to know that you are being diligent.

Case Study: Girls Cyberbullying Using Text Messaging

Type of Bullying: Cyberbullying using text messaging
Age of Onset/Gender of Target: Seventh grade, female
How Long Did the Bullying Last? Months leading up to the incident
Hot Spots: Cell phone
Did You Tell? If So, Whom? Mother of target reported incident to principal.

A few years ago, a new girl, Melisa, arrived in my daughter's fourth grade class. Her mother immediately reached out to parents because she wanted to prevent any further occurrences; her daughter had been bullied at her previous school. The mother was asking for guidance and support from parents so that this same scenario would not happen again to her daughter. A few weeks later at a sleepover, Melisa openly shared how she was bullied at her previous school. Her classmates received this information with a great deal of interest and, at the same time, horror about what exactly happened.

Two years later my youngest child, one of three children in our family, was still attending this same school with the same class-mates, in addition to Melisa, who had been bullied in the past. When our daughter was in sixth grade we gave an iPhone and a laptop to her. However, because of her young age, we limited her participation on social networking sites. My husband and I con-tinued to have many conversations with her about being careful and kind when she communicated and participated with others in the social networking world.

It became obvious that Melisa, the girl mentioned above, had psychological issues that created problems among her classmates. The other girls would comment about Melisa's size, how she was overweight, and how she lied. She would exaggerate her impor-tance by making bragging statements, such as, "Since I am so intelligent, I plan to attend Harvard when I graduate" and "I am going to be on Broadway since I have the best voice." Previously, her female classmates had tried to include her, but it became clear at a sleepover at our home that many students started avoiding her. She was not fitting in with the other girls. It was a close-knit class that had been together since kindergarten. I thought things were going smoothly because when things did occur that hurt Melisa's feelings, her mother would call my daughter and me and I would help to smooth everything over. My daughter, on the other hand, was so direct in her no-nonsense communication style that she created hurt feelings with Melisa and others. She would tell them how they needed to change, and her tone to a sensitive child was more times than not perceived as hurtful. I communicated numerous times to my child that it was not her job to dictate how others should act.

During the summer before my daughter entered seventh grade, Melisa and my daughter attended the same camp and shared a cabin. When problems arose at camp, the girl's mother would immediately call me to resolve the conflict. In return, I started asking Melisa and her mother to involve the camp counselor to assist with the conflict. This mother was a helicopter parent and was overly protective in helping her only child resolve conflict. When my daughter arrived home from camp, I made the mistake of sharing my frustrations with how I felt about Melisa and her mother. I was so frustrated with the number of hours that I had spent dealing with this needy family. The mother had interrupted me at work and home at all hours of the day.

One day the students in my daughter's grade were participating in a field trip. My daughter was playing games on her iPad because we had limited social networking apps. A friend was sitting next to my daughter, who was texting Melisa, who was at home at the time. She opted out of most field trips because it was hard for her to get along with her other classmates in such unstructured situations. For whatever reason, this classmate of my daughter's sent two mean text messages to Melisa stating she was "fat and stupid."

Melisa's mother immediately texted me a copy of the messages and said that my daughter sent these texts. I checked her phone and they were not there. Melisa's mother then said that a friend of hers who had colluded together to send the texts sent them. The mother reported the incident to the school as cyberbullying and cited that because my daughter and Melisa were having trouble getting along all summer, the texts were a way of getting back at Melisa. The mother also stated that my daughter had greater social power and forced the other girl to send the texts. In my perception, my daughter was in the middle of the social hierarchy and Melisa was at the bottom of the ladder. Putting this entire thing aside, if my daughter had something to do with the texting, I supported her having consequences. I did think my daughter owed Melisa a huge apology.

Soon I received a call from the principal, and the school found my daughter guilty of cyberbullying Melisa and gave her three days of out-of-school suspension. I asked the principal to review what evidence they had collected and they had none—just the story coming from Melisa. I asked if the punishment for the first strike was always this harsh because we found nothing in the handbook about three days of suspension. I asked if the school was open for any sort of restorative practices. The school stated that they had zero tolerance policies in place for any cyberbullying incidents and that the punishment had been determined and that everything was finalized. So my daughter and I spent three days at home. I tried to find community service and other activities that might repair the harm that she had created. I wanted productive activities that would help her to grow and become more respectful around other young women and herself. We concluded that it would be best if the two girls would stay away from each other in order to avoid any future problems. Unfortunately, both girls missed the sleepovers and the friendship that they had created, even though their friendship had been tumultuous.

Since this incident, my daughter has been very active in a youth drama group that performed plays in the community. Melisa had also showed interest in the same theatrical group since she was interested in performing on Broadway. The drama club had its first meeting, and we discussed how this might work. I communicated to my daughter that they would have to learn to coexist and learn to keep their distance. At the same time, I finally concluded that I would delete Melisa's mother's number from my phone so she could not send me three and four text messages a day. It was clear that it was very unproductive for me to be the referee.

POINTS FOR PARENTS

Parents should be aware of their child's personality. They should not deny that their child might have some part in bullying. Many parents are too protective of their children and don't see them making wrong decisions. Even though there was no physical evidence that this girl was directly involved, it is a possibility that she participated covertly if not overtly. It is much easier to face the consequences at this age than to do so later, when the scenario may be much more serious. It can be a valuable lesson learned.

Parents should talk about the possible roles for showing support for a friend. Discuss how a child can be part of the solution and not the problem when an inappropriate text is sent. When parents hand a child a cell phone, it is important to discuss all of the ways that children can be helpful and harmful, respectful and disrespectful, inclusionary and exclusionary, and appropriate and inappropriate using the phone and sending texts and pictures.

SUGGESTIONS FOR ACTION

- Talk about what active and passive bystander roles look like. Ask if they have ever taken on either of these roles.
- Discuss the consequences that would occur if children were to break their agreement.
- Coach your children on how to deal with different types of scenarios and role-play them. For example, if children text "JK" at the end of a mean text, explain to them that some children are cruel and say what they mean yet hide behind their statement by saying "just kidding."

Case Study: Boys Cyberbullying Using Meme Generator

Type of Bullying: Cyberbullying using pictures
Age of Onset/Gender of Target: Senior, female
How Long Did the Bullying Last? A month
Hot Spots: On the Web
Did You Tell? If So, Whom? Reported by target to principal

I have an eighteen-year-old son who attended high school in a large metropolitan area. At the point of this story, he was a senior and, if criticized by an adult like a teacher, he would turn inward, get angry with himself, and cry. He had an extremely sensitive temperament, which was overwhelming for him to control. He was a bright student and an all-around good son. He was motivated in school and enjoyed playing video games.

Recently, there was a situation that arose with a girl in school who represented an extremely wealthy sector of the students. She enjoyed informing her peers about it on a regular basis. As it happened, she was promoting a club that was not part of school. The school supported students being active in clubs and sports that were part of the school as well as the community. She communicated about her involvement in the club that was not part of the school on the school's Facebook page. She highlighted an upcoming event, which was focused on charity work, to everyone by encouraging them to participate and join the club as well.

My son and a friend were in a side chat about this event and noted how annoying this girl was. They said they were tired of feeling pressured and coerced about attending this event. They showed their disapproval in their attitude. One of the boys was familiar with meme generators on the Internet. These teenage boys took her photo and embedded the image into a meme generator. There were three images created: the photo of our nation's founding fathers signing the Declaration of Independence with George

63

Washington and Benjamin Franklin with her face superimposed as one of the founding fathers; a photo of Miley Cyrus in the audience after the music awards in her sexualized twerking dance with this girl's face superimposed as Miley; and the photo of a Precious Moment's face with the big eyes with teardrops and her face superimposed.

My husband and I were called in to the school because this act of superimposing a face using a meme generator was classified as cyberbullying. My son received the photo from a friend and shared the photo with another friend and posted them on the Web where other classmates could see them. The boys thought it was funny, and the girl was highly embarrassed that the boys took it that far. My son immediately apologized and took the pictures down the same day. That evening, however, the girl had contacted the principal and sent him a copy of the meme. She confided to the principal that she was shocked that they had embarrassed her. The principal labeled the incident as cyberbullying and treated the perpetrator with zero tolerance.

After viewing the pictures and consulting the administrative team, the principal was convinced that the boys were attacking the girl's physical appearance with the Precious Moment's meme. In my opinion, however, I thought that if the boys wanted to be cruel and mean, they would have created a 300-pound, ugly meme. Because the school agreed that this incident was horrible and egregious, they identified the following as punishment: suspension from school for a day, attending an upcoming Town Hall Community forum to explain what happened and apologize publicly for the harm that he had created, step down for a month from a leadership position in a school club, and write a cyberbullying policy for the school. Since my son had been involved in a sexist and rude act, I was very supportive of everything except the idea that a senior should be writing a legal document on cyberbullying. On the other hand, if they wanted him to research cyberbullying *and write an essay on various incidents, I would be supportive of that. This finally ended our cyberbullying nightmare.*

A month after this incident, my son, who was a senior, was pulled in to the principal's office after he crossed the street to go to a coffee shop. The principal mentioned that this was his second strike, referencing the cyberbullying as strike one, and stated that these incidents would appear on his permanent record. My son burst into tears fearing that he was not going to be accepted to college. He was beside himself. He never imagined that a dash across the street to a coffee shop would render him ineligible for college and that the high school would follow up and send discipline reports to the colleges where my son had applied. At the time, my son thought the high school was derailing his college aspirations.

My son made an appointment to see the counselor, and when he met with her, he questioned some information that he was told and quickly figured out that the principal had tried to be stern and use some coercion but that my son would not have his college aspirations detoured by the cyberbullying incident or his dash to the coffee shop. This was resolved, and my son was accepted to college.

POINTS FOR PARENTS

Parents often underestimate the extent to which their children engage in risky online activities. Parents who are overly relaxed or have a permissive parenting style, those who have difficulty communicating about online risks, and those who allow for private computing space are factors that contribute to risky online behaviors (Byrne et al. 2014). Most parents—including the one in this case—do not ever suspect that their child can or would ever be involved in any form of cyberbullying. They rely on the notion that their child is a good kid and has never been in trouble. "Meme" is an app that allows one to create a character that others can "like." The others can create their own version of the character with captions that say anything. There are no limits or oversight to their creativity, so literally anything can be said by anyone—regardless of whether they know the person.

The fact of the matter is that unless parents closely monitor their child's activity, they have no idea what their child is really doing online. There are new apps created on a regular basis. For example, "Yik Yack" is an app that is an anonymous social wall for anything and everything, and it is very popular among young people. Stories can be shared and voted on by others, and this can be done anonymously within a specific geographical area.

Young people are constantly looking for ways to find a private forum where they can do whatever they want. For the most part, students know their parents lack the knowledge or skills to keep up with the latest trends (Norton Online Family Report, 2010). Research shows that 62 percent of children report that they had a negative experience, while only 45 percent of parents believe it happens. Furthermore, there is a discrepancy between what parents think is happening and what youth are experiencing.

From our own personal experiences of talking with parents, we would guess that the percentage of parents who trust that their child is not engaging in any form of cyberbullying is actually much higher. In the words of the parent who told us this story, "Don't assume that the mean girl incident will not happen to boys and that mostly girls are involved in cyberbullying. Be knowledgeable of pictures and meme generators and the possibility that students may create humor that may turn into cyberbullying. Boys are more into meme generators (insulting or rude images that go viral and make fun of a person) or *reddit.com* (website with horrible misogynistic, racist, sweet, and benign material, along with "you ask me anything" dialogue with famous persons) and other online humor that is readily available. Parents and others may forget that boys have a juvenile type of toilet humor that may be funny until it is posted on a Facebook page or sent as a text message to an entire class."

SUGGESTIONS FOR ACTION

- Keep up with the latest trends. Regularly check Google and iTunes for the latest apps for kids of all ages. In addition, talk to other parents and listen to what their children are using for apps and websites. Sit down with your children and ask them to share the latest technology on the Web and on a phone, tablet, and other technology-related devices. Don't be surprised that they might tell you more than you might want to know. This is an excellent time to bond with your children. Set up a weekly time to sit down and share any concerns of the past week or the upcoming week.
- Check out which apps your child has on his or her cell phone, and try them out for yourself. If you are concerned, it is time for closer monitoring and a discussion about how it is being used.
- If your child is accused of cyberbullying in any way, listen to the facts before making a judgment. Keep in mind that you should be open-minded, regardless of the character of the target.

4. Physical Bullying

Case Study: I Am Jack!

Type of Bullying: Physical, name calling, exclusion, rumors

Age of Onset/Gender of Target: Twelve years old, male

How Long Did the Bullying Last? Two years

Hot Spots: School bus, recess, lunchroom

Did You Tell? If So, Whom? I was embarrassed and didn't tell anyone.

I am a mother totally committed to my children, a son and daughter; my children mean everything to me. However, I am an adult, and I get very caught up and occupied with adult responsibilities such as work, friends, extended family, hobbies, etc. Even if you love children and they know that you are there for them, they often do not have the experience to made decisions that are the best for them. At times, my son would ask me something, and I would say, "Later, Jack. I am busy." When one of his friend's parents called and said that his son could not play with Jack, I coincidently found out that my fourteen-year-old son was being bullied at school. My son was being targeted and called names. I learned that he had been isolated, pushed, and shoved until he felt alone in his school.

When I discovered this, I raced home as fast as I could to wait for my son to come home from school. When he came home, we talked and I found out that he had been bullied since he was twelve years old. He literally broke down in front of me. We both cried at the same time. At that moment, I actually thought I was going to die of pain. My son had gone to school every day for two years fearful for his life. Even though bullying is all about violence, my son had not told anyone, not even me because he said that didn't know how to tell me. Because he knows how hard I work, he felt that he didn't want to cause me any added stress. He was being brave and thought that he could deal with it by himself. Bottom line: he didn't tell me.

The bullying started one day when Jack made a stupid joke that went too far. He was just a twelve-year-old kid at the time. The joke was made to the wrong person at the wrong time. The other student was annoyed and started calling Jack names such as geek head. My son tried to do what he thought was the right thing and laughed at the name calling even though it was hurtful. The names persisted, yet my son continued to ignore the name calling. Subsequently, more people joined in.

Jack then tried to tell a teacher. The teacher was too busy, and my son shut down and told no one. More children joined in and sided against Jack. Both the boy and girl friends that he grew up with had turned against him and joined in with the majority. Jack was in danger because some kids went too far with their aggressiveness by spreading vicious rumors. Things escalated, and students who had never known Jack were influenced by the rumors they heard. The aggressors doing the name calling and rumor spreading thought all of this was hilarious. To this day, I do not know how Jack had the courage to continue in school under such harassment and intimidation.

Looking back, I saw behaviors that Jack was exhibiting that I should have noticed. The signs were in front of me, but I was oblivious to them at the time. Because of the bullying, my son started to develop tactics to survive at school. He tried to stay home more and be next to me. Jack tried to avoid the hot spots—such as before school, at recess, at lunchtime, or on the school bus—where bullying would occur. Since he knew that the most dangerous times at school were when adults and parents were not present or actively supervising students, Jack decided to come late to school. He felt safer being yelled at by a teacher than arriving early, when students could call him names and continually taunt him. Jack would then get detention and subsequently would lose a privilege like recess, eating with his friends, or riding the bus. This was exactly Jack's goal.

In school Jack would race as fast as he could to get into the bathroom to go behind the toilet to hide in order to avoid those kids. He found a spot to go to every day in school where he felt safe: the library. I thought at the time that my son was a genius because he was checking out books and describing the library and how he was fascinated with the different book titles. Little did I know that he was hiding himself in the library to protect himself from the constant humiliation of name calling, pushing, and the other cruel actions of his own peers.

The students who were bullying Jack were good students who reacted to a joke that had no malicious intent but was meant to be humorous. As this continued, the aggressors forgot that Jack was a decent kid who liked to tell jokes, get attention, and play football. What started out as a game turned into a nightmare for him. One day, they chased my son with a baseball bat and hit him. Again, it was not malicious, but it was all in the name of a game or playing around. Jack started developing psychosomatic illnesses and missing many school days. After missing school, Jack would be bullied more when he came back to school. He could not focus on schoolwork and would fail classes and get into trouble. Jack did not believe in himself. He was in a terrible place.

Once the silence was broken, I stood beside my son and became his protector and advocate. I went to the school and made the biggest scene. Jack couldn't be all that he could be because he was so frightened. When the school investigated the situation, they defended my son. I was so upset that I wanted to take my son out of school. One teacher truly changed the course of events and helped my son to turn around. He asked Jack if he would stay at the school a little longer and would assist him to make the school a safer place. Every morning, my son was asked to check in with this teacher when he arrived at school.

This teacher became my child's confidant and had his back. After the teachers talked with other students, most admitted that they were ashamed and really did not want to hurt Jack. The ringleaders did receive consequences for how they mistreated Jack. From that point on, they were closely monitored. After that, they were pulled off the playground whenever they used any type of aggression against others. Eventually, these students were less aggressive and began to show more empathy for others. Perhaps they discovered other ways to lead instead of by misusing their leadership powers to be hurtful to others.

Teachers have a grave responsibility to protect their students, but, at the same time, they have daily duties, obligations, and pressures to help children perform well academically. Because bullying is usually secretive and takes time to resolve, teachers may not notice the differences in behavior among kids who are involved in horseplay, fighting, or power-based bullying.

When a student is late to class, teachers may not necessarily be aware of a greater problem—being late for school may be just the tip of the iceberg. The teachers did not know that my son was avoiding school because he didn't feel safe. The bullying still continued but became less and less frequent when he had a person in the school whom he trusted and when, at the same time, the school was diligent in supervising areas where the bullying behavior was most likely to occur.

Our immediate family members all supported Jack. He became involved in activities outside of school. Jack started to believe in himself again. In the end, he won against bullying. Today my son is an amazing young man. If he saw someone in trouble, he would not just ignore it, and he has enormous compassion for others; at the same time, he knows how to stand up for himself. At the end, Jack loved his school and thought of it as a safe place.

POINTS FOR PARENTS

Busy parents can miss cues from their child—avoiding school, going in late, or coming home late can all be signs of a greater issue than may not be very apparent. In this case study, once the cues were pointed out to her, the mother readily recognized that she had not noticed changes in her son's behavior. Since these changes happened over time, it is understandable that they would go on unnoticed. Teens are often depicted as lazy, needing a lot of sleep, moody, and disliking school. So when a child is growing into adolescence, it is understandable that a parent would misinterpret behavioral changes. While it is easy to attribute these changes to adolescence, parents need to sharpen their observations and keep the lines of communication open in any way possible to get a sense of any issues underlying the changes in behavior. Many parents do not believe that their child can be the target of bullying. They believe that if their child has friends, there will not be any problems; however, what they do not realize is that children with friends can be targeted (Sawyer et al. 2011).

It is common for kids, particularly boys, not to talk about their concerns, especially when they have been targeted in school. The mother in the story said she was busy—but most of us are. The question is, do we know our child's style when it comes to conversation? It is possible that her son was deliberately choosing times when she was obviously not going to have the time to discuss his issues.

In her account, the mother said she "went to the school and made the biggest scene." For many reasons, the news that your child has been targeted for such a long time is certainly devastating and can fill a parent with rage. There is an expectation that the school will protect our children, and we all want to think of our children as perfect and definitely immune from being ridiculed, humiliated, and physically attacked by peers. So a furious response is practically instinctual because you want to protect your child.

Researchers have identified three stages of parent involvement in bullying behavior. The first is discovery, whereby—for any number of reasons—the parent becomes aware of a problem. Sometimes they recognize the early signs, but most of the time they find out through happenstance or when the problem has spun out of control. The second is the reporting stage, when the parent approaches the school with the issue. At this point, parents need to know whom to talk to about the issue, what will be done to rectify the issue, and what will be done for prevention. The third stage is the aftermath. This includes not only follow-up with those involved but also a general plan to prevent bullying behavior for everyone (Brown et al. 2013). To ensure a positive interaction, it is important to approach the reporting stage with the school in a way that will encourage collaboration on a common goal. After all, you are both invested in protecting kids from mean, hurtful, intentional behavior when students are unable to protect themselves.

One of the positive things about this story is that the parent immediately took charge and worked on positive ways to solve the problem. At no time did the parent suggest that the child simply fight back. Students who fight back are more likely to be targeted in the future. In addition, they are more likely to be aggressive in these "bully-victim relationships." In other words, they have been victimized but at the same time become aggressors. This only further complicates a problem rather than solving it (Giesbrecht et al. 2011).

Bullying behavior, including physical acts, can occur under the radar and be undetected by teachers. Sadly, research shows that bullying can be physical and nonphysical, with increasing intensity over time impacting the targets, the bullies, or the bystanders (Crapanzano et al. 2010). Most importantly, the impact of long-term victimization on the one being targeted can cause serious issues, as is demonstrated in this story (Storch et al. 2011). The intervention of the parent and the support of one particular teacher made all the difference for this young man.

SUGGESTIONS FOR ACTION

- Talk to your child on a regular basis, or at least leave time for your child to bring up any issues. We are not necessarily talking about having a specific time to talk—that would be like trying to force a flower to bloom. You have to give children an opportunity to talk on a regular basis, when they are free from distractions. Having dinner together is a good place to start, but that cannot be the only opportunity favorable to conversation. For instance, spending time in the car on the way to school or an event can work well. In a car you are isolated and free from distractions; no one can interrupt you. Of course, you will have to turn off the electronics and the radio!

  Some boys (and girls) talk in bits and pieces about things that are on their mind. One mother told us that her teenage son would walk into the kitchen and, while he was grabbing something from the refrigerator, say something that was on his mind and walk out of the kitchen. If she followed him down the hall to ask him a follow-up question, he would shrug it off and say "no big deal," and that was the end of it. But she learned that if she just waited, he would reappear looking for something else in the kitchen and talk a bit more. She learned that some kids have to talk on their own terms.

- Approach the school with the intentions of working with the school to solve the problem. Also, immediately work with the school to develop a safety plan for your child. This means that you have to figure out the areas and times when the child will be most vulnerable and then come up with a strategy to reduce risk. This may mean temporarily driving the child to school until the issue has been addressed or having additional supervision in areas defined as hot spots within the school.

- Identify a person or persons within the school whom the child feels comfortable talking to if he or she has the need. However, the issue goes further than that since the responsibility for the safety of a student falls on the adults. Therefore, those who are identified to support the student need to check in with the student to see how things are going and report back to the parent. This is extremely important in order to prevent retaliation and to reestablish a level of comfort and security for the student.

Case Study: Girl Gang

Type of Bullying: Physical, verbal, name calling, intimidation, assault, pushing, taunting, embarrassment
Age of Onset/Gender of Target: Junior high, female
How Long Did the Bullying Last? Through high school
Hot Spots: Neighborhood, hallways, bathrooms, and lockers
Did You Tell? If So, Whom? I told the school administration and law enforcement. They suggested avoiding places where I might be attacked.

When I was in seventh grade, I moved from an elementary setting to a junior high building. My dad was a fire fighter, and my mom was a stay-at-home mother. I had a best friend across the street with whom I spent all of my waking hours. We did everything together and were inseparable. At Thanksgiving, after my friend had a traumatic incident that shook the foundation of her family (her father had an affair and left the family), she told me that we could not hang out anymore. It was strange, and I was confused. She befriended a girl that lived around the corner. This girl had a questionable reputation and was into many high-risk behaviors. It seemed my friend had decided to associate exclusively with that girl and her rough friends. From my perspective as a twelve-year-old who did everything she was told, my old friend was moving to the "dark side."

It seemed to me that my friend and this new gang of girls had only one goal: making life miserable for other girls they randomly chose to target. They used physical and verbal bullying techniques and at times even asked boys to join in and participate in intimidation, taunts, and assaults on innocent targets. For example, one of the boys might stop a girl walking up the stairs and pretend to perform a sexual act in front of the girl just to get a shocked reaction from her and laughter from the gang of girls.

Any time they saw me, they would push me into the lockers, take my things, or knock my books on the floor. Much to my humiliation, this continued on a regular basis. Things escalated outside the school. The gang threw rocks through my bedroom window. My former best friend knew where my bed was positioned, and rocks would actually land on my bed. The gang would wait for me after school and follow me home, taunting and physically pushing me around. It was very intimidating and humiliating. I'm not sure if any of the adults knew about this—I just knew I was too scared to talk about this to anyone.

Finally, one of my classmates—a boy—started walking with me because this was the only way that I would not be tormented and tortured. I put up with these repeated, intentional, power-based behaviors for seventh and eighth grade and reached the point at which I thought I would kill myself. When my parents learned of this and of my desperation, they elected to send me to private school. However, I was still living in the neighborhood while attending private school. The summers were particularly difficult because when I did something as ordinary as going down the street to visit a neighbor, I would be called every name you could imagine. Until I graduated and went away to college, there wasn't one day when I left my home that someone didn't yell "slut" or "you're a bitch" at me out of their window. My parents reported these instances to the police, but the police told us to just avoid the trouble. The bullying and harassment finally ended when I left home to attend college. The last I heard, my friend, who was involved with that gang, ran away from home and became involved in an abusive relationship.

POINTS FOR PARENTS

With an emerging self-image, young adolescents are learning how to relate to their peers and develop relationships. At the same time, they are growing physically and their fluctuating hormones are impacting their emotions. Middle school can be a time of profound social and emotional development. Young people are learning how to understand their bodies, peer relationships, and their own world. It is a difficult time for them, to say the least.

The girls in this story clearly influenced their peers to exclude this student. The power of the social group clearly shaped the mean and hurtful behavior. As this happened, others joined in without having any apparent reason other than that they were following the leaders. These "leaders" were controlling their class through negative behavior. Peer contagion influences and escalates aggression (Dishion et al. 2011). The fear generated by that group dominated the entire climate. It was very unlikely that anyone would have been able to stand up to those girls to help the target without putting himself or herself in a vulnerable position. In other words, the group would very possibly turn on them.

Those who supported the leaders in the aggressive behavior would, over time, be likely to be aggressive on their own. Adolescents who associate with exceedingly aggressive peers tend to become more aggressive themselves over time (Marks et al. 2011). Aggressive behavior becomes part of their accepted behavior patterns and dominates how they interact with one another. This contributes to a hostile climate that can certainly be frightening and intimidating for other students. It also carries over to other arenas, such as the neighborhood, athletic fields, or other out-of-school activities.

Those who bully on a regular basis over a long period of time are more likely to engage in other more serious antisocial behaviors. Physical bullying in particular is more of a predictor of future delinquency and aggressive and violent behaviors (Bender et al. 2011). Stories like this are evidence that bullying behavior must be prevented. Bullying will continue and escalate when there is no intervention. The strategies used by the family—removing the girl from school and placing her in private school—were helpful in relieving the situation; however, the girl still lived in the neighborhood and had to live with the name calling and constant harassment right on the street where she lived.

By attending a school where she could be away from these aggressors, she was able to be successful in school. Every victimized student needs a place where he or she can be successful and have personal relationships with their peers. It helps them to grow socially and build their self-confidence, particularly when they are being mistreated in other aspects of their lives.

The real hero and example for us to consider in this story is the boy who walked her home. When he was with her, all the mean girls left her alone. He took it upon himself to stand up for her and defend her in the face of a very powerful social group. Bystanders are essential in influencing bullying behavior. They can, as with the girls in the group, also support the behavior. In doing so, they encourage it to continue.

On the other hand, the boy who walked that girl home was able to prevent the cruel behavior at least when he was with her. It takes a great deal of courage for an individual to stand up to a group under those circumstances, and we have to acknowledge that not every student has that kind of courage. However, we have to encourage that response from everyone. The research is clear—

bystanders are the key to stopping bullying behavior. Bystanders can and do influence the outcomes, either by intensifying the bullying by participating or stopping it by supporting the target (Salmivalli et al. 2011).

SUGGESTIONS FOR ACTION

- According to this story, by the time the parents learned of this girl's plight, the situation was very serious. Moving her to another school where she could safely learn was a reasonable alternative. Certainly, before parents make that decision, there are other alternatives, beginning with talking to and working with the school to protect and support the student.

- When one child dominates the bullying behavior, it is important to talk to your child about his or her feelings regarding that person. You want to help the child see how that person is really the problem, and the fact that your child is being targeted does not mean that he or she is inferior in any way. In other words, the problem is with the aggressor, not the target.

- When bullying spills out into the neighborhood, the home environment becomes uncomfortable and even hostile. A report to the police when the issue becomes physical is a good strategy but often there is little or no evidence for follow-through. However, reporting is crucial, even if all you do is create a record of the problem.

- The role of bystander is one that needs attention. The boy who walked her home is a wonderful example of how a bystander can make a difference. You can praise this student and even find ways to reward the behavior. Also, as a parent, look for ways to point out how the actions of one person can make such a difference for someone else. It takes courage to step up and speak up for a friend, and while you must be aware of that, you can still reinforce the message of empathy for others. By doing so, you are helping your child realize the importance of kindness and compassion. The goal, through all this bullying and victimization, is raising a child who can not only identify bullying behavior but also have the courage to be a proactive bystander.

Case Study: Parents Jump into Action

Type of Bullying: Physical
Age of Onset/Gender of Target: Near the end of eighth grade, male
How Long Did the Bullying Last? Through high school
Hot Spots: In the classroom when the teacher is present, hallway, after school, at home
Did You Tell? If So, Whom? He did not tell until he was caught smoking marijuana.

My husband and I have been married for more than twenty years. Our son attended middle and high school in a small town in a relatively affluent bedroom community close to a large metropolitan city. We were unaware that our son had been bullied, but we discovered later on that he had been bullied starting in eighth grade.

The first time the issue of bullying was introduced to us was when our son was sixteen, a junior in high school. The school called and asked if my husband and I would come in immediately for a conference with our son. When we arrived at the school that morning, both the principal and assistant principal informed us that our son had arrived late to school that morning and was stoned from smoking marijuana. This was shocking to us because we had no inkling that he was a pot smoker. He had never gotten into trouble, except for an occasional tardy day. This incident was a definite red flag that demonstrated to us that something more serious was troubling our son. The assistant principal had called him in to his office because when he arrived at school, he parked and locked his truck but forgot to turn the engine off. At that point, the staff noticed his unusual demeanor and questioned whether he might be under the influence of some medication or perhaps drugs.

The administration suspended him for three days, but at that time bullying was never mentioned. When we got home, we confronted our son and asked him what was going on. At first, he was reluctant to tell us anything. But hours later, he asked to talk with both of us. He stated that two students were constantly harassing him. They were twin boys who were in his grade, one of whom was the primary henchman.

During that conversation, it was clear that it was extremely difficult for our son to talk about what had been happening to him. He said that he did not feel confident about expressing himself to the principal because he felt ashamed that he couldn't stand up for himself. Thinking back, it took him four years to admit to us, his parents, that he was being bullied. This might have continued if it weren't for him being caught stoned from smoking marijuana.

At that time, we did not understand bullying behavior and, more importantly, that it could possibly happen to our son. He described being ridiculed and embarrassed on a regular basis. In addition, he told us that he had been hit, pushed, punched, and stabbed with a pen in his bicep. These incidents were occurring in the classroom when the teacher was not looking, in the hallways and after school. He mentioned that one of the twins was in many of his classes. I promised him at the time that I would handle this.

My husband and I, without our son present, asked for a meeting with the administration and grade counselor. We shared with the group that our son was being bullied by some of his peers. The main aggressors were twin boys and some of their friends in his grade. I wanted these aggressors out of his classes. The school stated that it could not do that at that time. I then suggested that since our son had a part-time job at an automotive store, I wanted him to be placed in a work-study program, something the school had never offered. I passionately demanded that our son would take only courses required for graduation and that for the remainder of his junior and senior years, he would attend school only in the morning.

The school finally adjusted our son's schedule after we persisted and persisted, and for a year and a half, he was in work-study, only attending school in the mornings. The school went along with our suggestion because we gave the school a choice: to either place our son in a work-study program or to pay private school tuition for him to enroll in a school specializing in students with learning disabilities (our son was labeled with a mild learning disability at the time). Our state has a provision that if school systems cannot offer an appropriate education, they must pay for one if requested. Through all of the negotiations, the school continued to deny that there had been any bullying because the security cameras had caught none of the instances of bullying behavior.

The bullying continued but happened less frequently. The twins and our son still had contact in the halls. During senior year, I noticed another change in our son's behavior. He was uncommunicative and became irritable and depressed. I contacted the school and asked for a conference and discovered that my son had again been scheduled in a class with one of the twins.

Even with my insistence, the school still refused to move the student. The counselor set up a meeting with the teacher, and we told him what had happened in the past. In the meeting, we were surprised to learn that the teacher and counselor both had noticed the interaction between my son and one of the twins, but because our son was laughing, they dismissed the possibility of any intimidation, coercion, or bullying behavior. At our insistence, they did increase adult supervision in the hot spots.

During the last semester of his senior year and because there was more active teacher supervision, there were no further inci-

dents. In the summer, however, the bullying took a different slant. Fruit (bananas, oranges, apples) was thrown at our house and mailbox. We reported this to the police, but the parents denied that their sons were involved and had an alibi for the time of each incident. The police said that their hands were tied because nothing could be proved.

The twins and their henchmen received no punishment from either the school system or the police. Our son completed his education, left the school system unscathed, and went on to college and graduated. The twins went to college also, but before the end of their freshman year, they were kicked out of school because of behavioral issues.

Because we would not give up and insisted on working with the school, we were able to protect our son. I think we were successful because we were proactive and demanded our son's safety at school. We leveraged the school by threatening an out-of-district placement if these issues could not be resolved. We continued with the consistent message to the administration that our son had a right to his education without being intimidated, coerced, or bullied.

POINTS FOR PARENTS

When confronted with a discipline issue, it is important to remain open to what the school is reporting. In other words, do not get defensive. It is so very easy to say, "My child would never do that," and argue with the school. It is hard to hear that your child is in some sort of trouble that requires a school suspension, particularly when the student has never been in trouble before that point. Even though the evidence was clear, these parents were not defensive, but they were keen enough to ask if this incident (smoking marijuana) was a symptom of a more serious issue.

However, since there is much confusion about the definition of bullying behavior, these parents—like most parents—did not know enough to identify bullying behavior or how to respond. Furthermore, without being told by the child who may be experiencing this aggressive behavior, it is unlikely that the parents would know.

When they asked the child if anything was bothering him, he was initially not up front with them about what was going on. Although they were very tempted to demand an explanation, they waited for him to speak up. The parents held back to give him some time to come forward on his own. In addition, they validated his feelings and were supportive in their responses to him. This is crucial, as responses that are not supportive can be harmful and can further isolate the child (Sawyer et al. 2011). This boy did open up to his parents on the same day, but that may not happen with most students. When students are talking about their problems with an adult, for the most part they are looking for help with the solution. They need to know you are listening and will support them; as this parent said, "I'll take care of this." While it is very important to teach all students to learn how to speak up for themselves so they can handle aggression, not only as students but for the rest of their lives, we must acknowledge that when we are talking about bullying behavior—repeated, intentional, mean behavior with an imbalance of power—we are talking about victimization. When someone is in that position, outside intervention is necessary to stop the behavior, prevent it from spreading, and protect the one who is victimized.

Most importantly, the parents recognized that bullying is part of a larger problem that would not necessarily stop when the aggressor was removed from their son's class. When they noticed signs of stress in their son after they had worked with the school to create a distance between their son and the aggressors, they immediately followed up and addressed the issue with the school.

These parents recognized that their child—and, for that matter, all children—has the right to feel safe in school. That right is universal for all children, and these parents were determined to make it apply to their son's experience in school. While it is important to trust the school staff, it is also important to be vigilant and to follow up with the school.

SUGGESTIONS FOR ACTION

- When called to the school because of a disciplinary issue with your child, first be certain the child is okay. In this case, the child was high on marijuana; in other instances, there could be physical injuries if there was a fight. This needs to be tended to first. Once you have determined there is no physical danger, listen to the school representatives to gather information. You will need to ask for all the details, including who was involved or discovered the problem, who else was present when the incident happened, and when and where it occurred. It is also a good idea to ask school staff if they have any idea why it happened and if they had any inclination that your child was at risk. This is important because the school—teachers and counselors who interact with your child on a regular basis—often can notice changes in behavior. This can include incomplete assignments, lack of participation in class, or a change in demeanor—perhaps sadness or anger and refusal to cooperate in activities.

- Feel free to take notes during the meeting with the school. It will help you to recall what they said and, more importantly, what they plan to do.

- Ask for a follow-up meeting. This will give you an opportunity to talk to your child to help you understand the circumstances and any underlying causes for the behavior.

- Talk to your child or—even better—listen to your child. This means giving the child an opportunity to explain himself or herself. This means you have to listen without judgment and ask questions that require more than a yes or no answer. These open-ended questions will help you get more of the background information.

- Follow up with the school. It is important to follow up with not only the administration but with the classroom teachers as well. Think of it as a team, with you as the coach—the one who coordinates all that happens in school. It sends a message that you are serious and expecting a safe environment for your child.

- Think of what you feel is the best solution for the problem, and present it to the school. Know what you're going to ask for. In this story, the parents wanted the aggressors out of the class. They demanded it and got it. They also suggested the work-study program and minimal classes to meet the graduation requirements. Even though it had not been done before, the school agreed to have this student do a work-study program at the request of the parents.

- When dealing with the police, you need to have facts, so you will need to be prepared with the history of these events, including dates, times, and other basic information. It is not uncommon for the police to be unable to intervene, as was the case in this situation. However, that should not deter you from involving the police. They keep records of all complaints, so by filing a report, you are establishing a pattern that may be helpful in the future should the situation escalate.

Case Study: Moving from Being a Target to Aggressor and, Finally, an Upstander

Type of Bullying: Name calling, physical, throwing food, threatening
Age of Onset/Gender of Target: Target: second grade, Aggressor: fifth through sixth grade, Upstander: tenth grade; male
How Long Did the Bullying Last? Target: one year, Aggressor: two years, Upstander: to present
Hot Spots: cafeteria, playground, recess, physical education, hallway, classroom
Did You Tell? If So, Whom? I did not tell because I handle my own business.

When I was younger, my family moved around often. We relocated to a large metropolitan area near the ocean. I attended one school in kindergarten and first grade, then moved across town and enrolled in another elementary school in second grade. At the new school, I found an extremely tight-knit, cliquey group of parents and children. It was hard fitting in when these families had been together since their children were in daycare.

In second grade, I was immediately targeted by a group of male students who later admitted that I looked like a portly student whom they used to make fun of regularly. They called me names and verbally taunted me in the classroom, threw food at me in the cafeteria, and threatened to beat me up after school. One specific day, a group of students followed me back to my classroom. They started throwing peanuts and crackers at me. Then suddenly, one boy who had been a spectator in the past came up from behind and grabbed my backpack and pulled me backwards, making me fall. I finally had enough and stood up and popped him in the head with my thermos. Finally, when I retaliated and stood up to the taunting of this group of boys, it set a precedent and they never picked on me again in elementary school. From then on, I do not remember ever being bullied again.

Looking back on my middle school years, I find myself moving from being victimized into being a bully. I had a next-door neighbor and another friend who lived down the street from me who were inseparable starting in fifth and sixth grades. We were close comrades. Another student in our class, Maxim, was odd looking, a little different, and had very few friends. My two cohorts were exceptionally cruel to him on a regular and daily basis. I don't know why and, to this day, can't figure it out. However, at times I would join in and hide his food, trip him when he was in the halls, and hide his backpack. One time, we even put dead flies in Maxim's hair. We were having a great time without considering in any way what we were doing to Maxim. This mostly happened when we were on the playground and during recess. One day, I remember vividly that I went too far, and just because I knew I could get away with it, I walked up and slammed Maxim's head against his desk as hard as I could. No one reported it. I felt bad for him that day, and somewhere deep inside of me, I knew it was wrong.

Adults intervened a few times, but not very often, because when our group taunted other students we did it on the sly. The adults weren't around or weren't looking so we got away with our actions. I do remember the time at the end of sixth grade when the principal had a conference with my two friends and their parents and teachers. However, they excluded me from the meeting, thank goodness. For two years I did bully Maxim, but I was not the main instigator—I was a follower. Most of the time I acted spontaneously and didn't put much thought into what I was doing because I was interested in keeping up with my friends. Finally, leaving the elementary setting and going to junior high school, I became so involved in sports that my attention moved away from those kids. I was busy, so my close friends became my next-door neighbor and the kids on my team.

I played football from seventh through ninth grades. When I entered high school, I continued to be active in sports. One day, when I was in my physical education class, I observed a new student who had just transferred in. He was in my same sophomore class, yet he was a year older. He was odd looking, overweight, not athletic, and Jewish. Another student in our class, Mark, who was in my new circle of friends, was exceptionally cruel to him on a regular basis— tripping him at the end of a mile run and calling him "Hebe" or "Jew" because of his heritage. One day in class, when he was using religious taunts against this student, I had enough of it. I yelled out to Mark that he was a loser and told him to leave this new student alone. From that point forward, Mark left the kid alone and all the kids in our group were nicer to him. As for Mark, he drifted away from the group and didn't hang with us much more after that day.

POINTS FOR PARENTS

This is a very interesting story, as one student moves from victim to one who bullies others to one who is a proactive bystander— not altogether uncommon as we have found when gathering these stories. Bullying behavior is about the misuse of power, and it is a learned behavior. This example certainly shows how boys view bullying, especially the view of the aggressor and his frame of mind. Those who bully others tend to choose times when they have the best opportunity to demonstrate their power over their target. It gives them the maximum opportunity for gaining peer approval and prestige (Salmivalli et al. 2011). That is why bullying behavior happens most often in groups of two or three, as was the case in this story.

A common response to bullying is to suggest that fighting back is the answer. That is what this boy tells us he did in the story. However, research shows that students who fight back are 2.6 times more likely than passive students to be targeted in the future

(Lodge et al. 2007). Furthermore, students who fight back are at a greater risk of perpetuating the bully-victim cycle. In other words, a student who fights back is more likely to be aggressive toward others who may be easily targeted.

In this case, the student learned that bullying would make him powerful and win him recognition and popularity from his peers. Since his friends were mean to others, he took on their behavior and, in his own words, "Most of the time I acted spontaneously and didn't put much thought into what I was doing. I was more interested in keeping up with my friends."

We are hoping that all students will be able to defend themselves by using many different strategies. It is very important that students know that we support them as they explore various alternatives to handle aggressive peers and that these alternatives are appropriate, socially acceptable, and safe.

Consider the uniform definition of bullying as set by the Centers for Disease Control (CDC) in 2014: "**Definition of Bullying Among Youths:** Bullying is any **unwanted aggressive behavior(s)** by another youth or group of youths who are not siblings or current dating partners that involves an **observed or perceived power imbalance and is repeated multiple times or is highly likely to be repeated**. Bullying may inflict harm or distress on the targeted youth, including physical, psychological, social, or educational **harm**."

This definition clearly discusses the observed or perceived power imbalance, which is key to these stories and all other stories of being targeted, fighting back, and being able to stop the bullying (take-out behavior). When victims are able to fight back, they are not being victimized; they are responding by defending themselves. The question is whether this is really bullying behavior. According to the CDC's definition, it is not. According to this definition, it was a fight between two students that settled a problem.

We are not suggesting, in any way, that the solution to aggression is more aggression. Rather, we are saying that aggression can only stop when there is a balance of power. By definition then, this story as described is a fight betwcen two students. The victim reached a point at which he had to stop the aggressor, and he did so by fighting. When this occurred, the aggressor stopped targeting the victim.

In cases where there is a clear imbalance of power and the target fights back, the targeted student is vulnerable to more aggression. Just think of all the ways in today's world that a student can be victimized. Then add the Internet and electronic aggression, and it is clear that we need to teach young people to be problem solvers.

This story is about group influence and how one person can influence his or her environment. Later in the story, when the boy was involved with his neighborhood friends, he adopted their tactics for being mean and hurtful to others. He even participated in the aggression. However, it is interesting to note that he did have a sense that what he was doing was wrong and continued because, in his own words, no one stopped it. Young people do look to us, as adults, to be responsible for creating a safe environment for everyone. The response, "No one did anything," is, in a sense, giving tacit approval to the aggressive behavior. Teachers not actively supervising or reacting to aggressive acts contribute to a climate in which no one seems to care about how students treat each other.

Finally, this student tells us that he became a defender when he was in high school. He became a powerful member of the team, so when he spoke, the others responded to him. He was able to be verbally forceful to protect the targeted student. Bystanders have a powerful influence on their peers. The student telling his story has developed empathy for the target. In his own words, he's had enough. The empathy he developed as he got older, perhaps from being a target or witnessing others being targeted, is driving him to intercede when he sees the new student as the focus of the cruel and racist behavior. His speaking up in the boy's defense stops the bullying and prevents it from escalating.

SUGGESTIONS FOR ACTION

- When moving to a new place or introducing your child into a new setting, it is important to set up a situation in which the child can make at least one friend. That can mean inviting someone in the neighborhood for a playdate or having your child participate in some group activity such as swimming, soccer, or scouting. You want to give the child an opportunity to have a connection to one or more of his or her peers so he or she will not feel uncomfortable and isolated from the group. Children who have friends are less likely to be bullied. Children who are loners are more at risk for being targets of bullying.
- If you think your child has not made any friends, look for opportunities to give them experiences with their peers. Talk about your concerns with the teacher, and ask for help to support your child.
- If your child is being victimized, ask, "What do you think the person wants? Why do you think he is doing that?" The answer is that the aggressor is getting something that he or she wants. Parents need to empower the target so that he or she does not have to engage in the encounter, thereby developing a pattern of behavior such as giving away a toy, crying, or screaming back. Stay away from labeling the behavior. Let the child label his or her own behavior and the behavior of the aggressor. This gives the child power and more responsibility for how he or she will respond in the future. When the child does not yell back or sulk, the child gains power. The goal is for the child not to give power away when responding to an aggressor's attacks.

- If you think your child is aggressive and may be targeting others, you might consider a nonblaming approach. Talk to your child in a way that is nonjudgmental, and take the opportunity to use a problem-solving approach. In other words, ask questions, but do not label the behavior. The ultimate goal is for the child to evaluate how his or her actions played a part in the incident. Remember, when we tell rather than listen, the child's thinking and point of view are not included in the process. When the aggressor labels his or her own behavior, he or she is more likely to own it. Ask, "What are you doing? What do you want from what you are doing?" He or she may respond that he or she wants a toy or to be in charge. Then ask how he or she wants to be in charge, and brainstorm different ways to be in charge without using aggression and coercion.

- When your child is a proactive bystander, when he or she helps someone being targeted, it is important to praise these efforts. As a parent, you want to not only encourage empathy but to also reward those gestures that are kind, helpful, and prosocial. You should do more than talk to your child—you have to model the behavior you expect of him or her. Kindness is something that is modeled and, when practiced, leads to empathy and compassion.

Case Study: Generational Bullying

Type of Bullying: Physical, emotional, name calling
Age of Onset/Gender of Target: Elementary grades
How Long Did the Bullying Last? From grade school through adulthood; male
Hot Spots: Classroom, lunchroom
Did You Tell? If So, Whom? No one, and I was never disciplined until I was an adult.

I didn't realize that I was a bully until I injured my adolescent son in 2006. I had had a difficult day at work and my son had had a bad day at school. I knew that I had used the parental discipline style that I had learned from my mother. Not understanding the harm that I was doing to my children when I was disciplining them, I intended to deliberately instill fear in them each time that I corrected their behavior. That day I became upset, and in my rage, I broke my son's arm. I was then prosecuted, and the children were taken out of the home. I am sharing my story because it took these circumstances for me to realize that I was an aggressive, intimidating, controlling parent who used bullying techniques.

With mandated family and individual therapy, I am thankful to God that I have acknowledged my evil ways and came to realize that I had been using intimidation and coercion to control my wife and my sons. I have two sons; my older son was twelve years old when I broke his arm, and my younger son was seven. They were removed for a year. Admittedly, this was a dark and conflicting time in my life. I had to evaluate who I was and what I was doing. Was I the person I wanted to be—a responsible parent with a good job and family? Or was I a disappointment to myself and, more importantly, to my family?

Looking back, I remembered laughing, making fun of, and calling children names in elementary, junior high, and high school. I targeted children, both boys and girls, who were not well groomed, wore dirty clothes, or were unattractive. I knew I was popular and had friends who would back me up.

Before the incident with my son and before I realized that I was an aggressor using repeated, intentional, and power-based behaviors, I thought back to my ten-year reunion. A former classmate who had always been obese came up and said that I used to pick on him and call him names about his weight. This left me speechless. I had no idea that my actions were so hurtful that they would be remembered for years. Now, I am so glad that he disclosed that information to me because it was something that I am sure he needed and wanted to do for years. And, it made a profound impact on the way I perceived myself and others perceived me.

I have been asking myself why I have bullied others. My mother became pregnant with me when she was fifteen years old. She was strict with me and called me names (e.g., ugly) and physically and emotionally abused me. She would use force and victimize me, and in return, I would use some of the same methods to victimize others. I would then feel good about who I was. However, inside I felt unloved and worthless. Neither my mother nor my father ever told me that they loved me.

My goal with my children was the same: to make them afraid of me. I used corporal punishment to create the fear. I rationalized my behavior by comparing it to the way my mother treated me. Since I had been successful, I was going to treat my children the same way. The bullying created a spider web of dysfunction in my family.

When I physically hurt my son and realized that he had done nothing to deserve that hurt, I then knew I needed help. I had gone too far. I had repeated what my mother had done to me. I have worked hard to change this pattern of behavior, and hopefully I have broken the cycle of abuse and bullying in our family.

POINTS FOR PARENTS

This is a tragic story of abuse and bullying behavior. While we cannot trace all bullying behavior back to family abuse, that is certainly a motivational factor in countless instances of cruelty and misuse of power. The research is clear that children who witness violence at home are more likely to bully others at school. Domestic violence is one of the highest risk factors predicting bullying behavior in children (Baldry 2003).

There are many causes of bullying behavior, and we know that this behavior is a social climate issue, occurring in an environment that perpetuates, allows, ignores, or even encourages the behavior. So when it occurs and is not stopped by peers, adults, or—in some cases—by the target, the bullying continues and escalates. When the origin of the bullying behavior is rooted in domestic violence, the apple will fall close to the tree. In other words, the behavior that is modeled may easily be imitated.

The great focus on the well-being of the target of the bullying behavior is highly appropriate. However, we cannot forget to consider the effect of this behavior on the aggressor. Research from as far back as 1994 suggests that approximately 35 to 40 percent of boys characterized as aggressors, using bullying behaviors by grades six through nine, had been convicted of at least three crimes by the age of twenty-four (Olweus 1994).

This alarming statistic has been upheld over the years and is a clear indicator that we have a responsibility to not only recognize and treat the target in these instances but to also treat the aggressor. A pattern of aggressive behavior that is allowed to continue through elementary, middle, and high school does not end with graduation. It can become a life pattern that can and does hurt others, and approximately one-third of aggressors have a criminal conviction.

This storyteller had no idea he was hurting others. It was a shock to him when, at the class reunion, a classmate confided that he felt victimized by the name calling and other repeated mean and hurtful comments made about his weight. Many aggressors go through life having no idea of the havoc their actions have had on others. Since the man's home life was so violent, he had grown up thinking that his family was normal and that normal people use coercion and intimidation. When you think about it, doesn't it make sense that domestic violence is a risk factor for bullying behavior?

To come to terms with his issue, he had to look deeply into why he was behaving in such an aggressive, angry way toward his own children. He used that as the rationale for the harsh way he treated his children. His feelings were often expressed as discipline and punishment.

There are many styles of parenting, and the most effective is known as an authoritative style, in which parents are connected in many ways to their children, consistently emphasizing reasonable rules and allowing for autonomy (Padilla-Walker et al. 2012). Let's break that down:

> *Connecting:* Listening more than talking to your child, being aware of your child's feelings, and showing empathy for the child and others.

> *Consistently emphasizing reasonable rules:* Rules need to be for safety and family harmony. Parents should emphasize the reason for rules and be clear on what those rules mean. Most importantly, rules must be consistent, with a clear agreement between parent and child about the rules and the consequences for not adhering to them.

> *Allowing for autonomy:* Taking the child's wishes or desires into consideration before making a decision. This can be a very simple thing. The idea is to—from a very early age—give children some choices. It is good practice for them and will serve them well as they get older.

In this story, as in many others, it is hopeful to note that patterns of abuse can be broken and can lead to positive change. In the words of the storyteller, "Parents need to apologize and say I am sorry and I love you. We all need to be thankful that we can have a second chance." That is the best advice for all of us!

SUGGESTIONS FOR ACTION

- The facts of this story are very serious, and the situation is one that requires professional advice. If you know of anyone in this position, the best thing to do is to urge him or her to get outside help before anyone is hurt.
- This story is a good example of how we all can learn and perhaps reflect upon our own parenting practices. While this case is extreme, it is important to remember that children are learning from all our behaviors, so we parents need to act like the people we want our children to grow up to be!

5. Kids Who Appear Different

Case Study: From Kindergarten to High School—Long-Term Bullying

Type of Bullying: Exclusion, verbal, physical
Age of Onset/Gender of Target: Kindergarten, male
How Long Did the Bullying Last? Through high school
Hot Spots: Hallways, transitions, bus, recess
Did You Tell? If So, Whom? I told no one because I felt ashamed.

In my family, I have one brother who is nine years older than me. For my brother, everything was easy; however, for me, I was challenged by the smallest problems. While growing up, I had many learning difficulties. I was diagnosed with dyslexia and a reading comprehension and auditory deficit disorder. In addition, I had delayed speech and was a stutterer. I attended private schools that had a special track for children with learning disabilities.

My bullying started as early as kindergarten. I did not have the verbal ability to communicate with my peers, nor did I have the hand-motor coordination to write and draw. Looking back, I don't think how the other students treated me was intentional, but their comments impacted my self-esteem. Because the other children made fun of my artwork, I felt embarrassed that I couldn't perform like my peers, and as a consequence, I became a target of taunts because I was developmentally delayed and had other disabilities.

According to my parents, one day in the first grade, I stood up for another student who was being bullied in the same way.

Standing up for someone else who has similar issues set me up as a target even more than before. I had a low opinion of my abilities, and I felt even worse. The other student I had stood up for left the school. From this time on, and for whatever reasons, I was made fun of and was bullied about once a week. Even though I attended a class for learning-disabled students, it seemed that bullying was a rite of passage and was passed along from student to student because at some time they had all been victims of bullying.

When I reached second grade, the bullying seemed to happen more often and with more intensity. Students learned to vocalize their thoughts with more words and, at the same time, became more covert in their bullying behaviors. They made fun of my speech, and any mistakes I made became a joke. I did not know how to respond to their bullying and knew I could not fight back. Subsequently, I told no one because I was ashamed of how I was treated. The bullying was taking an emotional toll on me.

By third grade, the intensity increased and the bullying became even more physical. I was typically pushed on the playground and in the classroom when the teacher wasn't looking; my book covers were torn and some of my belongings "disappeared." I seemed to be the biggest and most common target. By fourth grade, the beatings seemed to occur more often. Still, I did not report the bullying, but instead tried to befriend the popular students who were making fun of and taunting me. I thought if I could gain their confidence and they got to know me, they would ease up on their mean behavior. Instead, I became even more of a target. I started to avoid going to school because I knew that I was going to be physically mistreated at least every other day. In fifth grade, the verbal and physical beatings were occurring once a day. Students would threaten to kill me if I told anyone. At that age, I even believed them. Looking back at that situation now, I know that they were just trying to intimidate me. In any case, I was afraid and kept this all to myself, never letting on to anyone. On a ride home in the car one day, my parents asked me about the bruises and cuts. I finally broke down and told them how the students were bullying and physically attacking me at school.

My mother, who is learning-disabled herself, went to school the next day and shared my story. The school said that they would handle the situation. Afterwards, each time my parents called to check on the progress, the school would again state that they were handling it. Yet, from my viewpoint, nothing was being handled differently, except the teachers were discussing it with their students both individually and openly in class. This in turn made me more of a target.

In sixth grade, I became numb to the verbal taunting. I turned off my feelings and accepted the fact that I was going to be bullied at school every single day. I became depressed and put up a wall sheltering myself from students' comments. I just went to school, did what I had to do, and came home. In an attempt to help me, the teachers advised me to walk away, but that just simply didn't work at that point. During this experience, my family was composed of supportive parents and an older brother who all were advocates for me, but it was not enough.

In December of that year, I started studying martial arts. This became my saving grace because I thought I could save and protect myself from anyone bullying me. Even though I was a slow learner and had poor coordination, I worked very diligently to develop skills to defend myself. I remember one incident that was very scary for me and reminded me that I needed more training. Two weeks after taking martial arts classes in the schoolyard, a student tried to kick me. I grabbed his foot and threw him on his back. Then, he shocked me by yelling to the others to attack me. I didn't know what to do, so I started to run away and tripped and fell. I then curled up in the fetal position while six or seven kids continued to kick me. It felt like an eternity even though it lasted for only a few seconds until a staff member stopped it. At that point, I became more determined than ever to become more skilled in martial arts.

In seventh grade, I moved to a junior high school. Unfortunately, I still had the victim mentality. I carried myself in a way that exposed my vulnerabilities to others. I appeared weak. The bullying continued, but it was less physical because I had a growth spurt and was larger than many of my classmates. However, the students continued to verbally harass me, and for the first time girls joined in with the boys.

In ninth grade in high school, the bullying continued, but with less frequency. The hot spots were hallways, the bus, and transition times—such as during class changes, etc. I continued to be numb and to disconnect myself from my peers so that I would not feel any pain. I became detached and socially disconnected from all my classmates. The peer abuse had been so traumatic that if a student made a verbal attack on me, the act would highjack my emotions and I would retreat into my shell.

Up to this time, the other students (bystanders) would watch but would not react because they didn't want to be in the crossfire and then be victimized by the perpetrators. But they were also participants in the bullying. It was as if they were empowered by the boldness of others.

To add to my martial arts training and to increase my size and strength, I started power lifting. I wanted to see if this would affect how others treated me. By the end of tenth grade, I was obviously physically stronger. I started to notice that I was being bullied less and less. Martial arts and weight lifting made me feel good inside, but I still had a hard time responding to name calling. It was still deeply hurtful, and I was not able to handle the emotional turmoil of those verbal attacks.

With the support of my parents, I changed high schools between my sophomore and junior years. I wanted to change my social environment to see if a more liberal private school would be *a better fit for me to learn. The school had a great reputation in the area for both excellent academics and an accepting atmosphere. It was touted to be a warm, positive, caring environment where teachers were accessible and involved and students had responsibility for their education.*

During my last two high school years, true to the stated mission and vision of the school, this experience was the most positive for my growth. The bullying did not occur in this school where everyone was accepted for who they are. I started to feel my emotions and interact with my peers without fear of humiliation. I started seeing a therapist, and the experience was very eye-opening. I also had my first job, and it was a successful experience. My self-esteem rose considerably. In college, I chose to major in psychology and to become a therapist. I finally figured out how to relate to my emotions and understand more about myself and who I wanted to be.

Presently, I am in my thirties, married, and have a young child. I am a licensed social worker, and I plan to pursue my doctorate in the near future.

POINTS FOR PARENTS

This is a very sad story of long-term victimization. First of all, because it was so long term, the signs of the bullying became a routine and acceptable part of this young man's life because he had had limited positive experiences with his peers. When bullying begins so young, it becomes a part of a child's life, and the child feels bad all the time. It is hard to believe that something like this can go on for such a long time, yet it does. We could say that this is not a commonly occurring story, yet many people who have had a long-term experience would certainly disagree. But the fact of the matter is that students who have disabilities are more likely than others to be victimized by their peers.

In addition, some adults are unaware of the bullying that may be affecting a student because the victim never tells any adult. In particular, young boys are reluctant to tell their parents they are being bullied. A study of U.S. students in grades three through twelve showed that 38 percent of boys and 49 percent of girls did not report they had been bullied. (Limber et al. 2012). That means that fewer than half of all students who have been bullied tell a parent, and boys for a myriad of reasons are the least likely to tell. While this fact is startling, it helps to explain how parents could allow something like this to continue for such a long time. They simply did not know. In this case, as soon as they found out about the situation, the parents did go to the school on their child's behalf and believed the problem had been "handled." It is up to the parents to follow up with the school to be certain a plan is in place to protect their child.

The signs of a child under stress were clearly present after the parent went to the school for help. But this was a long-term issue. Many times, when signs of stress are attributed to personality type or emotional state, they are easily overlooked. Therefore, the underlying causes of shyness, timidity, moodiness, and irritability are overlooked.

SUGGESTIONS FOR ACTION

- Parents of students with special needs need to take special care of their child's school experience, particularly since their child is more likely to be bullied by peers. Children with physical, behavioral, or social issues that are apparent and part of their disabilities are particularly vulnerable, regardless of the issue that places them in a protected group. Therefore, any concerns about bullying should be addressed immediately, and ways of protecting the student should be part of the child's Individual Education Plan (IEP).

- When a child has unexplained headaches and/or stomachaches, sleeplessness, unexplained irritability, or changes in eating habits, parents must look for the source of the problem, as these behaviors may be signs that the child is being bullied. If you ask your child about this behavior and you cannot get a satisfactory answer, it is a good idea to bring the child to the pediatrician and tell the doctor about your concerns. The professional can examine the child for physical problems and then ask questions about social concerns.

- Other more obvious signs are unexplained bruises, torn book covers, and loss of friends. It is important for a parent to look deeper into the source of these problems and to connect them to other behavioral changes that may have emerged. As stated previously, it is not uncommon for boys to be reluctant to report that they have been bullied, and when they do, things have reached a boiling point. So it is up to the parent to actively try to get a sense of the problem. Again, this is about asking those open-ended questions in a nonjudgmental manner to get the information.

- The boy in this case did have some problems with his self-esteem and, given his experience, that was certainly understandable. The lesson here for parents is to try to focus on the big picture and put all the pieces together to get to the bottom of things. Any one of those signs would not necessarily have indicated a serious issue, but together they added up to a severe long-term problem, and the impact was devastating.

Case Study: Special Education Student

Type of Bullying: Exclusion, name calling
Age of Onset/Gender of Target: Fourth grade, male
How Long Did the Bullying Last? Months
Hot Spots: Playground
Did You Tell? If So, Whom? Parent

NOTE: *Mitochondrial myopathies:* A group of neuromuscular diseases caused by damage to the mitochondria—small, energy-producing structures that serve as the cells' "power plants." Nerve cells in the brain and muscles require a great deal of energy, and thus appear to be particularly damaged when mitochondrial dysfunction occurs. The symptoms of mitochondrial myopathies include muscle weakness or exercise intolerance, heart failure or rhythm disturbances, dementia, movement disorders, stroke-like episodes, deafness, blindness, droopy eyelids, limited mobility of the eyes, vomiting, and seizures. The prognosis for these disorders ranges in severity from progressive weakness to death. Most mitochondrial myopathies occur before the age of twenty and often begin with exercise intolerance or muscle weakness. During physical activity, muscles may become easily fatigued or weak.

I am the mother of three children, an older daughter and two sons. Our youngest son is eleven years old. He was born with mitochondrial myopathy, which is a neuromuscular disease that impacts his muscles, called hypertonia. Hypertonia is a condition in which there is decreased resting muscle tone. He uses a walker and cannot walk without assistance. He has delayed speech, slurs words, and repeats himself, as the words may be unclear and slow to develop.

After attending a private school established originally for special needs students through third grade and being homeschooled for a semester, my son transferred out of this setting in the middle

106

of the last school year into an elementary school in the public school system where we live. The story of my son having difficulties not fitting in with his peers began in fifth grade in December and has been continuing through April. The main locations for the name calling, rumoring, and exclusive behavior seemed to occur in the cafeteria and playground, where fewer adults are present.

One male student started picking on my son, calling him stupid, along with other names. This same male student would covertly get all of his friends to move away from my son at the lunch table, leaving him eating alone. It seems that the reason these incidents were occurring was because of a lack of active supervision by the few adults responsible for the students during the lunch period.

Just last week a different student, who was a friend of the aggressor, admitted to telling my son to grow up and stop depending on other people to help him carry his tray, etc. If you're using a walker, it is almost impossible to carry a tray. Last school year, this was not a problem because the teacher identified some students to assist my son in the cafeteria to carry his tray and sit with him. It seems that because he needed assistance doing simple tasks like holding a pencil, using scissors, etc., the other students were resentful that he could not handle his own duties.

During recess, which is immediately after lunch, my son walks around by himself using a walker. The different groups exclude him because he lacks the coordination to participate in their activities. He says he hates being out during recess because it is boring and that no one invites him to play. He wants to be exclusive with his best friend, but his friend wants to interact with the other classmates.

POINTS FOR PARENTS

This story is about a child who had an obvious physical disability. When a child who has disabilities is introduced to a school, particularly in the middle of the academic year, the other students in the school need to be prepared. This is a very serious matter because a child who has any disability is particularly vulnerable to mean, hurtful, and malicious behavior at the hands of peers. From the very beginning, schools need to be aware of the child's issues through an open and realistic dialogue about the capabilities and limitations of the child (Tremlow and Sacco 2013). Most importantly, parents need to have a clear picture of how the school plans to integrate the child into the school culture.

In instances such as this, parents need to be hyperaware of the child's surroundings and the actions of their peers. They need to be in contact with both schoolteachers and administrators about the child's academic and, most importantly, social adjustment to the school.

Bullying is a process—a social cultural phenomenon. We can set up an environment that will influence how children treat someone who is different by controlling the culture. In other words, by teaching kids about disabilities and how these disabilities impact the ability to perform ordinary tasks, we can develop empathy. For instance, the teachers can hold class meetings and talk to their classes about the physical limitations of the disability to help students understand the struggles of their classmate who needs a walker to get around the school.

Through a program called Understanding Disabilities, Inc., in one Massachusetts school district, trained volunteers go into the school and give all students the opportunity to experience firsthand what it is like to have a limitation. For instance, the unit on physical limitations gives kids the opportunity to do simple tasks with crutches or a walker. This experience goes a long way to developing empathy and is an outstanding example of building empathy through personal experiences.

Bullying behavior and the lack of intervention of the staff can be considered disability harassment, which is prohibited under the Rehabilitation Act of 1973 and Title II of the Americans with Disabilities Act of 1990. The U.S. Department of Education describes disability harassment as "intimidating or abusive behavior that creates a hostile environment by interfering with or denying a student's participation in or receipt of benefits, services, or opportunities in the institution's program" (U.S. Department of Education 2000). It is very important for parents to be proactive to prevent these issues from escalating.

SUGGESTIONS FOR ACTION

- Be in regular contact with the school and ask questions about its general strategies to prevent bullying. This can include questions about supervision, such as where the "hot spots" are (where bullying or mean social interactions might occur), who is usually present, and what is being done to supervise your child in those areas.

- Ask the school how it plans to introduce the child to the school and what its strategies are to talk to current students about this type of disability. The idea is to neutralize any negative feelings the other students may have simply because they do not know how to behave with someone who is disabled.

- In some schools, new students are connected to a "buddy" who will help them around the facility and introduce them to others. This is a good strategy to help a child develop relationships and find common interests with peers. Ask the school about its plan to help the child feel comfortable and make friends in this situation.

- Sometimes children with particular disabilities can feel hurt and excluded, even when there is no intent on the part of peers. As a parent, you need to consider your expectations and sharpen your observations so you can help your child recognize real bullying. In addition, you need to work with your child, through support and praise, to strengthen self-confidence.

- Remember, the best idea is to approach the situation as a partner in your child's education and in creating a positive experience at school. Therefore, it is best to cultivate a common interest rather than to approach the school with demands. That sets an atmosphere that is collaborative rather than adversarial.

Case Study: Asperger's Syndrome

Type of Bullying: Exclusion, name calling, relational aggression
Age of Onset/Gender of Target: Sixth grade, male
How Long Did the Bullying Last? Through middle and high school
Hot Spots: Bathroom, hallways, lunchroom, recess
Did You Tell? If So, Whom? Parents

When my son Luke was four years old, he was diagnosed with Asperger's syndrome. He was in group counseling and occupational therapy until he started kindergarten, when he was placed in a regular "inclusionary" classroom that extended through elementary school. There was a paraprofessional in the class who assisted students who had learning difficulties. Throughout elementary school, it was my perception that the other students were very tolerant with students who were different learners. In grades two through five, the school hired a young male teacher who shadowed Luke and similar students with special needs.

In middle school, it was a different environment, and there were fewer adults supervising the students with special needs. Since Luke had difficulties with casual conversation and was literal in reading social cues, it was harder for him to fit in. It was the culture for peers to isolate and exclude students who were different learners. When they made references to girls, for example, they could tell that Luke was clueless and didn't understand the meaning of their slang. They laughed and made fun of his naïvety. It was obvious that his classmates were maturing much faster physically, socially, and emotionally.

In order to protect him, I did not let Luke have access to the Internet and Facebook. I also did not let him ride the bus and tried to educate him about avoiding other places that were common hot spots for bullying in the school. However, in eighth grade, the bullying seemed to escalate because aggressors would strategically find ways to target Luke. They chose locations, such as the bathroom, where adults were not present, and on many occasions a student would threaten to hit Luke in the face. Also, because Luke did not like to be touched, especially by individuals outside of the family, students would pull on his backpack, tap his shoulder, or shove him to get a reaction. One time, when Luke was shoved, he reacted and pushed the student back. Then the aggressor punched him in the face. Because there was no eyewitness and Luke participated in the incident, the school used the zero tolerance policy to suspend both students. This happened on two separate occasions in seventh and eighth grades. Both incidences were written up as a fight.

Up to this time, boys were the aggressors and used physical bullying. However, a group of girls joined in the attack, complaining that Luke was calling them racial names based on their skin color. Because the school administration's policy was that an eyewitness was needed, they said their hands were tied and they could not do anything. It was not until two years later that a teacher was walking in the hall behind this same group of girls and overheard them taunting and ridiculing Luke. This was the same sixth grade group of girls who had been using racial slurs and intimidating Luke to get a reaction out of him. Finally, now that they had an eyewitness, the school intervened and the aggressive behavior ended. This type of bullying, girls bullying boys, was particularly challenging even though Luke has special needs because most people don't take this type of aggression seriously. Usually boys get into trouble bullying boys, but it is more unusual for people to believe that girls are bullying boys.

In middle school, Luke figured out that he was different from his peers. We discussed with him the issue of teasing and how we understood that it was difficult for him to understand this conduct. However, in high school, the conversations that students were having were more advanced and sophisticated than Luke's ability to comprehend. For example, it was difficult for Luke to grasp his classmates' meanings when they texted and sent pictures teasing and making fun of others. Some boys would coerce Luke into using a word that he didn't know would be embarrassing. It was a setup to intentionally hurt both innocent parties.

He continued to come home with very specific questions about words that his classmates used that had sexual connotations. One example was the word "gay." I explained to him the literal meaning and then how his peers were using it. At first, he was very defensive, but then he had a better understanding about how differently his peers might use the term. Despite those instances, things improved through high school. Most of the peers knew that Luke thought differently and were considerate of his feelings.

Two girls who had known him for many years befriended and protected him from some of the aggressors' attacks. With many special need students (e.g., Asperger's,) it is hard to get all the facts. Until Luke was in sixth grade, it was hard to acknowledge that Luke was two years behind socially and emotionally. He performed well academically, except in areas of comprehension, and socially and emotionally when he had difficulty reading social cues. In tenth grade, at sixteen years old, reading facial expressions and nuances such as sarcasm continues to be challenging for him, but with help and support, he is improving.

POINTS FOR PARENTS

Bullying occurs in many different situations, but most of the time it occurs under the radar and out of the view of adults. It is often subtle, covert, and hard to detect. It can happen in an instant with a mean look or a mocking gesture. It continues for many reasons, including the fact that others may not know the emotional impact that bullying can have on a child, particularly a disabled child.

Students with less obvious disabilities are more vulnerable to being targeted through teasing and bullying. Children with Asperger's syndrome have language and cognitive ability; however, they tend to be socially inept and naïve when compared to their peers (Sofronoff et al. 2010). They have difficulty understanding body language, subtleties of facial expressions, and the language of humor. It is their naïveté that leaves them easy targets for those who use bullying behavior. In this story, the victim was particularly sensitive to touch and sound. This in turn becomes a vehicle for bullying, as the peers understand that they can get a strong reaction when the student is poked, prodded, tapped, or touched in some way, particularly when he or she is not expecting it.

Students who have Asperger's syndrome more often exhibit less ability to understand or tolerate humor and are more ridiculed than their peers. They simply feel uncomfortable when people laugh at them, and once they understand, they avoid those situations. As a result, they are more likely to develop forms of social phobia (Samson et al. 2011). Clearly, many of these children cannot read social queues or understand humor as described in this case. This seems really repetitive.

In fact, whether or not the person is aware that he or she is being made fun of, he or she is still a victim. This type of behavior is particularly cruel because the victim not only does not understand the humor but also cannot laugh at himself or herself.

In this case, the peers coerced Luke into saying words that he did not understand and then made fun of him. The main components of bullying include repeated, intentional, and power-based behavior. When these criteria have been met, the result is bullying, whether the victim is aware of it or not. This is much more than the idea of "no harm, no foul" because it is hurtful—not only to the victim but to the bystanders and the entire culture that allows the bullying.

SUGGESTIONS FOR ACTION

- Since it is difficult to identify the signs of victimization in a child with Asperger's syndrome, the best thing is to think proactively. Work with the school and include prevention in the student's Individual Education Plan (IEP). This can simply mean that the staff is aware of the student's limitations and will heighten its observation of student interactions. It could also mean that the school counselor should periodically check in with the student to establish a relationship should there be any indications of stress or concerns about peers.

- Work with the school to bring information about disabilities, including Asperger's, to the children in class. Having discussions and giving all students the opportunity to hear about the struggles and difficulties of this disability is a good way to develop empathy.

- As a parent, you can give your student opportunities for experiences with children outside of school. This can be focused on the child's interests. But bear in mind that since social interaction is difficult, it is a good idea to find an area that is not only of interest to the child but one in which he or she can be successful.

- As a continuum, parents need to follow any recommendations regarding support and therapy and follow up with the school to be certain the IEP is executed as agreed. The key is to stick to the education plan, update your physician, and monitor your child closely. Most importantly, celebrate your child's successes!

Case Study: Accepting Autism

Type of Bullying: Intimidation, stalking
Age of Onset/Gender of Target: Sixth grade, male
How Long Did the Bullying Last? Through middle school
Hot Spots: Bus, to/from the bus, cafeteria, hallways, physical education
Did You Tell? If So, Whom? Parents, teachers

My husband and I have been blessed with two sons. When our first child was born, he exceeded all of the milestones for development. Basically, he rolled over, walked, and sat up early; however, he didn't talk. Friends and family told us that boys were slower to talk, but we became concerned when, at the age of two, he was not talking at all. To compensate for that, I taught him baby sign language so that we could communicate. That was working well until some of my friends informed me that I was hindering him from talking.

At this time I was in denial that anything was wrong. He didn't play with other children, but I didn't think that was unusual either. My husband and I were engineers but knew little about child development and raising children. Finally, I had friends telling me when my son was three years old and not talking that we should have him tested for free in the school system where we lived. At that time, they told me that if our son was autistic, there were many resources for children with special needs.

At the time I just wanted to prove everyone wrong, so I got him tested. After the testing, the psychologist informed me that my firstborn was found on the autistic spectrum. They pointed out that he had common characteristics, such as lack of eye contact and isolation from play with other children. Early on he clearly showed that he had no interest in making friends or interacting with peers. It took me a long while to accept his diagnosis because

115

I was in denial. When my second son was one and a half years old and displayed the same symptoms as my three-and-a-half-year-old, walking early and not talking, I had a profound epiphany that my husband and I had been chosen to be special parents for our two highly functioning autistic sons.

After learning that our firstborn was autistic and that a child with special needs was offered free preschooling starting at age three, we entered him into a neighborhood autistic preschool in the public school system where we lived. However, from what I observed, the staff had not been trained in working with children with autism, nor was the environment conducive to learning since my son modeled his behavior after the bad behavior of the other children. Since we were not pleased with his progress, we registered him into both a religious church school and then a Montessori preschool that didn't work out. Both schools were homogeneous and did not know how to work with students with special needs. So, when our second son came along, we never considered this path. Instead, we placed our two highly functioning autistic sons in a local preschool that had an inclusionary climate in addition to a teacher that offered extra support. This seemed to work well for both of our sons.

In school some students would call my older son "weird," but he just went his own way and dismissed them. On another occasion in first grade, a group of three boys coerced my son to pull down his pants. I went ballistic and threatened to call the police. Because of my son's lack of maturity, his social and emotional development, and his autism, I decided to hold him back and repeat first grade. This solved a lot of his problems because it removed him from his peers who were picking on him and influencing his behavior. His new first grade class was a much more positive influence on my son because it had a group of protectors, mostly girls. Because we held back our older son and it worked for him, we did the same for our younger son.

116

Our older son had very few problematic situations that arose. In third grade, however, a wealthy classmate took his lunch money. Because I was very involved with the school, I took it upon myself when I was at school one day to tell this child to never borrow money from my son again. He knew what I meant and repaid him. This was resolved and did not become a problem the rest of that school year.

In high school, after he had been in an affluent elementary and middle school, he found himself in a more heterogeneous situation with students from the projects. Last year, a student threatened to beat him up because he couldn't rap. Even though my son played tuba in the band, he could hardly play an instrument and march at the same time. The student threatened him during lunch and before school. The school made adjustments with the other boy's schedule, but soon afterwards, the boy's family moved and he transferred to another school.

Presently, my older son is sixteen, has a resource teacher in his classes, reads on an eighth grade level, and has an Individual Education Plan (IEP). Since we, his parents, chaperone many of his trips, we observed that he still isolates himself at times, but if you ask him, he will inform you that he has many friends. The only issue that continues to be problematic for him is that he purchases lunch for other children. He spends three times the money that he should be spending. He is highly empathetic, has clear speech, and is easy to communicate with, but he has horrible handwriting.

On the other hand, my younger son was a screamer and difficult to parent as compared to his older brother. He was clingy and difficult to understand, didn't like to be touched, and had immaculate handwriting. As a preschooler, he struggled with babysitters, preschool staff, and anything that was different. On the other hand, he loved to interact with other students in his own way. However, if the other students did not interact with him the way he wanted them to, he would scream.

He has always had a way with adults. Adults have always adored him. However, students didn't like him because he was bossy and screamed when he didn't get his way. These issues had been around throughout elementary school. He tried to control every aspect of every interaction and every game. Even though he didn't get along with his peers, he never hit another child; instead, he screamed. The teachers pulled him out of class for screaming more than once a week and took him to a resource room, where, as a consequence, he played video games. He figured out very quickly that if he screamed he would be able to play games. At the time, I had a very stressful job assignment and was not able to volunteer and stop by frequently. Instead, I communicated to the school not to pull him out of class when he screamed. I suggested for him to be taken out in the hallway instead. In fourth and fifth grades there was very little learning taking place except for my son manipulating his teachers. At the end of fifth grade, however, he finally stopped screaming. This was partly because in middle school, if you screamed in class, you would be sent to the principal's office.

In middle school my son thrived on changing classes and having different teachers. He loved the different notebooks and books for the classes. For example, he never forgot to bring home any of his class materials for homework. He was task-driven. His older brother, on the other hand, would forget his books regularly. My younger son got along with his peers better, but he still had social and emotional problems. When walking up to groups he would make comments that were out of place. He had done well academically, but these years had been cruel.

In sixth grade, when students merged from feeder elementary schools into one middle school, my son reported to me that a gang of boys was "bullying" him. He said that they were "staring" at him. I, as a parent, then started researching bullying. The definition used the word "perceived," so I reported to the administration using their language—that my son "perceived" that he was being bullied. Later, after an investigation, the school reported that he had misinterpreted the situation and was not being target-ed. I agreed with their findings because I knew that his perception could be skewed. However, later on in sixth grade, a group of African-American girls decided to start picking on my son. They started targeting him because of his speech. Then, they discovered that he reacted to loud sounds such as fire drills. Because my son was stubborn, liked things only his way, and was sound-sensitive, the girls would follow him to get him to react, to get upset, and to cry. They would surprise him from behind and scream in his ears to cause an outburst. This mostly happened when he was walking to and from the bus, during physical education class, and in the cafeteria.

One of his teachers wrote up the incident, but the assistant principal ruled that this was not bullying; thus, the girls received no consequences. However, they pulled the girls together and told them that if they continued to use "words" to target my son, they would label this action as bullying. So this group of girls made up words to intimidate my son and went as far as eliciting friends to do the same. In December of the sixth grade I received a call from the school that my son had hit another child. I was livid and left work immediately to talk with the school.

The assistant principal stated that my son had hauled off and slugged this girl in the face. After asking for details and talking with my son in the presence of the assistant principal, it was clear that my son flailed his arms when being screamed at from behind, accidentally hitting one of the girls in the neck. My son reacted to the screaming and was attempting to plug his ears to soften the sound. The school gave my son one day of in-school suspension for hitting the student. At this time, I went on a quest trying to find out if bullying could be classified as a group of girls repeatedly and intentionally provoking a sound-sensitive student from behind by screaming to illicit an outburst (i.e., crying or screaming).

My goal was for my son to be safe at school and to have a positive learning environment. I talked with the bullying prevention coordinator for the school system, researched our bullying state law, and checked out the federal government's website on bullying. I still did not find the answer.

In the meantime, we got our older son to role-play scenarios with his brother. Our purpose was to reduce his reaction in situations where he was screamed at or where there were loud sounds. Eventually, role-playing seemed to help as he continued through middle school. We convinced him to not react and to say very little back. One expression that we practiced was to say "So what?" Now, my son is fourteen and an eighth grader. He is reading on a fourth grade level and is still enrolled in speech therapy. He has found a best friend, another autistic boy.

POINTS FOR PARENTS

Every parent wants the best for their child, and they want them to be perfect to the rest of the world. Therefore, most parents have a difficult time when confronted with a diagnosis that says otherwise. Certainly there are many issues associated with autism that make a difficult road for any child. This story demonstrates how, when a parent comes to grips and accepts that reality, their strong support and diligent involvement can make a tremendous difference for their child.

This is a parent who, early on, recognized that these children's needs were not being met in school. She tried several situations before she was comfortable with the academic and social settings for her child.

When she was confronted with an issue that was labeled as bullying behavior, she gathered the facts, talked to her son, and discussed the situation with the school administration. Since the problem involved staring, she recognized that her child could possibly misconstrue the actions of other students.

In the situation where girls would startle her son to get him to scream and would also make up words to humiliate the boy, the school did not believe this was bullying behavior. The circumstances surrounding the instances where students would startle the boy to force him to react certainly can be considered bullying behavior. In this case, to deliberately startle a peer when they know he has a particular unusual reaction is mean and cruel. They did it on more than one occasion, causing the child who is being victimized humiliation, stress, and eventually punishment when his reflex action struck one of the girls.

If you think back to the definition of bullying—repeated intentional behavior that involves a power imbalance—all those elements are present, so it is clear that what happened here is bullying. When bullying is not stopped, those who perpetuate the behavior will continue, and often the bullying will escalate. This is exactly what happened in this story.

The response of the mother to talk to the bullying prevention coordinator and to gain a clear understanding of bullying behavior is right on point. Parents need to not only be aware but also be proactive in understanding any challenges their child may be facing. This parent took things a step further by role-playing instances with her child to give him the opportunity to try out different solutions to a problem in a safe atmosphere. This is an excellent strategy to help students build confidence and to take control of a situation. It helps equip them to better handle situations by having a repertoire of effective and safe responses.

SUGGESTIONS FOR ACTION

- Set up for a list of your expectations for a school. Consider questions such as:
  — Does my child need an Individual Education Plan (IEP)?
  — Can the school properly execute the requirements of the IEP in the most complete and efficient manner?

— Is the staff qualified to work with a child who has special needs?

— Is there a mechanism for regular communication with the school?

— Is there a plan to assist children who have social issues or are less mature than their peers?

— How do they help all students develop empathy, understanding, and acceptance of others?

— Does the school have a systemic approach to bullying?

Once you have developed those criteria you can determine if your child's needs are being met in that setting.

• Know the policy for bullying prevention in your district. This can be found on your school's website. If you cannot find a policy, go to your state's website, since most states have laws to protect children from bullying, and look for the bullying prevention law. This will give you the working definition of bullying behavior that schools in your state must include in their policy.

• Talking to your child about how to handle situations that are difficult is important; however role-playing is also very effective. Not only does it give them the opportunity to try out responses, but it also enables you to coach them so they can learn how to best react. In this case, they were able, to some degree, to desensitize the child to reacting to loud noises.

Case Study: Cranial Deformity

Type of Bullying: Physical (throwing rocks/books), stealing food, rumors

Age of Onset/Gender of Target: Eighth grade, male

How Long Did the Bullying Last? One year

Hot Spots: On the way home from school, hallways

Did You Tell? If So, Whom? I reported it to a teacher, and the bullying increased.

My son attended the local elementary school in our neighborhood. We have lived in this community for more than twelve years. He entered the school system as a kindergartner and attended the same school through fifth grade. During the summer before sixth grade, another school opened up in a neighboring area. This new school focused on computer technology. We talked it over as a family and elected for him to attend this charter school; however, after seventh grade, the school system decided to draw new boundaries. My son had to withdraw and enrolled back in his neighborhood school in eighth grade.

Background on my son: My son has a cranial deformity. When he was in utero he was positioned such that when he was born he had a cone-shaped head. He had to wear a cranial helmet that was adjusted periodically to reshape his skull. He wore this cranial cap for two years. Afterwards, he had an asymmetrical look in which one eye was lower than the other. As he grew older, it became more pronounced and noticeable to his peers.

Until now, eighth grade was one of the most difficult times for my son. He was trying to assimilate into a group of students who had already formed cliques and factions. In addition, he was more sensitive and self-conscience about his facial deformity than he had been in the past. One African-American boy in the neighborhood had it out for my son. He lived six houses down the street and had previously been friends with my son. However, suddenly and without reason, this young man and his Hispanic friend ganged up to terrorize him at school and on his way home.

They would throw rocks as he walked or rode his bike on a sidewalk through the back of the greenbelt area of the neighborhood yards. In the hallways at school, this gang would book-check him, knocking his books to the floor. In the cafeteria, they would intimidate him by taking his food. They attacked him just because he looked different from the others. And, since he was taught not to fight back and the school reinforced that if you fight back you're equally part of the problem—called zero tolerance—my son did not react. The response by the teachers was to "just walk away." He did and the bullying intensified.

To make things worse, my son chose an adult at school to share and report his story to confidentially. Then, the male staff member told his daughter who attended the same school and was friends with some of the boys. In return, she shared the information with the perpetrators. At this time, we never imagined that the situation could escalate. However, things got worse, and my son was labeled a snitch for reporting the information to a teacher.

I immediately made an appointment with the principal and was told that he could not do anything about the situation with the teacher. Being exasperated with the situation, I thought I would start keeping a log. With the log in hand, I met with the teachers to inform them about the one student who was our neighbor and the instigator and the need for active supervision. Since the eighth grade was small, it was more challenging to have the school separate students into different classes.

A short time afterwards, I received a call from my son's math teacher, who reported that there was a rumor going around in the hallway that two students were going to jump my son after school. Because there had been a similar threat and severe beating of a girl walking home from school just the previous week, I was even more scared. I called the school and told my son that I would pick him up and not to ride his bike home. In the meantime, I had been delayed at work and he rode his bike. In the greenbelt area, our neighborhood friend and a cohort threw a rock that knocked my son off his bike, and they then continued to beat him up.

I called the school first and no one from the administration was able to take my call, but I left a voice message. I then called the police and they were there immediately. When the police arrived, they took pictures of my son's shoulder, which was hit by a river rock as he was riding his bike, and his lips, which were bleeding from the fall. The police asked where the perpetrator lived, and I pointed to his home. The police visited the home and talked with the father and son about the incident. The perpetrator told the police that my son was the aggressor and that the neighborhood boy was innocent of all charges.

The police recommended that we not file charges unless we were planning on moving soon because of the repercussions that it would cause. I did not file a police report. However, the police suggested that the school prevent the students from having classes together. They changed my son's schedule, not the aggressor's. I told the school and the police that if there was a future incident, I would file a police report.

We avoided passing the home of the perpetrator and never drove in the area of the home. With this all happening from the beginning of eighth grade to December, we made it through the next five months with only one episode that took place between the same two students and my son in the cafeteria. My son reacted by throwing a slice of pizza at one of their faces. All three students received a day of in-school suspension on the same day, in the same room. When I was called about the incident, the administrator recalled the restraining order and immediately restructured their punishment.

After my son finished eighth grade, a high school was com-

pleted right across from our subdivision. Our neighborhood was zoned for this new high school. However, since my son wanted to continue his focus in computer technology, I applied for and received a variance for my son to attend the high school where his friends from sixth and seventh grades were scheduled to attend. Presently, my son has just completed tenth grade. He is still getting bullied occasionally, but now he has friends who will stand up for him. He is active in many computer organizations, from STEM (Science, Technology, Engineering, and Math) to Robotics.

POINTS FOR PARENTS

A word about zero tolerance: This is a term that is widely used in context with bullying prevention. It grew out of the war on drugs in the 1970s. There were instant and harsh consequences for the use, sale, and possession of illicit drugs under zero tolerance laws. That concept has been carried to the schools to mean that there is a severe, predetermined punishment for the breach of a policy and a violation of the rules. This consequence is usually punitive, is applied unilaterally, and does not allow for any extenuating circumstances. When it comes to issues related to bullying behavior, there is no evidence that the zero tolerance approach is effective.

Suspending and/or expelling a student does little, if anything, to change behavior. In fact, it is associated with further negative outcomes for youth (Peterson and Schoonover 2008).

Schools need to have an array of discipline options that are flexible to encourage a positive school climate and promote school safety. These alternatives must be flexible and common sense based on the facts of the issue (Reynolds et al. 2008).

This case is an excellent example of how zero tolerance does nothing to get at the real issue—bullying behavior. When the boy who was being targeted by his peers struck back, both he and the perpetrator were suspended from school. This boy, who was struggling with many issues—not the least of which is communication—had reached a point of frustration and retaliated by throwing a pizza, was given the same punishment as his peers.

The boy's action, throwing the pizza, was clearly inappropriate. However, an investigation by the staff would have revealed that this was a long-term problem involving a student with special needs, and that it was not going to be resolved with an in-school suspension. Had the parent not intervened, the student would have been treated the same as his attackers.

Regardless of the zero tolerance policy, the parent was correct about fighting back. Violence is never a solution to violence. It can, and most likely will, escalate the problem—making it worse and even placing your child in a serious position in which he can be harmed.

To complicate this matter, when the student had enough trust in an adult, his confidence was violated when the teacher passed that information on to his own daughter. The word "snitch" is one that kids use to describe someone who has the courage to report aggressive and dangerous behavior. In a school where there is positive school climate, students are confident that they can rely on adults to support and protect them in these situations. In a supportive school climate, students are more likely to ask for help and—more importantly—speak up for their peers (Elliot et al. 2010). We want all of our children to be in a climate where bullying behavior is not tolerated and one in which adults and bystanders will take mean, hurtful behavior seriously.

SUGGESTIONS FOR ACTION

- Consider the policies of the school. If you hear "zero tolerance," offer other alternatives for dealing with bullying problems in school. In the case of a special needs student, there needs to be accommodations in the Individual Educational Plan that specifically address any consequences that may be necessary and how they will be handled. You may need to be very vigilant and consider the signs or changes in your child's behavior that may indicate he or she is being bullied. The key here is to consider solutions that are safe for your child and follow up with the school to be certain that the plan for safety has been followed.

- Work with your child to help him or her think about solutions to situations he or she may encounter when it comes to someone who may be mean and hurtful. Fighting back is never the answer. Violence only escalates the violence. The child should not just walk away. When the threat is real, children need to know whom they can trust. In the absence of such a person, it is your job to be their advocate.

- Reporting can be helpful, but sometimes it can make things worse. Many children are afraid to say anything because they do not want to be labeled as a snitch. That is not only a disgraceful word to them, but it can also mean that they are vulnerable to retaliation. This can be an opening for to you to talk to your child about courage and what it takes to do the right thing. Talk to your child to see what they think of the word "snitch." When it comes to kids, it can have a variety of meanings.

- Recording behavior is a good strategy to establish a pattern of behavior. When dealing with the school, if you have a history with dates, times, locations, and persons involved, you can establish a pattern of mean, hurtful, and intentional behavioral patterns and assist in both the investigation and the safety plan for your child.

- We have described bullying behavior, and it is important to note that bullying behavior can lead to assault. In this case, the attack on the boy on his bike is just that—assault. This is an example of how bullying can escalate to that level. When this happens, involving law enforcement is necessary. However, even though it is their responsibility to deal with the assault, the bullying behavior will continue without intervention. Therefore, it is crucial to involve the school and, as we discussed, follow up on a regular basis to ensure your child's safety.

Case Study: Battling with the School System over a 504 Plan

Type of Bullying: Gender-based name calling, physical, exclusion, assault
Age of Onset/Gender of Target: Second grade, male
How Long Did the Bullying Last? Until the beginning of seventh grade
Hot Spots: Bus, playground, recess
Did You Tell? If So, Whom? Parents (occasionally), counselor, assistant principal

Our son is presently twelve years old and one of four children. He has a sixteen-year-old sister and two younger siblings who are not yet in school. When he was two years old, I thought something was wrong when our son stayed awake for days at a time; although he had cousins that were a few months older, he showed no interest in playing with them. The pediatrician suggested that he might have a form of autism and wanted us to have him tested. The first individual we saw said our son wasn't autistic but instead referred us to a speech therapist. After further testing, our son was diagnosed as being on the autism spectrum and was evaluated to have a pervasive developmental disorder not otherwise specified. He had this diagnosis until about five years ago, when a doctor added borderline Asperger's to his condition.

We had moved across the country from a liberal state that offered many resources to a state that offered very limited accommodations. Unless a child had a full-blown diagnosis, the chances of the child receiving help would be limited. Although it was suggested many times to place our son on a 504 plan, we were told that he would not be placed on the plan unless his condition worsened. In sixth grade, he was three years behind his peers socially and emotionally but appeared very intelligent. He could logically move from A to Z, but moving through it was very confusing.

We have never discussed with our son that he had a form of autism. In second grade, however, he realized he was different. He was excluded from playing with other kids during recess because they recognized him as being different. He could not differentiate students who were in the mild or severe range on the autism spectrum and did not understand the exclusion factor. He treated everyone like a human being with dignity and respect, even if they were different. On the other hand, his peers who were not in special education would shun the children who were different.

In third grade, our son transitioned to a more academic elementary school and was not picked on. In fourth grade, a larger boy in fifth grade started picking on him on the school bus. The aggressor would call him "gay" and physically push him and knock him down. The aggressor was very athletic and was a popular student leader who was looked up to by peers in his grade.

At the time, my husband and I didn't know how to handle the bullying and told our son to just let it slide off his back, not to worry about it, that it wasn't true, and to just stand up for himself and say something smart. Since it was spring, the bullying lasted for only a few months and then school was out for summer. Thank goodness we did not see many behavior changes at home. I did discuss the situation with the school, and they said that they would address it.

Fifth grade was an awesome year, probably because our son was in the oldest grade in his third year in this elementary setting. He seemed to have grown and matured and for the first time appeared more socially accepted by his peers. For the purpose of advancing his social skills, we continued having him participate in youth football and baseball like most boys in his grade. He definitely had a year that was less stressful than most. In the past, the stress of being called names and exclusion had created massive meltdowns in our home and, at the same time, affected him academically.

In sixth grade, he continued to play youth football. Because his father was his coach, there was little or no bullying on the football field. Unfortunately, the bullying started again on the school bus with the same students calling him "gay" and "stupid." Near the end of the football season, the bullying was less frequent and not as bad. However, when he came home and would discuss the day, he would describe to me how some of his peers had been taunting him. I would then tell him to stand up for himself, dismiss it, not let it bother him, tell himself that it is not a big deal, and stand up and just say something back. The suggestions seemed to not make an impact and made it worse most of the time. As soon as football ended, however, the bullying worsened. We knew something was happening because his grades were falling. The frequency of the bullying seemed to increase to several times a week.

I was adamant that our son would not be able to strive academically, nor would he be able to feel safe at school, unless he was placed in a protected class through a 504 plan. Because some of the state laws contradicted the federal law, parents with students with disabilities had an uphill battle to fight. I personally had been fighting with the school and school district for months as they continued to deny his eligibility in a 504 plan. I even described the impact of the bullying incidents, how my son had been in tears, and how his emotionality affected him physically. I could tell from afar how his day had gone by watching him walk with his eyes down and with slumped shoulders. He looked broken.

We continued to work with him and role-played how he might react differently to the students who called him "gay." He became more baffled and could not understand exactly how he could stand up to the continued harassment. Having the courage to do something was one thing, but what could he do to stop it was even more paramount. Calling my son "gay" originated from this older, popular fifth grade boy who targeted our son in fourth grade. The mimicking of his behavior by his friends and other bystanders targeting our son after three years had a snowballing effect. It became the norm and a common occurrence.

All along I had contact with the school and described the bullying of my son. I soon became known as "that parent" because I was at school so frequently. I asked for the school to intervene and talk with the perpetrator and inform him that his behavior was inappropriate. I strongly believed that any perpetrator should be educated and told that calling a student "gay" was not permitted, and that if it continued there would be consequences. After persistence on my part, the school suspended the aggressor. This slowed the bullying down, but it picked back up after Christmas break. The damage was making a lasting impact with our son. His self-esteem plummeted, his grades worsened, and his confidence plunged. The bullying continued to worsen because more bystanders became part of the problem instead of the solution.

Then, not surprisingly, our son started not confiding in us about the bullying. We thought the bullying was happening less frequently because we were not being told about it. I was continuing to fight for the 504 plan. However, his grades were not improving, his handwriting was on a third grade level, and he was so literal that he was not able to move logically from point A to point B to point C. His thinking was illogical. I was concerned because he would not be able to pass the eighth grade exam or the writing exam in high school if he failed the sixth grade exam in middle school.

Once again, I asked the school-based leadership (SBLT) team to meet to discuss a 504 plan so that my son could qualify for *special education. When I walked into the meeting, the assistant principal pulled me aside to tell me how proud she was of my son because he was confiding in her that he was being bullied two or three times a week. He had quit playing outside because he was bullied there. The assistant principal emphasized again how proud she was that he was describing when, where, and how often the bullying was happening, and how he was handling it. At that moment as a parent I wanted to die inside. Our son stopped coming to us, his parents, because our suggestions didn't work.*

Both my husband and I couldn't understand why our son did not take our advice to stand up for himself. We knew that there was little supervision on the bus, and thus, it was a good place for bullying to happen. We knew that the severity and frequency of bullying was intensifying. Lastly, we knew that if things continued taking a toll on our son emotionally and psychologically, he might do something unfathomable.

Now it was February in the school year. Nothing had changed. Everything was continuing as usual. The school had not developed any accountability standards to address and prevent any future bullying occurrences that we had previously encountered. Thus, I continued to pressure the school to have a regular meeting every thirteen days to address placing our son on a 504 plan and bullying issues. At this next meeting, the principal reported after his investigation that our son had not been bullied since he had no proof that it had happened. I commented that if my son was lying, we had a bigger issue. The principal stated that our son was the most openly honest student that he had ever been around because he had previously admitted when he was in the wrong. He further commented that if he didn't have proof, the school might be liable.

I knew if there were no intervention in the situation, our son would be further victimized. It was more than one boy who was orchestrating the taunting. In addition, his henchmen and their friends participated in the bullying they saw modeled by their pop-

133

ular, athletic classmates. If students felt bad about who they were or wanted to control others because they were controlled at home, then why not pick on a weaker student who was passive and would not fight back?

Days later, when the boys in my son's class were playing two-hand touch football during recess, my son blocked a pass, got tangled up in the play, and when he stood up was pushed down by another student. We had told our son that if someone came into his personal space, he had the right to push them back but not hit them. When he pushed the other student back, the student slapped our son across the face. My son just stood there. Then the same student slapped him again. My son just turned around and walked away. During this time, the principal had turned around and saw some of the incident but did not react.

After recess, my son, who was very upset, went to physical education class and then asked to see the counselor. At this time, the school had enacted a 504 plan for our son, and the counselor was responsible to make contact at least a few times each week to oversee my son's social anxieties and help him to be more assertive and sit and stand taller. The counselor called to report to me how everything was progressing and stated that there had been an altercation involving our son. I was not told that the same student slapped him twice. When my son got home about an hour after school was dismissed, I called the school, but there was no answer. I then called the superintendent's office, and she was reported to be in a meeting. I was so upset that I told the secretary that she had one option—to get someone to talk with me on the phone about a student who had assaulted my son, or I would have the student arrested and give the school system some unwarranted publicity.

On Monday morning, after the principal and central office administrator had conferred, the principal pulled both my son and the aggressor who had slapped my son twice into his office to mediate the conflict. Both students were warned about their behavior.

*Two days later, the same aggressor who had been warned assault-
ed another autistic student by slapping him in the face, bloodying
his nose after a horseplay incident. The only way the family knew
of this similar incident was because I reported it to the parent after
a school employee told me about the incident.*

*The following day, the other parent of the victim and I met with
the principal and shared with him a sixty-page document from
pacer.org, a website whose purpose was to advocate for families
and students with disabilities. I explained the objectives of getting
the bystanders on board to fix the bullying problem. Then the principal admitted that there was a bullying problem at school that
needed to be addressed. I was still angry about the situation, and
so was our son. The main reason was that the aggressor was not
punished for either incident. His consequence was that he was not
allowed to play football during recess.*

*Reading more about disabilities on pacer.org, I learned that
parents could address bullying by including this information into
the student's 504 plan. The following week I shared this fact with
the SBLT, and surprisingly, the principal denied my request. Immediately, I informed him that by federal law, my son had the
right to an education and to be safe at school. I then engaged in
a screaming match with the principal. The principal stated that
my son had grabbed the other boy's neck and had thrown him to
the ground. This information had never been shared the numerous
times we had met until now. I suspected that the principal was
trying to coerce and intimidate me and had another agenda. The
principal further stated that in all of the bullying cases involving
my son, they had no clear, concrete evidence that he had been
bullied. Then it was mentioned that there had been only four cases
identified, but I knew the number was near twenty. So, there was
a huge discrepancy between the records that the school had kept
and reality. I abruptly dismissed myself from the meeting and went
to the main office and asked for a copy of all of the incidents of*

bullying involving my son. The school only shared four reports. I was furious. I kept my own records and knew better.

When I left the office, I told the principal that I was going to file a police report against the perpetrator who assaulted my son. When I made this report, the police encouraged me to follow through with the charges because of the numerous conversations they had with other victims' parents of bullying from the same school. When I came back to school to sign in my son, I ran into a postal worker acquaintance of mine. As we were talking, she reminded me that there were cameras situated throughout the campus. Then she told me that I should ask to see the footage of the incident in question in which my son threw another child to the ground.

I turned around and asked the secretary for the video of the incident. As I waited, I was told that there were no cameras around the area of the incident. Then I was told that parents cannot see footage in which other students are on camera because it violates privacy laws. I then asked for the administration to put the information that they told me in writing on school letterhead. They refused. I was told that only the superintendent could give me the right to see the video, so I requested for the administrator to call the superintendent. He stated that the superintendent was out of town. I then went home and called the school board.

I told the person at the county office that she would have to let me see the video that I was requesting or have me meet with the interim superintendent, and if she did not, I would go to the media. The interim superintendent spoke to me and said that he would review the footage of the incident. and when the superintendent came back into town, she would address it with me. I waited for a phone call and it never came. It became April and the bullying continued. Now, since my son had been a target for bullying for so long, when an aggressor was punished for bullying my son, there was another aggressor in the wings that took his place.

*Days later, the bus broke down as my son was being trans-
ported home from school. With the chaos on the bus, a student
decided—just because he could get away with it—that he would
hit my son in the back of the head while he was waiting for another
bus to take him home. When I heard about this physical attack on
the bus, I called the principal. Without any hesitation. he believed
what I reported and stated that this student had been cited for
multiple discipline referrals and would be suspended from school.
However, because our son was nonviolent and we didn't want him
to get hurt or for this to continue, my husband elected to take
our son to the home of the perpetrator to discuss with the parents
what happened. With both families present, my husband shared
insight into our son's disability and how their son was picking on
a child with autism. The parents looked at their son and asked if
this was accurate and he said it was. These parents then disclosed
that their child had been suspended for fighting, not bullying. The
parents were grateful for the meeting, and it was made clear that
their son would not pick on this student ever again.*

*The rest of the year ended with no incidents. Interestingly
enough, the eighth grade student who started the name calling
three years ago befriended our son for the first time. In seventh
grade, school started with our son being a little anxious, but this
was not unusual when entering a new situation. A girl that always liked our son and tried to watch out for him ran into me at a
school event. As we were talking, I asked how our son was doing
this year. She went on to say that our son was bullied relentlessly
every day by the same two students. When I asked about this year,
she said that little was happening until yesterday, and that they
started calling him names again and intimidating him. I noticed
that yesterday he was very aggressive and irritated when he came
home. Finally, I put together that one of the aggressors played
football and was a defensive star on the team with our son; our
son had to answer to him on the football field since he was the*

defensive leader. That was the reason that our son did not tell us about the bullying.

I then went to school and had an impromptu meeting with the football coach and athletic director and discussed with them how our son was autistic and how it was a pervasive disorder with an Asperger's condition. Similarly, the football coach had an older child with the same diagnosis. I explained the history of the bullying, and the coach and athletic director made it known that it would stop immediately.

The young girl who observed the bullying also made it known to the principal what she had observed last year and this year on the bus. A zero tolerance policy was enacted in the school. The principal called the two perpetrators in his office and stated that this was their last warning and that this behavior must stop immediately. From this day on, there was no further bullying during the last five months of my son's seventh grade year. He is thriving at school.

POINTS FOR PARENTS

This very detailed story is really about how a parent persisted with the school administration. Parents are often labeled as "that parent"—the person who is constantly after the school in order to protect their child. However, it is the school's responsibility to ensure that every child gets the full education that they have a right to under the law. This parent first has to fight to get the support services for her child and then to protect her child from the cruelty of peers who singled him out because of his disability.

Violence prevention efforts for children who have any level of disability are difficult and require not only intervention but also support from professional staff. It is complex, to say the least, and in a situation such as this, the schools appeared to be ineffective, and the problem continued for years (Rosenberg 2012).

Children who are in special education, by definition, require support and individual plans for their education. Anything that interferes with that plan needs to be addressed. It goes without exception that anything that involves violence and victimization needs to be handled in a way that does not, in any other way, further stigmatize the child or further separate him or her from his or her peers (Rosenberg 2012).

If a parent has made a difference in how his or her child is being treated and can advocate for the child's safety, then the parent has done an exceptional job. Don't be afraid to be "that parent." It will bring something good to a child.

SUGGESTIONS FOR ACTION

- When there is a problem, document everything, including what your child tells you, conversations and meetings with the school, and any other relevant information.
- Think of your child's safety first and identify a "go-to" person in the school who is available for your child during the school day, should they need someone to talk or to go to if there is a problem. Be sure to talk to the classroom teacher to be certain that the child will have access to that person. Work with the school to determine guidelines for this so that this will be used without disruption to the class or others.
- Think about the issues that disturb your child. For example, if he or she is worried about being to close to others, talk about how his or her needs can be met during times when children are in proximity to him or her.
- Check to see who is monitoring students' behavior in unstructured areas and hot spots of the schools—lockers, halls, stairs, etc. Be sure they are aware of the issue, and ask the teacher to check in with them regularly to be certain there are no problems. This school had cameras. This is a good way to docu-

ment an incident after it happens, but in terms of prevention, it is better to have an adult presence in those areas.

- Ask the school administrators to detail how they plan to prevent future instances, and then follow up with them periodically.
- Get the details for reporting, investigating, and preventing retaliation. Most importantly, ask what steps they have in place to support rather than blame the victim.
- This school tried mediation to resolve the issue. Bullying is about victimization. Mediation is not a tool to handle these issues. Ask how the school staff will be educated about the school's bullying policy and what their best practices are for bullying prevention.
- Role-play with your child to develop skills such as not reacting or avoiding hot spots and stressful situations.
- Ask the school to work on empathy and understanding with all children so that they will understand their peers who may have disabilities. Educate all children on how to intervene non-violently and how different types of disabilities can intensify bullying.
- Suggest that the school share information with all parents about disabilities and peer acceptance.
- Most importantly, don't worry about becoming "that parent" because you are advocating for your child. Parents need to listen to their child and to the school as well. Persist and follow through with the school, and look at this as a partnership with the school with the common goal of the education and well-being of your child.

6. Kids Who Have Weight Issues

Case Study: I'm Seventeen and Trapped in a Seventy-Year-Old's Body

Type of Bullying: Exclusion, harassment, intimidation, emotional, verbal (name calling)
Age of Onset/Gender of Target: Elementary grades, male
How Long Did the Bullying Last? Through elementary and middle schools and through tenth grade
Hot Spots: Lunchroom, cafeteria, hallways, playground
Did You Tell? If So, Whom? Adults

I'm seventeen years old and a junior in high school. My story begins with introducing you to my family. My father and mother had a tumultuous relationship, and in the summer after my third grade they divorced. My father continued to live in our small farming town; however, my mother had the responsibility of raising my younger sister and me but delegated that duty to my grandparents. She remarried two years later.

After my father left my mother, I became depressed. I used food to feed my depression and gained over 100 pounds during the fourth grade. For the first time, I was called names about my weight and appearance and told that I should go ahead and die. During these two years, my mom focused her attention on dating my future stepfather; my sister and I were not part of my mother's life. So, my grandparents stepped in, and we lived with them. Even after my stepfather came into the picture, we lived with my grandparents for the next five years. I did harbor resentment with how my mother pushed us aside. However, we won the better of the two

*worlds by living with my loving and wonderful grandparents. Be-
cause my grandfather had a passion for politics, gardening, and
50s music, guess what my passions became? Today, I call him my
father.*

*Living in a farm community, we were somewhat isolated from
other peers when not in school. As you might imagine, I connected
well with adults. In fifth grade, I joined a youth leadership club at
school, and this became my shield and protection. I also showed
a great deal of interest in honors history yet struggled in honors
math. My peers labeled me a teacher's pet. On the other hand,
students called me unusual and weird, maybe because they could
not relate to a preteen who had the same hobbies as their parents
or grandparents. Nor could they relate to a student who wore but-
ton-down shirts and khaki pants instead of blue jeans and a t-shirt.*

*A fifth grader even called me gay and sent a rumor around that
I wore mascara. I happened to have long, dark eyelashes. Whatever I did or didn't do seemed to get negative attention. It appeared
to me that I was a scapegoat in the school. At the end of fifth grade,
right after my mother got remarried, I was so distraught at school
that I scribbled on a paper towel that I was going to kill myself. I
was so serious that I took the key to my stepfather's large gun cab-
inet and removed a gun. Just then, my grandmother walked into
the room as I threw the gun on the bed. My grandmother saw what
happened, but instead of quizzing me, she placed her arms around
me, gave me a big hug, said she loved me, and took my hand to
watch a movie with her in the living room. By the grace of God, I
have never felt that desperate again. However, after this incident, I
self-disclosed details about how I was being bullied at school and
how horrific and humiliating it has been.*

*Going into middle school, I was optimistic that I would have
a fresh start. However, the same students were passed from fifth
grade to sixth grade. The administration had divided each grade
into two groups: the "Brady Bunch" and the "Genius Gang" as*

we called them. I was in the Brady Bunch, and the students who were doing most of the bullying were in the Genius Gang. Because the school pushed competitive activities and I could not compete in athletic games, the bullying seemed to escalate throughout the year. One day during physical education class, we were asked to walk around the track. There were two large oak trees that blocked the view of the adults. One student came up to me and called me a fat ass and pushed me down and kicked me. That was the only time that I remember being physically bullied. I did report the incident to a teacher and my parents but did not feel comfortable sharing the name of the student. I thought that there would be retaliation if I did. This same student had bullied me verbally throughout the years, but this was the only incident where he attacked me physically. I had done nothing to him.

The bullying in middle school continued throughout the three years. Students called me names based on my weight and made fun of my clothes, my hobbies, my interests, my eyelashes, etc. Because I knew that I was not coordinated and that boys made fun of me when I played sports, I hung around mostly girls. Because of this, I was called gay and a fag and other such names. One day in eighth grade around the Christmas holidays, I was eating by myself in the cafeteria, and three black students were told to sit down next to me. While eating, these students taunted and criticized me about what I ate and my weight, calling me fat, stupid, and gay and then describing homosexual acts with a fat boy in great detail.

I was humiliated, embarrassed, and hurt about their remarks. I then broke down emotionally and started crying. I got up, left the cafeteria, and went to the library, where I found a quiet corner and isolated myself for about 45 minutes, trying to calm down. During this time, only one teacher came and asked me what happened. I was so embarrassed that I said very little. Later, the assistant principal called me into his office, and again, I didn't share many details because I was ashamed and mortified by the three students' sexual references. What bothered me the most were the unsuitable sanctions delivered to the three students: they had to wash the table in the cafeteria for a day.

Summer passed rapidly as I continued to be active and volunteer in the youth leadership program. When ninth grade started, I again had high hopes for a fresh start and to put the bullying behind me. During this last year, I had opened up with my grandparents and the adults who led the youth development program about the bullying and that I had thoughts of killing myself because of the pain and suffering from being harassed. Moreover, the students who were aggressors seem to have grown up, and the frequency and severity of the bullying was less. I was befriended by two science teachers and opened up to them about my past and being a target for bullying. In addition, I began connecting more with my peers. I had more friends and felt more connected with my school.

In tenth grade, the bullying started to slow down. At the same time, I became active on the board of directors of the youth development club in our region. I am now in eleventh grade and feel depressed at times when I think about how my father doesn't communicate with me and how students had taunted and bullied me in the past; however, even with the hurt, my life is better and is improving. I have forgiven those who have mistreated me. I believe that most of these students have grown up and hopefully aren't involved in mistreating others. I have noticed that some of the aggressors have dropped out of school, and who knows where they are or what they're doing.

Presently, I am running for a state office in the youth leadership organization that I belong to. I am active in my church and continue to teach Sunday school. I am hopeful and pray that bullying has ended for me. I am offering my assistance at church and elsewhere if a student is being bullied. I plead that parents will support, listen to, pay close attention to, and advocate for their children.

POINTS FOR PARENTS

This story is about a boy who was trying to overcome his emotional problems and resorted to comforting himself with food. While his emotional issues most likely stem from his home life, these issues were exacerbated by the fact that he was overweight. Overweight children whose parents are under stress or, as in this case, absent often have difficulty coping. As they become depressed, they feel self-conscious about being active and participating in sports or other activities with their peers.

These children are the ones chosen last or not at all for teams. They worry about being embarrassed and do all they can to avoid these uncomfortable situations. This worry becomes a barrier to physical activity, which is a key factor in reducing obesity in youth (Gray et al. 2008). In this boy's own words, "Because the school pushed competitive activities and I could not compete in athletic games, the bullying seemed to escalate throughout the year." The boy tells us he was victimized in particular during gym class.

His grandparents were very loving toward him, and he even considered his grandfather his father. They gave him an opportunity to develop personal interests. However, they were not the typical activities for a preteen, which further isolated him from his peers. The grandparents were not aware of the boy's struggles. When he was in extreme pain, his grandmother wisely comforted him and listened to his story of victimization at the hands of his peers.

Overweight and obese school-aged children are more likely to be the victims of bullying behaviors than their normal-weight peers. They are at greater risk of developing medical and emotional problems. In addition, these tendencies may hinder their short- and long-term social development (Farhat et al. 2010).

In recent years, we have become aware of the increase in overweight and obese youth in America, and this has become a focus of a national discussion. It is estimated that in the United States, approximately 19 percent of youth ages six to eleven have been classified as obese, with a body mass index (BMI) that places them in the 95 percent of the Centers for Disease Control (CDC) average growth charts (Baker et al. 2007). This leaves children vulnerable to physical limitations such as heart disease and diabetes. Not only do these children have to contend with physical issues, but they are also vulnerable to the persistent meanness of bullying behaviors from their peers. Being overweight is a stigma that becomes material for peer cruelty. These children are outcasts and become isolated, fearing further humiliation because of their size and appearance. Two states, New York and New Hampshire, have identified obesity as a protected group in their respective state bullying laws.

Obese and overweight boys are two times more likely to be targeted with physical and relational aggression. They are at greater risk of social consequences simply because of how they look. Furthermore, those who do not retaliate may experience other negative consequences such as isolation, depression, and social anxiety (Kukaswadia et al. 2011). It is heartbreaking to hear about the abuse this boy endured for such a long time. The harassment extended well beyond being called fat. He was called gay and stupid to add to his humiliation. Once again, homophobic terms are part of a bullying story. These terms are such a collective part of the culture that they have become a common way to demean someone.

When the boy disclosed to a teacher that he had been targeted for such a long time and was feeling humiliated, he felt unable to disclose the names of the aggressors. The same thing occurred when he was asked by the assistant principal to reveal the names. Then he was angry that the perpetrators were given such a minimal punishment. This is understandable to some extent; however, if the adults had put a safety plan in place, it would not have taken long for them to witness the bullying behavior and, in turn, deal with it appropriately.

Students who have been victimized are often afraid of retaliation, and that fear is a very real concern. When the adults in the school are not aware of the extent of the problem, there is no incentive for the bullying behavior to stop. Even when there are some consequences, the behavior will continue unless the adults in charge monitor it closely in order to protect the victim.

By the time the boy was in tenth grade, he tells us that the bullying had decreased. There can be lots of explanations for this phenomenon; however, it most likely is, as he said, that he developed more friendships in and out of school. He felt more connected to the school and had reached a point at which he was able to understand that he was much more than the names he was being called. Because of his experiences in the leadership organization and the love of his grandparents, he was able to overcome his difficulties, be successful, and develop self-confidence.

We are not, by any means, suggesting that he simply grew out of his victimization and that is why he is better off today. No one should ever, at any point in his or her life, feel so desperate that suicide is an acceptable alternative to end the pain. The fact that he has gone beyond these horrific experiences is a testimony to the love of his grandparents and his ability to overcome these obstacles. But we cannot forget that the research is clear: Bullying can have a long-term impact on the target, and the victim may, on some level, be affected by this abuse.

SUGGESTIONS FOR ACTION

- Parents of children who are overweight or obese need to consider that their child is at particular risk for being targeted. Here are some questions you can ask yourself to get a sense of whether your child is experiencing any problems:
  — Look at your children's friends—are they the same ones they have been associating with, or have there been any changes?
  — Do your children avoid social situations?

— Do they avoid physical education classes?

— Are they participating in athletics or club activities?

- Whenever you discover others have targeted your child, it is important to meet with the school to discuss the matter. The most important outcome of that meeting should be the development of a safety plan for your child. That means discussing not only the students involved but also the times and places of the bullying and creating a plan to protect the child. That plan should at least include:

  — Increasing supervision in vulnerable areas (hot spots) that were identified.

  — Having a safe adult in the school whom the student can check in with and talk to on a regular basis.

  — Scheduling a meeting to review progress with the school; call every other week to see how things are developing.

- Activities outside of school are an excellent way to help build self-esteem. By giving the child an opportunity to meet others with a common interest, you are giving him or her a place where the child can develop relationships and explore interests and talents.

- Keep the lines of communication with your child, and above all—like the grandmother in this story—be nonjudgmental. In that nonjudgmental climate, the boy was able to talk about his pain and accept the support that got him through this difficult time.

Case Study: Did Being Physically Larger than My Peers Make Me a Target?

Type of Bullying: Verbal, name calling, physical
Age of Onset/Gender of Target: Fifth grade, female
How Long Did the Bullying Last? A semester
Hot Spots: Physical education, classroom, hallways
Did You Tell? If So, Whom? Teacher, parent, principal

In fifth grade, a male student who was in class with me targeted me. He was athletic and seemed to have many friends and followers. I presume he targeted me because I was nice to others, had pink hair, had a pet snake, and was larger than most of the other girls and boys in my class.

One day in the spring, and without prior warning, this student started calling me names such as "fatty," staring at me and making animal sounds when I walked by. He repeated this same behavior again and again. Then, in physical education class, we were playing dodgeball, and this same male student threw the ball multiple times and hit me in the face. He and his friends laughed. So, I decided to take a friend with me who had observed what had happened and together, we reported the incident to the teacher.

After we repeatedly reported this student's aggressive and hurtful behavior, the physical education teacher told us that the student didn't mean to hurt me and to go back out there and participate in the game. At the time, I was wearing glasses and didn't want to get my face bruised or have my glasses broken. Overall, I reported these incidents to several teachers, and they all dismissed my assertion that I was being targeted and bullied by the student.

As the bullying continued, I didn't know what to do. I told him to stop it, but that didn't work and things worsened. I had one friend who stood up for me and told him to stop, but he continued to taunt me. Finally, after I could not take it anymore, I told my mom. My mom thought something was up because I was avoiding school, which was uncharacteristic of someone with perfect attendance. Eventually, she and I made an appointment with the principal and the counselor to discuss my fear of going to school. After I shared my story with the principal, he was understanding of my predicament and moved the student who had been bullying me out of my class. Immediately, things got better; however, he still called me names, stared, and laughed at me when we crossed paths in the hall.

The school year ended, and our family moved from the South to the Midwest, where I attended school for one and a half years. Everything went smoothly as my classmates treated me very respectfully. Then we moved back to the South at the beginning of the second semester of seventh grade. I attended the same middle school where I would have matriculated if I had not moved; the boy who had taunted me was also in the same grade. He continued to give me strange looks when we saw each other in the halls, but he usually ignored me. However, I still felt unsafe at times and fearful and that he might attack me the following year. This time I feel more confident than ever that if something does happen, I will immediately report it to the principal. After discussing the situation with my mom, I am contemplating having a conversation with the principal to prevent us from being in the same classes. Next year, I think I might log any future incidents in a private diary and share it with the principal if I feel intimidated, harassed, or bullied by any student.

Presently, I am not sure that the bullying has ended; only the future will tell. However, I am excited about going into eighth grade and hope that with the support from my mom and my principal, I will be able to overcome any obstacles that might arise.

POINTS FOR PARENTS

We have talked extensively about the research and the impact of bullying on students. The most recent research in 2014 from the U.S. Department of Health and Human Services shows that the impact of bullying on those targeted lasts longer than the incident. We are referring to children who are frequently hit, pushed, or called names once or more per week. This can cause long-lasting health effects well after the bullying stops. In fact, those who had been bullied showed low scores on measures of physical and emotional health. When this is considered, it is not possible to overstate the urgency in dealing with this problem as early and thoroughly as possible to prevent the long-term impact of bullying.

This story is one in which the parents and the school administration together were able to relieve a bullying situation in order to protect a student. But it was not easy. Let us examine what worked well in this story. To begin, the girl took a friend with her to the teacher to report the bullying. Bringing a friend for support is an excellent strategy when reporting bullying behavior. It gives the target support and adds validity when reporting the incident to the adult, whether that be a teacher or administrator.

When the parents and the girl met with the principal to discuss the problems she was having in school, the discussion centered on problem solving. The solution was excellent because the perpetrator was moved to another class. So often the one being victimized is the one who is moved or has to make accommodations to separate from the aggressor. When this happens, it is as if the message to the victim is that because of him or her, there is a problem. The victims are the ones tasked with readjusting their lives. When you look at it that way, it seems absurd; however, in most cases, the victim is the one moved to another class, a new bus, or even a new school to provide relief from the bullying.

It would have been even more helpful if there were a plan to reduce the opportunity for the aggressor in this case study to have access to the girl who was being bullied. She tells us that he would call her names, stare, and laugh at her whenever their paths crossed. To reduce the possibility of retaliation, members of the school's administration must follow up with both the target and the aggressor to be certain there are no reoccurrences.

The most uplifting part of this story is how the girl is moving forward. Upon her return to school, after her time in a different hometown, she feels more confident than ever before. She has a strategy to report the incident immediately should she be confronted with any aggression. In addition, she is planning ahead and requesting that she be placed in separate classes from the main aggressor. In addition, and most importantly, she is planning to keep a diary. This is a great way not only to document any issues but also to record her growth socially and emotionally. Just a few written words per day can show progress on a journey free of fear and intimidation.

SUGGESTIONS FOR ACTION

- Bringing a friend when reporting a bullying incident is an excellent strategy. Two voices lend validity to any story and provide support for the target.
- Increasing active supervision is a first strategy when there are bullying issues. However, when a plan is in place and changes must be made, the aggressors—rather than the targets—of bullying should be moved and uprooted from their setting, whether it be the classroom, a bus route, or wherever the problem occurs.
- Planning ahead to be prepared for any reoccurrences or retaliation. This girl is planning to report any bullying acts immediately to the principal. This gives her comfort and courage, which lessens her fear of attending school where she feels frightened and intimidated.
- Documenting with a journal or log. This gives you a written record while providing an outlet for feelings. She can see how her feelings and attitudes evolve over time, and this will give her self-confidence as well as a place for her private thoughts.

Case Study: Fighting Back

Type of Bullying: Intimidating, threatening, physical (pushing, shoving), name calling
Age of Onset/Gender of Target: Sixth grade, male
How Long Did the Bullying Last? Through tenth grade
Hot Spots: Hallways, physical education class, riding bike home
Did You Tell? If So, Whom? Told parents, made a police report

When I was in the sixth grade, I was a normal kid in all respects, except I was larger than most of my peers. I was average height and weighed 200 pounds. There was another boy in my grade, however, who was a bully. He didn't like me and would say something mean to me, and in return, I would say something back. I don't remember a single event that made him start taunting me. He would shove and push me into a locker, or he and his friends would walk by and call me names always related to my weight, such as fat ass, porky boy, fatso, tubby, boob boy, bag of dough- nuts. The list of names went on and on. It even became a contest between those kids to think up new mean names for me.

I was convinced that their plan was to make my life miserable. I went to my parents and asked them for advice because I knew that if I fought this guy, I would be suspended from school. I was taught to turn the other cheek and that violence does not solve anything. So I thought I would do what was morally right and not fight and continue to report what was happening to my parents and a trusted adult at school. Over time, the bullying got worse because I did not give them what they wanted—I did not break down and cry or fight back. I think because I didn't stand up for myself, this group of boys thought they could get away with it, so they continued to make fun of me.

One evening I remember going to a school dance on my bike since I lived close to school. When the dance was over, an aggressor and his henchmen chased after me and threatened to "kick my fat ass." One other time they had rear-ended my bike with their bikes and made me crash. Once again, I felt harassed and consumed with the thought that I had to look over my shoulder wherever I was and that I couldn't get away from them. I was terrified and believed that they would hurt me if given the opportunity. When I arrived home, I told my dad, who was a local police officer. I thought that he could advise me the best. My dad suggested filing a police report, and I did just that. Not surprisingly, I heard nothing from the report. I don't think there was any action taken. I think it was just considered a legal log just in case there were future incidents.

In the following month, there were fewer incidents, but then everything started up again. At school, if this aggressor and his friends saw me alone at break in the hallways, they would continue to call me names and threaten to hurt me; however, if the aggressor wasn't with his henchmen, they did and said nothing. It was only when they were with this aggressor that they attacked me as a gang. This intimidating, harassing, and bullying behavior continued through middle school into high school and occurred two to three times each week. Most of the incidents happened at school where adults were not present at the time. These students were very savvy about where and when they chose to call me names and push me against the lockers. After putting up with bullying for more than four years, everything seemed to be routine. I would come to school and continue to avoid these same students who had harassed and taunted me since middle school. However, in the summer before ninth grade, I became interested in martial arts to see if this activity might increase my confidence level. So I became very involved in developing my skills in self-defense.

In the fall of tenth grade, I had just been told that one of my grandparents had died over the weekend. On Monday when I arrived at school, I was so preoccupied with what was happening in my family that I was not thinking about avoiding the perpetrators who made my life miserable. As I was leaning on my locker waiting for class to start and not paying attention to anything else, the usual aggressor passed by and shoved me into my locker. Without thinking, I called out his name and tackled him to the ground. He got up and tried to tackle me without much success, then a teacher intervened and broke up the fight.

I felt so guilty that I had let the aggressor get to me and that I had attacked him. It was out of character for me to attack another student, but after four years, I guess I had let my anger build up and could not hold it in anymore. I had been taught that fighting doesn't solve anything and that sitting down and talking it out was the preferred method to resolve conflict. I was brought up to the office, and both of us were sat down next to each other. The vice principal called the aggressor into the office first, and his parents were asked to come and pick him up since the school had a zero tolerance policy. I was then called in. The vice principal knew my mother since she had worked for the school system as a consultant for the last ten years. He asked me to tell my story. He then gave me the same consequences—three days of out-of-school suspension. On a lighter note, he stated afterwards that he was proud that I had stood up for myself, and that if he had the authority he would not have suspended me.

I found out that I was not the only person whom this aggressor was harassing at school. He had been to the office many times for the same behaviors, and the vice principal made it clear that this aggressor had a track record for being suspended many times. When my mother picked me up, I knew she was disappointed because she had always told me that violence was not answer. I knew that she understood how this same student had tormented me in the past; nevertheless, she wanted me to work it out through non-physical means. She was proud that I had stood up for myself but asked that I choose a different, peaceful method next time.

It was intense for me since this was the first time that I had actually pushed back. It did seem to get better. The aggressor did not pick on me anymore, except once or twice in physical education class, when he was aggressive while playing a sport. However, since I had stood up to him once, it was easier for me to stand up to him again. He understood that I was not going to put up with his intimidating and coercive behavior and that I would stand up for myself.

Once I graduated from high school, there were no more incidents. I have run into him twice since graduation. We acknowledged each other in the room, and we each went our separate ways. I have heard from friends that he has been in legal difficulties and has an arrest record.

POINTS FOR PARENTS

This case study is about a boy who was repeatedly, over several years, harassed by being called mean names. Bullying is repeated, intentional, hurtful behavior directed at a person who is not able to defend himself or herself. In this story, because of the number of people involved in the intentional persecution and the fact there was no one who would help the victim, we can say with certainty that he was a victim of bullying.

This boy attempted several strategies to deal with this problem. The boy is the one who repeatedly talked to the school administration. His parents indicated that he should solve the problem himself, and when it became physical with the bicycle incident, the parents went to the police. According to this story and until that point, they never involved the school. To the police, this was an incident that would be part of a legal log to indicate a history in the event of another incident.

There are many coping strategies you can use when confronted with repeated, hostile actions that leave you feeling defenseless. There are the problem-solving coping mechanisms such as self-defense, standing up to the bully, seeking social support, and distancing. Distancing is an emotion-focused coping approach that includes seeking social support, internalizing, tension reduction/externalizing, self-blame, and focusing on the positive (Tenenbaum 2011).

Problem solving is the most common form of coping with bullying behavior for targets. Initially, this boy did exactly that—he tried to ignore the bullying and then tried to ask his parents for help. Finally, he reached a point at which he could no longer problem solve, and he stood up to the bullying behavior that had evolved into harassment. For him, fighting back was a last resort because he believed that nonviolent problem solving was a better solution.

It is sad that he had to reach that point. Many coping mechanisms had failed; if things had been handled properly early in the story, the boy never would have reached the point at which he had to physically attack the aggressor in order to stop the bullying.

One of the greatest failures in the system that did not stop this bullying incident is the response of the vice principal. He said he was proud of the boy for standing up for himself. That is absurd, as it is the school's responsibility to provide a safe environment for all students. The fact that the boy had to fight his tormentor was in no way a credit to the boy; rather, it is an embarrassment to the school.

In fact, the consequence of a suspension did apply to both the boy and the perpetrator because the boy did break the school rule by starting the fight. The boy had to suffer the same consequence for the incident, and the perpetrator was left to believe that the victim was equally to blame. Even the boy, after all he had been through, recognized that fighting was not a way to settle a dispute.

Yet the vice principal's comment, "Glad you stood up for your-self," actually is reinforcing violence as a solution for this type of an issue.

At the end of his account, the boy tells us that he had heard that the student who was the aggressor had "legal difficulties and an arrest record." This is, again, a failure of the school to deal with this bullying behavior. As we analyze these stories, it is clear that it is quite common for the long-lasting effect on the student who bullies is negative. Everyone is affected by this behavior. Bullying is a key risk factor for delinquency and antisocial development (Baker et al. 2007). The schools have a responsibility not only to the one who is victimized but also to the aggressors as well.

SUGGESTIONS FOR ACTION

- Sit down with your child to discuss how to handle bullying and other coercive behaviors, especially if they have been repeated for months or years and can't easily be worked out by the usual means. Suggesting to children that they should just walk away may not work.
- Take the next step. Parents can be an essential link between the school and the child. When there are issues that are making school difficult for their child, it is important to consult with the school immediately. This should always be the first step before the police are involved. In some serious instances, it may be necessary to involve both simultaneously, but in any case, the school should be included.
- Calling for an investigation. Even though the boy had to accept a consequence for striking the other student, the parents need-ed to call for an investigation of the bullying. Clearly, the vice principal's comment shows that the school knew about the in-cident. Therefore, the school is responsible for making certain that there are consequences for past behaviors and taking steps to prevent reoccurrences.

7. Bullying, Harassment, and Protected Groups

Case Study: Peace at Age Thirty

Type of Bullying: Verbal, threatening, controlling, gossip
Age of Onset/Gender of Target: Early elementary grades, female
How Long Did the Bullying Last? Through elementary, middle, and high school
Hot Spots: Cafeteria, playground, homeroom
Did You Tell? If So, Whom? I reached out to several teachers and my parents. When the authorities scolded the aggressors, the bullying got worse. After a while, I took whatever was thrown at me and counted down the days to summer.

I remembered that bullying started when I was six or seven years old. It might be because I was the smallest in my class and one of the smallest in the school. When I entered third grade, it appeared that everyone increased in height except me. In those earlier years, I was an outspoken, outgoing kid and didn't let anyone push me around. I would describe the bullying that occurred as threatening, controlling, and overpowering.

If the bullying had been only at school, I might have been able to deal with it; however, it occurred in my home, too. I had a rough upbringing in my family. My father had chronic pain, didn't work, was depressed, and had anger outbursts. Consequently, we struggled financially. I referred to my dad as Dr. Jekyll and Mr. Hyde. All of this had a huge impact on the way that I viewed my life.

I unfortunately absorbed it all. Because my sister was six years older and usually out with her friends, I had no one in whom to confide and felt alone. When my father had outbursts and my parents fought, I internalized the hurt and pain and blamed myself for their transgressions. I reluctantly changed into a soft-spoken, introverted, and quiet individual who didn't know how to be assertive and stand up for myself. I became a magnet for bullying.

Bullying and meanness toward me increased in severity during my middle school years. The hot spots seemed to be the cafeteria, playground, and homeroom when the teacher was out of the room—which was most of the time. They called me names like dyke, queer, and weirdo. Bullying became more pronounced when, in seventh grade, my friends and I tried out for the drama program and were selected to act and tour around the area. For some reason, perhaps because some students were jealous and envious of us, the bullying became harsher.

The school was diverse with a blend of student cliques, yet there was a sector from a low socioeconomic area that added its challenges. The bullying occurred in groups and was accepted by all adults because the attitude was that "boys will be boys" and "girls will be girls." The adults even suggested that those words were just names, and I should just ignore them. That same group would surround my friends and call us drama geeks and even threaten us. They would throw things, spit on us, kick us, and use crude sexual slurs. I was frightened that if I said anything back in retaliation, I would be pounded and beaten up. The unwritten rule in this school was: "This is the way we do things." After a while, I was so miserable that with the support of my parents, I started seeing a social worker outside of school to help me cope. In seventh grade the drama geeks supported each other and attended the same classes. However, with a change in schedule in eighth grade, we were spread out in different classes in school. Things definitely changed for the worse when I had no contact with or support from the other drama students. A few adults did know what was going on. Even though they seemed to understand, they were not able to stop it.

At some point in eighth grade, I decided to react and threw a chair at one of the aggressive boys using foul language. However, because of the understanding adults who knew what I was going through, I did not get into trouble. I was aware of some bystander support because they told me that they thought these incidents were serious.

Because I was in so much pain and emotionally drained, I started cutting myself. When my parents found out, I was placed in a weeklong intensive inpatient treatment children's home. I became even more scared in this setting because of the stories I heard about the other kids in the facility. After I was released, I did stop cutting, but I have to say that I was never suicidal. I cut myself because I wanted attention and help so I could get some relief from all the pain. I had left clues for others to pick up that I was hurting. However, when I returned to school, it was rumored that I tried to commit suicide, and some taunted me by giving me the nickname "suicide."

When I entered ninth grade, my parents and I chose a high school out of my district. Some of my drama friends attended the same school, which was well known for its intolerance toward bullying. When I entered this new school and community, there were fewer cliques, and students in general were more inclusive. It was a place where I could start a new school life.

However, it was not surprising to me that even in that environment, the ostracizing, intimidation, and harassment continued. This time the aggressors were a group of popular students. To fit in, I decided to become reactive and even proactive. If someone mistreated me, I would lash back and begin attacking him or her. I was feeling terrible about myself. I also started drinking and smoking marijuana. Because this behavior wasn't really me, and at the same time I seemed to feel more anxious, I decided that I had to change my ways.

Unfortunately, like a pressure cooker, my emotional state of mind became so unstable that I dropped out of school during October of my senior year. I was treated for a serious anxiety disorder that resulted from the bullying and consequently became agoraphobic. My parents requested that the school have an exit meeting with the principal and counselor in which I explained to them my situation. They understood that I was too anxious to attend school and agreed for me to drop out. I was a very good student, but because I had so many absences because of fear that others might mistreat me, it was unlikely that I could graduate because I was behind in credits. Even though I dropped out of school, I continued to pursue my GED and graduated with my class.

It seems that most of the drama students were affected by the bullying, but that I was the one who was impacted the most. As recently as five years ago, I have had reoccurring dreams in which I was not able to stand up for myself. I would wake up and pray that if confronted, I would be able to stand up for myself. I also never had an expectation that the student bystanders should have stepped in because I knew that they were just as scared as I was. I am presently seeing a social worker monthly who specializes in bullying and anxiety. I work full-time, am married, and am eager to start a family. Bullying does end. I made it, and you can make it, too. I am comfortable with myself and continue being involved with the theater. I am at peace with myself, and since I cannot change the past, I accept what happened. It has been a tough journey, but there is hope on the other side. I have forgiven those who mistreated me, and I am grateful for those who helped me along the way. I just wish there had been more of them.

POINTS FOR PARENTS

The young woman in the story had a very difficult experience in school from the third grade to the end of her school career. At the end, she clearly has gained wisdom. It is so sad that she had to experience those years of victimization. There are many levels to her story, beginning with the victimization because she appeared different. From a very young age, she was singled out by her peers and ridiculed. This is her story, her own experience, and clearly it has had a profound impact on her life. For many reasons, she was vulnerable, and that may be a key to why she was victimized for most of her school life.

There has been a great deal of research to understand why students pick on one student relentlessly. Some call it moral disengagement. "Moral disengagement refers to such sociocognitive maneuvers, which permit people to disengage from moral standards without any feelings of remorse, guilt, or self-condemnation" (Thornberg and Jungert 2013). Essentially, some people are able to ignore their personal moral standards. Basically, when in a group, individuals can do things that they would not do as individuals. In addition, they can do it without feeling badly or any remorse at all.

The groups in this story just continued on a path that separated themselves from other groups. She describes them as the "popular" students who picked on others who were different. The "popular" students called the others the "drama geeks" and had no respect for them, even when the "geeks" had success and some recognition.

The level of disrespect included homophobic slurs. It does not matter if these students are lesbian, gay, bisexual, transgender, or questioning; the simple fact is that they are being humiliated and victimized because they are not part of the general stereotypical population. Using this language is a way to gain social dominance (Poteat and Rivers 2010). These "popular" students are using their meanness to establish dominance and a social hierarchy. Poteat's research recommends that biased language such as this is prejudicial and should be discussed as part of bullying prevention (Poteat and DiGiovanni 2010).

This girl went through a very difficult time that gave her serious anxiety. This condition is thought to be very common—perhaps the most common psychological disorder of childhood and adolescence. We now are learning that anxiety does not diminish as children and adolescents go into adulthood. Often, as in this case, childhood anxiety extends long into adulthood (Cartwright-Hatton et al. 2006).

Agoraphobia is a form of anxiety that includes panic attacks with intense fear and serious physical symptoms. It is known as a panic disorder and is linked with other forms of anxiety in adolescents. Anxiety took a toll on this girl as she endured the bullying behavior for so many years. It led to her use of alcohol and marijuana. As she said, "I was feeling terrible about myself. I also started drinking and smoking marijuana." This is not unusual, according to the National Institute of Health (NIH). "Collectively, an emerging body of work suggests reliable associations among panic-spectrum problems, social anxiety, and problematic alcohol use behaviors among adolescents" (Blumenthal et al. 2011).

Another aspect of the impact of bullying on this student is the fact that at one point, she resorted to self-harm. Students who are exposed to bullying on a regular basis are at higher risk for self-harm. Other risk factors include serious issues in the family environment, symptoms of depression, problems with conduct, or borderline personality characteristics (Fisher et al. 2012).

Moving to another school only gave this girl temporary relief. She was able to make friends in a similar group and then found that some peers in that school also targeted them because of their particular interests—for example, athletes; academic achievers; and band, drama, and even self-described geeks. They all find their place in a school. There is often little interaction and, at times, tension between the groups. The casual comments and negative communications that occur between students can contribute to a hostile atmosphere. The more it happens without intervention, the more likely it is to continue and escalate, as it did in this story.

This is almost a universal phenomenon. When the girl went to a new school, she had similar, albeit less intense, bullying experiences. This situation existed even though the school was described as "well known for its intolerance of bullying." This is a perfect example of why bullying prevention in schools needs to be systemic—including all stakeholders—and ongoing, involving continual training and evaluation.

SUGGESTIONS FOR ACTION

- When confronted with bullying issues, parents need to consider the safety of their child as the primary goal. If the bullying does not stop after reporting the incident(s) to the school, setting up a safety plan, documenting the problem, and following up to ensure progress, an alternative placement should be considered.

- An exit interview with the school must include a detailed conversation about the reasons the child is leaving the school. While that seems obvious, many people feel it is not worth the time. Many people feel that it makes no difference, but it does. Schools need to have a clear understanding of why a student cannot continue his or her education. Furthermore, we suggest documenting the conversation by taking notes. These notes may be helpful should you ever need them in the future.

- If it reaches the point at which anxiety is severe, outside help should be sought through a referral from the family physician, school counselor, clergy, or local social services agency.

Case Study: A Neighborhood Fiasco

Type of Bullying: Name calling, threatening, emotional
Age of Onset/Gender of Target: Seven-year-old, male
How Long Did the Bullying Last? Throughout elementary and middle school
Hot Spots: After-school care
Did You Tell? If So, Whom? Parents

I am the mother of Michael, an only child who is now fourteen years old, in eighth grade, and adjusting well. When in elementary school, my son did not have any issues with other children during the school day, but he did in the after-school program. One specific aggressor, Adam, was never in class with my son during school. They were in summer camps together and lived in the same subdivision. However, the administration seemed intuitive enough to never place these two boys in the same class.

Adam's home could be characterized as one with parents yelling and screaming while the children ran amuck. Adam continued to aggravate other families in the neighborhood and to invite himself to play in our homes. When he did come over, he was a handful. In addition, there was a hostile older brother who added to the mix and whom the neighborhood children feared. Thus, the other children were apprehensive going to Adam's home to play because of the dysfunction of the family.

Early on, when Michael was four or five years old, he had separation anxiety when I left him. Therefore, I always picked him up early from after-school care. By second grade, he was adjusting well to attending school. However, during those earlier years when both my son and Adam were in after-school care and Adam could not get my son's attention, he would call Michael a crybaby. Even though my son asked him to stop at the time, he continued. Thank goodness he only had to endure this taunting for an hour each day. Adam was one of the last to be picked up. I wondered who else he chose to ridicule after my son left.

Because Michael was our only child, I would usually have another child in my home to help entertain him. When Adam came over, usually unannounced, he would appear jealous and started to create havoc until he got everyone's attention. This continued into third grade, but the name calling progressed from "crybaby" to "gay," "queer," and "fag." Most third graders may not know these words, but my son did. I am sure that Adam heard these words from his older brother, who dressed in the hardcore punk style called "goth" and the "emo" look. Things stayed status quo through the fourth grade until the summer, when things escalated. Michael tried ignoring Adam and staying out of his way in after-school care and when playing in the neighborhood.

At this time, we learned that Adam's parents were going through a divorce. Adam's mother would call and ask if Adam could come over and play with Michael and would hint that it would be helpful to her if he could spend the night. Because Adam had a foul mouth and had torn up some of my son's possessions, Michael wanted to have nothing to do with him.

During the second week of fifth grade, Michael came home from school tremendously upset with Adam calling him names. I called Adam's mother and confronted her with her son's behavior. I was emphatic that the name calling had to stop. We would not tolerate another year of this torture and harassment. I asked for a meeting of both boys and parents at my home the next day. We had crossed paths with Adam's parents but had tried not to interfere and to let the boys work it out—until now. Before Adam's parents came over, we rearranged the furniture in order to make the setting more inviting. We role-played with Michael and discussed how we, as a family, should be respectful, be assertive with our responses but not aggressive, and have an inclusive and accepting attitude. When Adam and his parents walked in, Adam

167

looked down and never could look at us. Michael, on the other hand, was courteous and polite. Yet, we stated unequivocally as a family that Adam could not continue taunting Michael. However, Michael asked Adam if they could be friends or at least be friendly to each other. The father spoke for Adam and stated that this would never work.

A few weeks after this meeting at our home, it began again. This time it was Adam staring at Michael when they were eating their snack. When Michael came home and described the staring to me, I suggested he say, "Why don't you take a picture? It will last longer." The next day when Adam started staring at him, Michael repeated this to Adam, and it set Adam off. When Michael stood up from the table, Adam tripped him. Then Michael said firmly, "Stop it, Adam! Stop it! I have had enough from you." Adam then said, "When I get home, I'm going to come over to your tree house and shoot you dead." He used his hand like he had an imaginary gun. Michael was frightened and scared when he left after-school care, not knowing what Adam was capable of.

When I heard about this latest incident, I e-mailed the principal, assistant principal, and counselor and asked for a meeting the next morning to address the threat that Adam made to my son. I had kept a log of the past incidents along with the minutes from the meeting in our home. I brought all of this documentation to their attention. As an advocate for Michael, I discussed how Adam's past behavior—in addition to him making a death threat—can be addressed in our state law addressing bullying, intimidation, and harassment.

The school followed up by asking the school resource officer to investigate the incident. After examining the facts, Adam's parents were called in to the school and informed that Adam would be suspended for three days. It was further mandated that if there were any reprisals or retaliation, Adam would be referred to the juvenile court system. In October the principal called my husband, Michael, and me into her office and shared that she would recommend to the middle school administration that Michael never have a class with Adam during his middle school years (sixth, seventh, and eighth grade), nor will they ever be on the same academic team.

Michael had an uneventful middle school experience, with only a few exceptions. During the sixth grade, Adam and Michael rode the same bus to school. The bus driver and other students constantly reminded Adam that if he was mean to anyone or called any student a name, any acting out would be caught on tape by the video and audio surveillance cameras. This alone brought Adam's behavior under control.

Presently, Michael continues to be on the honor roll each year in middle school. He is in Boy Scouts, plays soccer, and is first chair trumpet player in the band. Michael has just taken a growth spurt and stands six feet, three inches tall at fourteen years old. Adam, on the other hand, struggles academically and seems to be left out and not cared for or respected by his peers. At fourteen years old, Adam is five feet, seven inches tall. During middle school, Adam continues to be aggressive and has been called to the principal's office at least twice for beating another student up.

POINTS FOR PARENTS

This is a mother who tried several approaches to helping her child overcome the bullying he was experiencing. Meeting with the parents of the aggressor was one of her strategies, but it provided only a temporary solution. Within a short amount of time, Adam was back to his previous aggressive behaviors. While this meeting seems like a logical place to start, it is one that can be very precarious. Adam's parents could have easily denied the issue and blamed Michael for the problem.

Parents have told us that when they took the problem into their own hands, they found themselves in an adversarial situation with the parents of the aggressor, inadvertently igniting a neighborhood conflict. Most parents, by nature, are protective of their children, and it is rare for them to acknowledge that their child can be the cause of a problem. This is true even if you feel you have a relationship with the other family. This mother described how she took special care to arrange the furniture and make things comfortable. However, talking about your child's behavior is very emotionally charged, and regardless of the setup, parents can be very defensive. Without a third party there to assist, meanings can become confused or twisted and intentions misunderstood. This is crucial to consider, particularly if these are people with whom you have a relationship or have to encounter daily in your neighborhood.

If you think that you must speak to the parents of the aggressor, it is a good idea to do this in a nonconfrontational way—perhaps by stating only the facts and asking the aggressor's parents how they think they can help to solve the problem. In a less dramatic way, you are then aligning with them to address an issue in the interests of both boys.

Generally speaking, the best avenue through which to deal with these problems is to bring them to the attention of the school. By involving the school, you have that third party that will take on the role of addressing the issue with the parents. Also, any problem—whether or not it originates in the neighborhoods—will surface in the school, and the school will have to deal with it. If the school is made aware of the situation, it can sharpen its observation of the students. It won't take long for the school to see what you know is happening in the neighborhood. It can then deal with the student, and you will avoid any potential hard feelings in the neighborhood.

When meeting with the school, as this parent eventually did, it is a good idea to approach the situation with the intention of working with the school to develop a safety plan. The main goal of this meeting is to ensure the safety of the child. Once you have worked out the details with the school, you need to set up a method for communication. Be specific about how and when you will check back for progress, and, of course, how you wish to be notified if things escalate in any way. While all this is happening, it is important to log all contacts with the school. In order to document progress, Michael's mother kept notes on all her conversations with the school, including outcomes and expectations.

Because there was a threat, the parents took the correct action by taking it seriously and bringing it to the school immediately. The school, in turn, involved the school resource officer who made it clear that there would be serious consequences if the threats continued. What is impressive about that action is that retaliation was also mentioned as a factor that would result in serious consequences.

It appears that Adam is a boy who has a number of problems. Whenever emotional and behavioral problems exist, we need to extend our concern to the aggressor. Failure to attend to these problems can mean that the bullying and aggressive behavior will continue (Leiner et al. 2014). In fact, in this story, this is exactly what happened because Adam "continues to be aggressive and has been called to the principal's office at least twice for beating another student up."

The process of eliminating bullying needs to go beyond protecting the target and disciplining the aggressor. We have a responsibility to adequately treat both parties to stop the escalation of violence and aggressive behavior.

SUGGESTIONS FOR ACTION

- Talk to your school. Ask for help! Let your child know that you are going to talk to someone you trust (such as a teacher, counselor, or administrator) so the adults can create a plan to stop the bullying.
- When talking to the school, make it clear that the bullying

behavior is occurring on the bus and that any strategy needs to include bus safety.

- Document everything—conversations, visits, and—most importantly—any incidents of bullying behavior.
- Stress with your child that the use of words like "gay" and "fag" are not acceptable under any circumstances. Not only are they hurtful, but they also demonstrate a prejudice that is hurtful, demeaning, and detrimental to others.

Case Study: A Teacher's Perspective

Type of Bullying: Racial, name calling, exclusion, cyberbullying (social media)
Age of Onset/Gender of Target: Middle school, female
How Long Did the Bullying Last? Throughout middle school
Hot Spots: School and home
Did You Tell? If So, Whom? Mother

A petite eighth grade girl was transferred into my class during second semester, and I immediately knew something was wrong. She was a beautiful, biracial girl who could not make eye contact. She appeared to be so fragile, with so much pain and sorrow behind her eyes that I tried to give her extra space while handling her with kid gloves. Some days she would work up to her potential, and other days she did very little.

A few weeks went by, and I felt compelled to check in with the mother regarding her daughter's progress in class. The mother was very emotional and shared with me that her daughter had been severely taunted and bullied at her previous school. Her road to recovery had been an uphill battle. A group of girls targeted her because she was biracial. They called her racial names, excluded her in school and continued to use social media to cyberbully her at home.

Her personality changed from that of a sparkling child who loved school to that of an unhappy child who refused to go to school. Her grades plummeted, and her personality turned inward. She refused to leave the house.

After my conversation with her mother, I was wondering if I could help with the healing of her daughter and, at the same time, prevent this from happening in my class. So, I addressed three different things. First, as we were reading a class novel, The Old Man and the Sea, *I decided to have an open discussion on how exclusion, rumors, and other mean behaviors related to each of the characters. Secondly, I assigned each student to create a cartoon and describe how important it was to embrace one's own culture. She described an individual who was faceless, all alone, and depressed. Lastly, I asked permission from her mother for her daughter to read a book that I had written about bullying and to ask her daughter if she could elaborate on the main character. She shared that the main difference between her and the main character was she felt invisible in a crowd.*

At the end of the year, I saw a drastic change in her demeanor. She got her voice back. She would laugh and ask questions. She smiled and seemed to enjoy school. She became the girl I had always thought she could become. She trusted in me, and I in her. Presently, she is a high school junior and exceeds academically, socially, and emotionally.

POINTS FOR PARENTS

Under circumstances such as this, where the child is entering the school because of a history of bullying and harassment, it is clear that the parent must be hypervigilant. This parent was successful in working with the school and alerting it to the previous issues.

This could not have been possible if it were not for the mother getting involved, changing her daughter's school, and forming a bond with the new school and teacher. It took a team effort. Talk with the teacher, and let him or her know what you need. Ask the teacher to keep the lines of communication open, and make it a point to check in with the teacher on a regular basis.

The teacher was able to reach out to the child in an attempt to make her comfortable. She was able to engage all the members of the class by asking them to look at their own experiences through literature that was part of the curriculum. This is an excellent approach and part of a systemic method of addressing bullying behavior. It is about prevention. Rather than waiting until there was a problem, she used a classic piece of literature to generate a discussion about exclusion and rumors. She followed that up with lessons about embracing culture and additional student discussions. This is a great example of how a curriculum can give students the opportunity to understand themselves and others. It is essentially a path to building empathy.

These classroom lessons and discussions are central to bullying prevention. This is the opportunity for students to have discussions about their concerns about bullying as well as to learn how to handle the bullying. The most successful approaches to prevent bullying behavior are systemic. That means prevention must be multifaceted. Just dealing with the individuals is not enough because peer support and underlying cultural attitudes often fuel bullying behavior. Successful prevention programs include everyone in empathy development as well as a clear understanding of agreements, supervision, and consistent intervention. It is also important to point out that these efforts must continue: bullying prevention and empathy development are not onetime events; they are part of a process that must be ongoing.

SUGGESTIONS FOR ACTION

- Talk to the school about your child's history and your concerns. Schools know that a child's academic success is directly related to social and emotional development. If a child is lonely, isolated, and disconnected from peers, it is likely that his or her academic performance will suffer.
- Find out about the classroom teacher's plan to introduce the new child to the class.
- Watch to see how the child is developing new relationships, and talk to the classroom teacher about strategies to encourage new friendships. Also, provide opportunities for relationships out of school—e.g., sports, dance, or any other interest that the child may have.

Case Study: Bullying, Discrimination, and Harassment

Type of Bullying: Gender, verbal, name calling, physical, threatening, excluding, rumors
Age of Onset/Gender of Target: Fourth grade, male
How Long Did the Bullying Last? Elementary, middle, and high school; college
Hot Spots: Various
Did You Tell? If So, Whom? Parents

My story begins with me being raised by a single mom. My parents divorced when I was young, and I was raised in a Hispanic home with a younger sister. My role models were females. I enjoyed activities that girls were mostly involved in, such as shopping, playing an instrument, gymnastics, dancing, etc. I didn't associate the activities with a certain gender but just enjoyed them.

I attended a private, church-related school in a large northern metropolitan city. The school was rather small; it had about 75 students in first through eighth grades. When I entered the school in fourth grade, I joined the band and gymnastics. I noticed that students started to make fun of me because I played the flute and was practicing gymnastics. The harassment progressed as other students mocked my feminine tendencies. I was called sissy, girly, gay, and faggot even though at that time I didn't know what the words meant. To be more specific, when I was in fifth grade, six or seven individuals, a combination of girls and boys who were the older students in my class would push me and take my lunch away. It was done in a joking manner, but it humiliated me. They were having fun at my expense.

The rest of the class observed this happening and seemed to be afraid to speak up because they thought it would happen to them. It seemed funny to the perpetrators but hurtful and embarrassing to me. This progressed from taking my lunch to excluding me in groups with friends, punching me, and taking my possessions (clothes and books) to the girls' restroom and leaving them there. I was scared to go into the girls' restroom. I was also germophobic, and the students taunted me for this by making up anecdotes of urinating in my shoes. I became very anxious when these incidents started happening on a daily basis.

Because I was close to my mother, I told her what was happening. I also told my stepfather, who came into my life during the time I was being bullied. My parents went to school and addressed the situation with an administrator. His response was "to toughen up." Because this didn't work, I started internalizing the taunting, harassment, and bullying behavior. My grades were being affected, and I dreaded going to school. One day when I went to school, a girl in my class placed a finger puppet on her middle finger and presented it to me. Not knowing its significance, I discussed the incident with my mom. After each of these incidents, I became even more anxious because of the cruelty inflicted upon me by classmates.

I then had a full-blown psychotic break in fifth grade when I reached ten years old. I lost touch with reality. These were the darkest and scariest days of my life and my family's life thus far. I would wake up and make no sense to my mom. One evening I woke up and saw that I had no face. I woke my parents and asked them to read the Bible to me because the devil was coming after me. I was extremely paranoid. My family had to take down all of the picture frames and cover up the television, and I "stayed safe" by crawling under a comforter throughout my home. I was suffering from severe depression and anxiety and was eventually placed in an inpatient (two weeks) and outpatient psychological hospital (four months). I was prescribed antipsychotic drugs. In addition, I was checked for sleep disorders and any brain abnormalities. It was a very exhausting experience for my family and me.

Everything came crashing down. I officially withdrew from school, and my mom agreed to homeschool me. I continued therapy to address the depression and safety issues that were caused as a result of being bullied for two years. I truly believe the bullying contributed to 95 percent of my breakdown, and the absence of my biological father to the remaining 5 percent.

After considering our alternatives, my family decided that to get a new start, we would move to the South, where I would enroll in seventh grade in a similar religious school. The school was much larger, with three seventh grade classes. However, with my interest in clothing and fashion, playing the flute, and gymnastics, I continued to be targeted and teased by other students. Because things didn't improve as much as we were hoping, our family moved to an adjoining southern state a few hours south, and I attended another religious school. The eighth grade was uneventful.

Until now, my peers had told me that I was gay and a faggot, but I now admitted that I had always been attracted to females. Going through puberty and acknowledging that females were moving through this tumultuous time faster than males, I was relieved that

I was not responsible for choosing my sexuality. What a relief to me at the time! I then shared my thinking with my closest friends.

I admitted readily that my peers had bullied me, but now the rumors and gossip seemed to pass to faculty and the administration. During my freshman year, I was totally excited about everything. I was involved with student senate, chorus, and gymnastics, among others. However, beginning with my sophomore year, four or five peers spread rumors around the school that I was sexually active with other males. Even though it wasn't true, the school staff judged me as guilty because I looked the part. During a gymnastics match, a school administrator came up to me and reported that a decision had been made to dismiss me from the school because I was bisexual and had committed an act with another student. At the time, no one would listen to my story—it was a done deal. This was another shattering moment when I didn't know what to do, and I was scared.

Because the school was directly associated with the church, the school had biblical guidelines regarding homosexuality. Since homosexuality was considered a sin, the church felt justified in discriminating against me. I withdrew from high school my sophomore year and was again homeschooled. During this time, I was taken off of my antipsychotic medication and was placed in therapy to change my sexuality. I again felt very depressed and confused because I was being punished for being sexually active, which I had not been. I worked with a Christian therapist who delved into the roots of my sexuality, which made me more depressed.

In my junior year, my family attempted to re-enroll me into the same high school from which I had been "released." However, the school asked me to sign an agreement that I was a heterosexual before I could re-enter. Since I could not comply, I was denied enrollment and prohibited from attending any activities on campus. I was threatened with law enforcement being called if I were ever seen on school property. The only time that I was on campus was six years later at my sister's graduation. From then on, I was not only barred from the school but also "excommunicated" from the local church even though our church didn't practice excommunication.

When I tried to attend church, the looks and whispers were very evident. I could not participate without stares and glares from the congregation. When I ran into the pastor from my academy's church, I recognized him and put out my hand, which he refused to shake. The nonverbal taunting and harassment came more from the adults. I had not been sexually active; this congregation supports homosexual individuals if they do not act on their sexuality. However, I was found guilty without any proof—not only by my peers but also by the administration at school and at church. As a reminder, I was living in a small, conservative town in the Bible Belt that was limited in its views on sexuality.

Not only was I rejected; my family was rejected, too. During a conversation with my mom, a longtime family friend stated that she understood why my mom was disappointed and upset with me. My mom quickly took offense. She emphatically told her how proud she was of me.

During these two and a half years when I wasn't in a regular school setting and was being homeschooled, I took a part-time job in the community at a local fast food restaurant. One day after work, I walked over to my car and discovered that someone had written the word "faggot" on my windshield. Before I reported it, I found out that the manager of the restaurant was bragging that he had written it on my car. The manager felt it was justified because of my sexuality.

I felt very anxious during this time of my life because I was not in my structured environment. All of my life I attended a private religious institution that pushed me academically and kept my mind focused on learning. It was more challenging for me to push myself with little interaction with peers. I was more isolated but did get involved with some community projects. My biggest concern became asking myself if I will graduate from high school. Would a GED hinder me from being selected by a university of my choosing? After discussing this situation with my family, I studied for the GED for three weeks and passed it. Because I tested well and had taken some preliminary course work for college, I was accepted into college with no problem.

When I entered this auspicious institution, I was terrified that if I disclosed my sexuality, I would again be excommunicated from attending this church university. I was convinced that I would not be supported.

During my freshman year, I befriended a student whom I kept at a distance because I feared that our friendship might jeopardize my university standing. If the university discovered that I was bisexual or gay, I would be barred from the university and the church affiliation. During this time, this young man started having psychological problems and was stalking me. I was so confused and bewildered that I started fearing for my life. My only out was to ask for help and acknowledge to the university administration my dilemma. In the back of my mind, I only had memories of how the church overreacted to my situation without any facts and had scorned me by barring me from attending school.

When I approached the administration, to my surprise and amazement, I was listened to and supported regarding my journey and its struggles. The stalker was confronted, and I was relieved that the perpetrator was detained. I was openly accepted by the university and not excluded because of my church's position on theology and sexuality. The church became open about my plight and others in my same quandary.

Presently, I am in my last years of attending this university, where I am majoring in pre-law and international business. I am actively involved with implementing policy changes for the university, the church, and the LGBTQ (Lesbian, Gay, Bisexual,

Transgender, and Questioning) population. I am personally involved with liberating students who are entering this or similar university church settings, who are depressed and suicidal, and who need emotional support from the LBGTQ community. Many of these students have lost support from their families and are receptive to a compassionate university setting that is empathetic and nonjudgmental. I am very hopeful that the tide is turning.

POINTS FOR PARENTS

This is a story of courage in which this young man had to overcome egregious bullying, harassment, and prejudice. He was able to overcome all of this even though he paid the price by having serious emotional problems.

We need to be very clear here—this is more than just a story about prejudice and harassment based on sexual orientation or perception. It is about an unequivocal violation of this student's civil rights. It is about Title VI of the Civil Rights Act of 1964, which prohibits discrimination on the basis of race, color, or national origin, and Title IX of the Education Amendments of 1972, which prohibits discrimination on the basis of sex. Schools are in violation of these civil rights statutes when peer harassment based on race, color, national origin, sex, or disability is sufficiently serious that it creates a hostile environment and when such harassment is encouraged, tolerated, not adequately addressed, or ignored by school employees.

Through a 2010 correspondence sent to all educators, the Office of Civil Rights (OCR) in a "Dear Colleague" letter defined bullying, harassment, and the school's responsibilities under the law. In the letter, the OCR used an example eerily similar to this story. They were very clear that not only is this type of behavior unacceptable, but that schools also have a fiduciary responsibility to protect all students.

The letter states: "As noted in the example, the school failed to recognize the pattern of misconduct as a form of sex discrimination under Title IX. Title IX prohibits harassment of both male and female students regardless of the sex of the harasser—i.e., even if the harasser and target are members of the same sex. It also prohibits gender-based harassment, which may include acts of verbal, nonverbal, or physical aggression; intimidation; or hostility based on sex or sex stereotyping. Thus, it can be sex discrimination if students are harassed either for exhibiting what is perceived as a stereotypical characteristic for their sex, or for failing to conform to stereotypical notions of masculinity and femininity. Title IX also prohibits sexual harassment and gender-based harassment of all students, regardless of the actual or perceived sexual orientation or gender identity of the harasser or target.

"Although Title IX does not prohibit discrimination based solely on sexual orientation, Title IX does protect all students, including lesbian, gay, bisexual, transgender, and questioning (LGBTQ) students, from sex discrimination. When students are subjected to harassment on the basis of their LGBTQ status, they may also, as this example illustrates, be subjected to forms of sex discrimination prohibited under Title IX. The fact that the harassment includes anti-LGBTQ comments or is partly based on the targets' actual or perceived sexual orientation does not relieve a school of its obligation under Title IX to investigate and remedy overlapping sexual harassment or gender-based harassment. In this example, the harassing conduct was based in part on the student's failure to act as some of his peers believed a boy should act. The harassment created a hostile environment that limited the student's ability to participate in the school's education program. Finally, even though the student did not identify the harassment as sex discrimination, the school should have recognized that the student had been subjected to gender-based harassment covered by Title IX."

In simple terms, schools can violate the civil rights of their students by not protecting them from gender harassment. It is never acceptable to use cruel names and to tag a student because of his or her real or perceived sexuality. However, in some environments, this discrimination has been tolerated more than in others. The law is clear that all students have a right to an education free from fear, intimidation, and harassment. The notion of an environment free from harassment extends to the workplace. The comments and actions of the boy's supervisor contributed to a hostile work environment.

The school in this case study not only allowed this prejudicial behavior but also encouraged it by ignoring it. When the parents told the school about the bullying, the administrator's response was that the boy should just toughen up. Sadly, the boy told us in his narrative that that strategy did not work. Of course that did not work! Without any discussion with and consequences for the perpetrators, they had no incentive to stop the bullying and harassment. Why would they stop if no one addressed their behavior?

The fact of the matter is that LGBTQ youth have to deal with social exclusion, including social rejection and isolation, diminished social support, and discrimination as well as verbal and physical abuse. Furthermore, teachers and adults often lack the understanding, knowledge, skills, and willingness to appropriately address the issue (Milburn and Palladino 2012). In this case study, the adults' prejudicial behavior of wanting the student to change his sexual preference was part of the problem.

Expecting the person who is being victimized to change his or her behavior further sends a message that the problem lies within the victim rather than the behavior of the aggressors. The victim cannot ever be blamed for being a victim, including how he looks, talks, or acts. The climate must be one where everyone is accepted for who they are, and—most importantly—everyone must be safe.

SUGGESTIONS FOR ACTION

- Talking to the school and reporting bullying behavior in this case is simply not enough. When there is blatant homophobic aggression and the schools have failed to make the environment safe, parents need to demand that the school protect the student from harassment. Furthermore, parents need to insist that the schools adhere to the district policies regarding discrimination.

- In addition, it is reasonable to demand that staff be trained to appreciate inclusion and to work with students who may be LGBTQ.

- If the parents do not believe that these demands are being met, it is recommended that they contact the local antidefamation league, the local chapter of the Gay, Lesbian, and Straight Education Network (GLSEN), or the local Attorney General's office for more incident-specific guidance. This is a very serious issue and must be handled in that way.

- Above all, the safety and welfare of the student is paramount. Therefore, parents must give their children all the support necessary to help them navigate through these situations. This can include a counselor to help process feelings before there is irreversible damage to a child's emotional health.

Case Study: A Broken Nose

Type of Bullying: Physical, verbal, staring, intimidating, racial

Age of Onset/Gender of Target: Fifth grade, male

How Long Did the Bullying Last? Seven months

Hot Spots: Physical education class, classroom, bathroom

Did You Tell? If So, Whom? Yes, I told my teachers, counselor, principal, and parents.

I am presently a seventh grader attending a public school. The bullying that I describe below took place in the fall of fifth grade and continued into the spring of that year. I attend an intermediate school composed of fourth and fifth graders. I live in the community where I attend school and ride with my parents to and from school each day. This first incident of bullying started in my math class when a student walked by my desk and pushed my math book off my desk and onto the floor. When he walked by me, more often than not, he would push or bump me and whisper the word "bitch" in my ear. Whenever he walked toward the back of the room to sit at his desk, he would continually stare at me. Anytime I turned around, he would have a mean look on his face.

This behavior started in October, and he continued to intimidate and bully me almost every single day. The teacher didn't confront the behavior because she was busy addressing other concerns, wasn't looking in my direction, had stepped out of the class, was absent with a substitute present, or was attending to another group as our class was involved in cooperative learning teams.

I told my teachers about the bullying numerous times, and they told me to stay away from him. I had four scheduled classes with him each day, one of them being physical education, a class that had nearly 100 students. When he did mess with me, I would tell him to leave me alone, but that seemed to not work. I was perplexed about why he would call me a bitch because my friends didn't use that word referring to other boys.

I was not the only person with whom he was aggressive. He had confrontations with other students and was suspended for being in fights. He and his friends usually did not mix with my friends. Their style was to intimidate others, usually in groups. He actually looked somewhat older and was taller and larger than his peers.

I feared being in school each day because I didn't know what to expect. I didn't know if he was going to threaten me with some

*type of intimidation, physically push me, or call me names. I be-
came moody and stressed, especially at home, and feared going to
school. It was hard for me to concentrate, my grades were affected, I cried easily, and I didn't want to eat.*

*My parents became concerned and told me to stand up to him
and to report the bullying to my teachers. I had told my parents
about the bullying the first time, after they confronted me about not
wanting to go to school and not eating. This was about a month
after he started bullying me.*

*My grandfather found out about me being bullied and e-mailed
a county office administrator asking him for help. After conferring
with the principal, the county office administrator assured my parents that the principal was aware of the situation and would keep
an eye on it. He continued to say that this problem was not unique
to me, nor was this bullying situation the only discipline issue that
our public school system had to deal with.*

*As time went along, my father addressed the bullying issue at
least five times with the school. My dad even came and observed
my physical education class. He couldn't believe the chaos and
the lack of adult supervision with over 100 students coming and
going from class. However, nothing seemed to change, except it
provoked the problem children to retaliate even more. The principal continued to remark that there was no bullying at his school.*

*One morning in the spring, I went to the bathroom along with
a group of other boys. As I was leaving, the bully and a group of
onlookers surrounded me. He called me a bitch and acted like he
was going to pummel me. I asked him to leave me alone, told him
that I had done nothing, and then walked out. When the bell rang,
I went to the counselor's office, where I had previously stopped
to talk about the bullying and reported how this student threatened me in the bathroom. The counselor seemed concerned about
the bathroom incident and convinced me that she wanted to confront him in her office and asked me to be present. When he came*

into the counselor's office, she asked him about the confrontation. His response was that I was a snitch. The counselor asked us to stay away from each other. After he left the counselor's office, she asked me if I felt better and I emphatically said, "No."

In the afternoon in physical education class, the teacher asked our class to walk eight laps around the track. Usually, students pick their friends and start walking leisurely. A friend walked with me. As we started walking, the same aggressor came jogging by us and called me a snitch. He continued to bump into me and asked me if I wanted to fight. A couple of laps later, I leaned over to tie my shoe, and he pushed me as I stood up. I tried to push him away, but instead he hit me twice in the face, breaking my nose. I blacked out, and the next thing I knew, my friend was escorting me outside the gym. My teacher asked me to go to the bathroom to clean the blood off of my face. I then was taken to the office to be confronted by the principal, counselor, and the aggressor.

Both of us were suspended for one day each for fighting. The principal sent us back to the same chorus class, and then we were dismissed to go to the car and bus line. When my mom picked me up, she saw the blood on my clothes and parked the car to speak with the principal, who was in his office. My parents were never notified of the incident that happened at school that day.

Since that day, my parents have been working with the school to guarantee my safety in school and were very upset by the lack of communication and basic concern for me after that incident. Presently, I am a seventh grade student in the same school system.

POINTS FOR PARENTS

There are many ways to look at this story. The boy is called names that are biased. The use of these terms is both humiliating and demeaning. The continued use of these terms may appear incidental to the children not being targeted, but the one who is targeted may perceive them as hurtful and demoralizing.

The fact that the adults did not respond may be part of what is known as attribution error. "Social psychologists are persuaded that we are all guilty of overestimating the influence of personal characteristics on behavior and underestimating the influence of the situation itself. In fact, this tendency is so widespread that it has been called fundamental attribution error and has been recognized as a component of research and theory in social psychology (Kennedy 2010). In other words, researchers are just as likely as lay people to attribute behaviors to personal qualities rather than to situational influences."

Kennedy's research goes further and suggests that even teachers are likely to make attribution errors, drawing a quick, inaccurate conclusion about what is happening between students based on their own experiences and assumptions about what is actually occurring at the time. Another way of representing an example of this comes from William Powers and his work with perceptual control theory.

By definition, attribution error occurs when we observe a situation and, based on our own personal experiences, make a judgment error about what we think had occurred. For example, when observing a dispute, an individual might make an inaccurate supposition that since the students are the same size and age, there was no power imbalance and therefore no bullying. However, to find out if there was attribution error, asking the target how he or she felt might determine if he or she was unable to defend himself or herself and if he or she felt bullied. Without that information, we cannot necessarily make assumptions about the situation.

This condition describes the internal references that a person uses to form a judgment about what he or she is seeing or experiencing. Attribution error is such a common occurrence that researchers recognize the condition as a widespread component of social research that determines accurate observations of behavior. The goal is to ask questions in order to gain a better understanding of what is happening without interjecting one's own assumptions.

There are a few steps you can take to avoid attribution error (Kennedy 2010):

- Consider how you perceive the person's situation. In other words, consider if your conclusions are based on your assumptions of how a person should behave. In this case, it is understandable that, without more information, you might assume that being called a bitch is not so bad. Ask questions that require a descriptive answer rather than a yes or no. Basically, try to get a sense of where the person is coming from. These are questions that get at the *why* or *what* is behind the behavior. In this case, since these epithets can be considered biased language, it would be important to ask if this has happened before and if anyone else is involved. This will give you an understanding of the extent of the behavior and scope of involvement.

- Form expectations of how a reasonable person would act in that situation. In this story, an idealistic response would be for the boy to tell the aggressor to stop by saying something like, "This is homophobic language, and it is unacceptable." Of course, when you look at it that way, it seems absurd to expect a fifth grader to say something like that. Considering that we are talking about peers and a target who may not have a strong sense of self-esteem and who may feel intimidated, the boy's options are more limited. He can ignore it, as he did, but it only continued. He can confront the aggressor, but it did no good. Or he can ask an adult for help.

- We can interpret the boy's behavior. For example, we can think he is overreacting to simple exchanges with his peers and choose not to do anything because we want to send a message that students need to learn how to deal with these "little" difficulties on their own. In doing so, we are sending a message that all students need to learn how to handle their own problems.

- We can infer the cause of the behavior based on some personal characteristic. In other words, we can decide that the boy is fragile and whiny. He cannot take a joke or communicate with his peers. While this seems shocking, it is a very common practice for adults to jump to conclusions about a situation based on an assumption about our knowledge of what we believe is a particular personality style. The repeated reports—"I told my teachers on numerous occasions"—could place that boy in the category of a complainer who cannot solve his own problems.

This story is a good example of attribution error. There were two different perceptions: the observer/teacher made a judgment different from how the victim perceived the situation. The teacher and young target in the story compared their perceptions to a past reference rather than looking at the situation from the perspective of the target. The teacher concluded that "kids were just being kids," while the young boy concluded that he was being "ganged up on."

In the meantime, the student was experiencing cruel and hurtful bullying through that one word—"bitch." In one syllable, this aggressor was repeatedly able to humiliate and attack the target's own sense of identity. He is just one of many students, regardless of their sexual orientation, who face gender bias, bullying, and a hostile school climate that allows the behavior. Biased language is associated with the use of words like "gay," "fag," "bitch," and so on. The use of that language is a major component of homophobic language that is a form of discrimination (Poteat et al. 2013). The continued use of these words contributes to an environment that encourages prejudice and becomes so acceptable that people do not even acknowledge that it is a form of aggression. That sets up a perfect climate for attribution error—the behavior is so common that it does not appear hurtful—while, at the same time, this form of bullying is actually a serious gateway to discrimination.

The next component of this story that must be discussed is the incident itself. The act of hitting a boy and breaking his nose in the way it happened is clearly an act of assault and battery. The threat is to harm; ability to do so constitutes the assault. The punch was battery, as it was harmful and involved physical contact. The boy was intentionally threatened, resulting in a broken nose. The parents are well within their rights to involve the police, particularly since the school did not appear to take the incident seriously.

SUGGESTIONS FOR ACTION

- A recurring theme in these stories concerns the role of the school after the parents report the problem. The parents assume that because the school says it will take care of things, the problem is solved. However, the parent absolutely needs to follow up with the school. The parent's job is to advocate for the child. This means checking back with the school to see what steps it is taking to address the problem and keeping a detailed log of every conversation. Furthermore, parents need to continue to check in with their child through conversation and behavioral observations. Talk to the child, ask those open-ended questions about how things are going, and look for signs of distress, sadness, or avoidance of school.

- Be aware of any language that implies homophobia, and stop it immediately. It is not, under any circumstances, okay to refer to someone—particularly a boy—as "bitch." In many ways, parents are the standard bearers for how we treat one another. so it is very important to be certain to model appropriate behavior. By the same token, we can point out to the child our rejection of that type of language when we hear it in other places. That language is a sign of disrespect that, in the long run, supports homophobia in our culture.

- The fact that the assault on this boy resulted in a broken nose brings this problem to a level that includes battery (attacking a person with the intent of inflicting bodily harm). This assault and battery is no accident; the threat of harm was present when you consider all the previous hateful incidents. This is a police matter. The school, as a partner in the solution, should be primarily involved in this issue. Therefore, the parents need to file a formal report to the police.

- Follow up with the school to develop a safety plan for the child to ensure that the child will be able to attend school without the fear of retaliation from the aggressor or any other person, whether it be students or staff members.

8. Different Perspectives

Case Study: A Target, Then an Aggressor

Type of Bullying: Exclusion, gossip
Age of Onset/Gender of Target: Fifth grade, female
How Long Did the Bullying Last? Through middle school
Hot Spots: Classroom, playground
Did You Tell? If So, Whom? I didn't tell.

I came to the United States as a new immigrant from Mexico. I could not speak English and initially enrolled in fifth grade. When I moved to the United States, I had to live with my sister until my mother got settled. I attended the elementary school zoned and closest to where my sister lived, which was located in a large Caucasian neighborhood.

Because I only spoke Spanish, I didn't understand a word the other students were saying. I felt singled out because I was new and not able to speak a language that more than 95 percent of the school population spoke. Because of my circumstances, I appeared quiet and reserved; however, I had leadership skills. But without a way to communicate with my peers and to integrate, I seemed inferior. I started to feel sad and embarrassed and thought that something was wrong with me.

Girls in the classroom would laugh at me, probably because of what I wore or how I sounded when I spoke. On the playground they excluded me from playing with them just because I was different. One girl, who appeared to be the ringleader, would give me a look, and the others would follow.

On one occasion, the teacher asked a question, and the majority of students held up their hand and said out loud, "I know."

In Spanish, when you scream that same sound out loud, that is an expression that students use when someone is hurt. I would then find myself staring at my classmates in amazement. Students would continue laughing as I struggled to use my broken English. I felt alone, with no alliances on the playground where students were staring at me. I continually asked myself if I should be there.

Looking back at the situation, I never thought I was being bullied because I didn't know the meaning of the word. I do remember, however, how I felt when students repeatedly, intentionally, and in a large group would make fun of me. I felt excluded, embarrassed, sad, hurt, scared, and inferior. I hated school; however, fifth grade was ending and summer was beginning. I also had just found out that I would be transferring schools because my mother found a place to live and I would be moving in with her.

In sixth grade, I moved in with my mother in the projects, which was located in a totally different area of town than where my sister lived. The projects were composed of mostly African-Americans and Hispanics and had very few Caucasians. So, when I went to school, I could relate and speak with the majority of the students because they were Spanish-speaking. We would always hang out. I got into three fights that year, mostly walking on my way to and from school, but was never suspended for a violation at school.

Several months after school started, a new Hispanic girl, Stephanie, enrolled. She was quiet, dressed very conservatively, and spoke limited English. So, for whatever reason, it became my mission to make fun of and be mean to her. I unequivocally told my friends to not talk or hang out with her and to not invite her to be part of our group. I was a leader who had a lot of influence. I am not sure why I singled Stephanie out, but it might have been because I was in her same situation the previous year and she was no better than me. I was modeling the same behavior—intimidating my friends not to play with her. At recess, Stephanie ended up standing alone, leaning on a tree on the playground.

Several months went by and the school year ended. Stephanie left the elementary school to attend middle school, and I never saw her again. Most of us were dispersed into different middle schools.

Middle school was a difficult time for me. I displayed a tough girl demeanor and was angry and didn't realize why. It was a defense mechanism because I didn't want to be hurt again, so my goal was to have my peers fear and respect me. I was suspended three times. Twice I was defending a friend. Teachers were confused because I had great potential; however, I had an aggressive attitude with a tough exterior.

In high school, I made the most positive changes in my behavior. During the summer, I had requested to attend a different high school than my friends because I knew that I needed to be around students who were more academically oriented and had a positive influence on me. My mother finally consented. During high school, I hung around ten or twelve Hispanic girls and boys my entire four years. We elected to not be part of the mainstream and did not participate in clubs or sports. However, we never caused trouble, and no one had issues with us.

POINTS FOR PARENTS

While this case seems to be about aggression focused on race and ethnicity, we are discussing it in this chapter because we are looking at it from the perspective of one who has been victimized and then becomes the aggressor. This is not an uncommon outcome for someone who has been bullied. Certainly, some people who have been bullied become silent, withdrawn, or depressed and experience the impact of long-term victimization in many aspects of their lives.

Students who have been bullied, without any intervention from either peers or adults, can become aggressive and bully others in turn. Research suggests that the risk factor for violence increases by one-third (Ttofi et al. 2012). That means that one of the negative outcomes for a student who has been victimized is that they are at risk for becoming aggressors themselves. This is one of those stories.

This girl tells us that when she was targeted, she felt excluded, embarrassed, sad, hurt, and inferior. When feelings such as these are allowed to continue because of the victimization, it can have a serious impact on the person who is targeted. In her own words, she describes feeling angry when the new girl comes to school. The new girl is quiet and withdrawn and speaks little English—which is very similar to the storyteller. She tells us that she feels resentful and angry and is mean to her and does not understand why. She tells us that she was modeling the same behavior that she had experienced. She further explains to us that she had an "aggressive attitude and a tough exterior."

When victims of bullying do not have a social support network to help them handle or overcome the hurt of victimization, they are more likely to have poor outcomes (Rothon et al. 2011). Support from peers and family can have a buffering effect from those consequences of bullying victimization.

We need to protect children from bullying victimization for many reasons. We can do this by helping to stop the bullying, teaching resilience, and encouraging empathy. There is a connection between the moral development of a child and the inclination to bully others. Bullying and aggression are directly associated with certain kinds of moral reasoning that relieves guilt. This is called moral disengagement theory (Perren et al. 2012). When you look at this story, in this context it makes total sense that this girl, after being the victim, became the aggressor to a girl who was similar because she was new to the school, was quiet, and spoke little English.

This is an example of another reason why it is so important for us to work with children and young people to stop bullying behavior and to replace it with inclusion and understanding.

SUGGESTIONS FOR ACTION

- Once again, we are bringing up the "golden rule" of the importance of talking to your child and acknowledging your child's perception and perspective. Clearly, the girl in this story was unhappy. It is important to understand why. If your child will not tell you, consider the possibility that this alone may cause distress. In this story, it is reasonable to assume that because she was in a new school that was not diverse, her ethnicity could be a part of the reason. This can be a starting point for the discussion. Try something like: "When I'm at school, I've noticed that there are only a few people who are Hispanic. It makes me feel a bit like an outsider. Have you ever felt that way?"

- This is a child who was a leader and had influence over her peers. Be aware of how your child is using those skills. If you feel that your child is using his or her skills in a negative way, you need to redirect those skills. For example, give the child an opportunity to lead in a positive way. This might mean involvement in a club or something else that interests your child; for the girl in this story, she could join a club that celebrates Hispanic heritage. Of course, praise children for their effort to reinforce the value that you are trying to teach.

- When you see a change in behavior—going from quiet to outgoing and even aggressive—it is important to consider the reason and respond accordingly. In this case, the girl began associating with aggressive girls. She says that even the teachers were confused by her behavior. Remember, the sooner there is social support, the more likely the child will benefit. Working with children from a young age is crucial to making changes that will prevent future bullying issues.

Case Study: Relational Aggression: A Mother's Perspective

Type of Bullying: Relational aggression, gossip, rumors, cyberbullying (texting)
Age of Onset/Gender of Target: Seventh grade, female
How Long Did the Bullying Last? Through middle school
Hot Spots: Hallways, class, home
Did You Tell? If So, Whom? I didn't tell anyone.

When we moved to the south, my daughter, Sally, was starting seventh grade at a neighborhood middle school. Because we had moved before, Sally was even more reluctant to be thrown into a group of students in the middle of the school year. She knew it was difficult to be the new girl in class with everyone looking and staring at her every move. Months went by, and Sally seemed to be looking for a group of girls that would accept her for who she was. Eventually, in eighth grade she found a group of three students (Joy, Madeline, and Rebecca) who seemed to be a perfect fit for her to be around. My recollection was that all of the girls seemed really nice. Among the girls, Sally seemed to choose Rebecca to associate with more than the others. They spent countless hours in both homes and at school and shared some of the same classes.

Looking back, I noticed early on that my daughter appeared withdrawn and sad even though she had a group of friends that surrounded her. I thought that her moodiness came from her moving across the country and trying to acclimate herself to residing in a new state, attending a new school, and reaching out to new friends. I had heard that Rebecca had a boyfriend, yet he was showing interest in getting to know Sally. Suddenly, Rebecca, Joy, and Madeline were no longer a group.

One day, Sally came down the stairs sobbing profusely. I was shocked in all honesty and had no idea what was going on. When she calmed down, she shared with me how her friends did not like

198

her, were being mean to her, and said that she was too clingy and not a good friend. They alluded that Sally had stolen Rebecca's boyfriend. From that point on, Rebecca and her friends excluded Sally from associating with them and being in their inner circle. This was devastating to my daughter and devastating to watch. It was scary for me because I had no control over what was happening. I tried to talk with her, tell her that it would all blow over, and support her, but I could tell that what I said made no impact on how she felt.

When I thought back to previous talks with Rebecca, I picked up subtle references that she thought Sally was clingy and needy. With this information, I believed Sally when she said that Rebecca continued to influence her friends and classmates to dislike and exclude her. She spread rumors that Sally had stolen her boyfriend and that friends don't act in this manner. This relational aggression continued for the next two years. One girl, Casey, who appeared to veer away from Rebecca and befriend Sally, became a ray of hope for my daughter. Because Casey and Sally were in a theater troupe together, they got to know each other in a different way. During their freshman and sophomore years, Casey and Sally became close friends. At one time during this juncture, Casey apologized for letting the things that Rebecca had said destroy their relationship.

Years later, my daughter took the advice to follow her heart and find her sense of confidence and self. She learned to never give her power away.

POINTS FOR PARENTS

This is a story of a parent who was communicating with her child, yet her child was still being excluded and victimized by her peers. Friendships are of particular importance in early adolescence. It is how children are learning to define themselves.

Adolescents have to learn about the difference between gossip and general chitchat. Girls (and boys for that matter) need to understand that fear, vicious rumors, and gossip are damaging and impact everyone. One mother told us that she stressed with her daughter that whenever she was participating in rumors and gossip, she was setting herself up to be targeted in the same way. Kids need to recognize that same group that is talking about someone will just as easily be talking about them. The interesting fact about these issues is that in many cases, the student who has been victimized frequently stays connected in a relationship with the aggressor (Remillard and Lamb 2005). Looking at a group from afar, you will view laughter often masked by humiliation and embarrassment.

When the culture allows this type of behavior, everyone is vulnerable. Social support from peers is critical to helping a student navigate through these instances. These behaviors can include getting others to exclude someone, sharing mean or untrue stories, using lies and confidential information to get back at someone, and forwarding mean messages or embarrassing pictures. The list goes on and on—just ask your adolescent and they can fill you in!

Adolescents often internalize relational aggression and translate it to critical appraisals of themselves. They see themselves as the problem rather than the aggressors. The mother in the story identified this phenomenon when she referred to the impact on her daughter's self-confidence. This type of behavior can appear relatively benign, yet it can be devastating for a child.

SUGGESTIONS FOR ACTION

- Give students the opportunity to have friends and mentors in different areas of their lives. This could be through clubs and other activities in and outside of school, such as religious activites. It helps anyone to be able to put things into perspective if there is a problem in school or elsewhere. Knowing they have other friends makes it less catastrophic for them and helps to shift their focus to other peers.

- Talk to your child about how relationships change over time, and even talk about your own experiences with friends when you were their age. It is comforting to hear that there is a commonality to having issues with friends. However, it is important to point out how to recognize the difference between relational aggression and moving on in a friendship.

- Role-play the incidents that your children struggle with and worry about. Then practice responses to mean statements and actions. If a child has the opportunity to think through possibilities that are safe and socially acceptable, he or she will be able to make better choices when confronted with a difficult situation.

The next two case studies are linked in that they discuss the same story. The first is from the perspective of the child, and the second is from the parent.

Case Study: Homeschooling to Avoid Bullying: The Child's Perspective

Type of Bullying: Physical, emotional, name calling
Age of Onset/Gender of Target: Sixth grade, male
How Long Did the Bullying Last? From sixth through eighth grade
Hot Spots: Classroom, hallways, physical education classes
Did You Tell? If So, Whom? I told no one at school because I feared that I would not be able to play sports.

Bullying for me started in sixth grade. A group of four boys in my class made fun of the clothes that I wore and began calling me names such as "gay." They would follow me down the hall and hit me in the back of the head and try to trip me. I was taught to not fight back at home and in school. Also, being on the wrestling team, I knew that if I were disciplined for fighting, I would have a good chance of being kicked off the team. I think their goal was to destroy my image and get other students to not associate with me. This constant ridiculing and intimidation continued through eighth grade until I didn't enjoy or want to go to school.

During one class in the spring of eighth grade, a student that most students feared continued to call me names. He was a football player and the leader of the group of four that had been harassing me. He was somewhat popular but seemed to always be in trouble for being in a fight. The taunting escalated until he walked by, started hitting me, and then slammed my head into the desk. My head was bleeding, but the teacher ignored the entire scene and kept teaching class. He denied my request to go see the nurse. When the bell rang, I went to my next class, which the aggressor was also in. I couldn't hold my anger in any longer, and he and I started fighting. I was disciplined with three days of in-school suspension for defending myself, and the perpetrator received the same punishment. When I came back to school after my suspension, the teacher who had done nothing to stop the harassment was joking with the class and the other students about the incident.

Because of this incident and the school's mishandling of the taunting, intimidation, and aggressive behavior of this group of students, my parents decided to homeschool me in ninth grade. Then in tenth grade, I transferred back into the neighborhood high school with the same students who attended my middle school. However, since my mother had previously discussed this situation with the administration, this student and I were placed in different classes and in different hallways. The staff was alerted to actively supervise any contact that the students might have.

Case Study: Homeschooling to Avoid Bullying: The Mother's Perspective

Type of Bullying: Gender (faggot, gay) and racial names, physical (hitting on side of head), threatening, rumors, gossip

Age of Onset/Gender of Target: Sixth grade, male

How Long Did the Bullying Last? From sixth through eighth grade

Hot Spots: Classroom, hallways, physical education class, locker room, bathroom

Did You Tell? If So, Whom? Parents, teachers, administration

My son was bullied starting in sixth grade. Since we lived in a rural community, my son dressed ahead of his time. He dressed very artsy in his skinny jeans and had a "mod," trendy haircut different from his peers. Some students would call him faggot and gay and other gender slang terms. One student would slap him upside the head as he walked down the hall. The boys in his class knew they could mess with him because they knew he would not fight back. If you were in sports and were found fighting, the coach would dismiss you from the team. Because he did not know how to defend himself without being physical, the bullying continued to escalate.

In eighth grade, in front of a teacher during class, a boy walked by my son's desk and slammed his head into the desk. The teacher did nothing and said nothing. The teacher asked both students to go outside the classroom to talk it out. At that time, the other student attacked my son, and they fought it out in the hall. Both students got suspended even though my son was defending himself.

As parents, we were confused as to what we should do. We continued to address the name calling and physical mistreatment by addressing it with different teachers. We sat down with the administration numerous times and reported each and every inci-

dent. The school said that they would address the name calling and physical taunting, but their intervening strategies made the problem worse. They chose to dismiss my son early from class so that he could get to his next class without having to endure any encounters. This action made my son more of a target. We thought the better strategy would be to ask the aggressors to be isolated instead of isolating the target. The year was long and strenuous and ended with the bullying continuing and increasing in frequency.

Starting in ninth grade, since I had not received any cooperation from the middle school, I homeschooled my son. I knew if he had been placed in the high school with the same middle school students, the name calling and physical bullying would have gotten worse. Since no one seemed to intervene effectively, I suspected that nothing would have been done about the harassment, taunting, and targeting of my son. As a parent, I did not want my child to be unsafe and in danger.

The bullying had been intensified in sixth grade, and by eighth grade, my son had dropped out of every athletic program he had ever been part of. He also had gone from an A and B student to straight Fs. In sixth and seventh grades, the bullying occurred in the locker room, physical education class, and hallways. They would typically steal his wrestling and regular clothes. In sixth and eighth grades, the aggressor was one specific boy, yet a different one in each grade. In seventh grade, the perpetrator was a group of African-American boys who threatened—through texting—to bash my son's head against the wall in a certain bathroom at school. It was so emotional for him that he would come home and sob about how students were mistreating him. By eighth grade, he had given up and perceived himself as a target. My husband and I had many teacher conferences and were told that these incidents happened in middle school and that it was impossible to supervise every inch of the campus. We shared the texts, and the students who sent the texts were given in-school suspension.

My son has been a leader and active in sports, band, and clubs in middle school. After being homeschooled in ninth grade, he asked to go back to high school. Because he is a people person, he wanted to go back and participate in athletics, band, and clubs. The same students that taunted him in middle school were around in high school, except for a few of the aggressors, who are in a separate alternative setting. My son is not reporting any bullying in tenth grade thus far, but we are monitoring things closely.

POINTS FOR PARENTS

When you look at these stories, the facts are similar. The perception of both the student and the parent involves a serious problem that the school is unable or unwilling to deal with to protect the target and stop the bullying from occurring. The story of the boy's head being smashed into the desk appears to be assault. There is a point at which bullying crosses a line and becomes a police matter. Certainly, it is essential to bring the incident to the attention of the school, but any instances where there is physical harm needs to involve the police as well.

The mother was very aware of the pain her child was experiencing on a daily basis from the actions of his peers. She did report the incident to the school, but we do not know how it was delivered or if she followed up. If she kept a log of what the child was experiencing and brought it to the attention of the school, there would be more of a structure for them to use in their investigations. Furthermore, with a log of incidents, they can adjust supervision of students in areas where there are cameras.

The mother's solution was to remove the student from school and homeschool for a year. While this may protect the student from further bullying, there are other hidden risks to be considered. One of the goals for schools is to help children learn to socialize in a group. Homeschooling in itself cannot offer that experience. Many parents who homeschool reach out to the community to give their child social experiences, but we do not know if this student had this opportunity. We do know, however, that this student needed to be protected from this hostile environment, and for that reason the mother chose homeschooling.

Part of any training for this child needs to be focused on developing social skills. In other words, bullying must be dealt with from different angles. We need to make the environment safe, teach bystanders to reject the bullying behavior, and work with the targets to develop self-confidence.

SUGGESTIONS FOR ACTION

- When physical battery is involved, call law enforcement. This can be done within the school with the school resource officer. He or she should conduct the investigation and be part of the safety team's discussions with the school.
- Document, document, document! Log what is going on—write details about the incident, date, location, and who was involved. This helps things to become concrete. The more specific details the better. Collect all of your correspondence (e-mails, texts, letters, notes).
- After reporting an incident to the school, it is your job to follow up if the school does not. Don't assume that the problem has been handled. Check on progress. While the school cannot tell you about the consequences for the aggressors, it can update you on the strategies being used to stop the bullying behavior. When conferring with the school, be rational, specific, and unemotional, and list choices for the school instead of making demands. Also, try to find common ground and build on it. Say, for example, "We both are interested in learning and keeping all students safe. How can we achieve this and have this be a win-win for all parties involved?"
- If the school is resistant or does not seem to have the strategy to address the issue, feel free to make suggestions—for example,

moving the students into separate classes to limit their contact or adding active supervision to "hot spots."

- If you make the decision to remove the student from the school to homeschool, be certain that the student has a social outlet— for example, sports, music, drama, clubs, or religious activity.

The next two case studies are linked in that they discuss the same family. The first is a mother's account of her childhood, and the second is about her daughter.

Case Study: Mother Was Bullied Growing Up

Type of Bullying: Exclusion, name calling
Age of Onset/Gender of Target: Fifth grade, female
How Long Did the Bullying Last? Through eighth grade
Hot Spots: Classroom with teacher present, bathroom, playground, walk home
Did You Tell? If So, Whom? I told my mother and teachers.

My first experience with bullying was when I was in elementary school. I distinctly remembered that I got into some trouble in first grade for talking too much and in second grade for fighting and talking back to the teacher. However, in third and fourth grade, things changed and I settled down. I really liked both of my teachers. In fifth grade, things became a little turbulent and the bullying behavior started, but in sixth grade, it intensified. I remember being in the bathroom, and I accidentally stepped on a girl's finger and she threatened to beat me up. When the teacher heard about the incident, she asked for both of us to go outside and "beat the stew out of each other." I was shocked by how the teacher wanted two fifth grade girls to handle the incident that happened in the bathroom.

There was a group of marginalized girls who were mean and

whose goal was to make my classmates dislike me. They would exclude me whenever possible during group projects in the classroom or playing games on the playground. I never knew what sparked the pettiness and meanness, but I vividly remember how horrible I felt when I came home every day and told my parents how I hated school. I dreaded going to school each and every day because I didn't like being ostracized.

I had stomachaches and felt physically sick. Adding to the mean girl group was a gang of boys who liked these girls. They would make fun of a pimple on my nose or anything else they chose to notice. There was no way for me to hide the pimple. They then called me "Rudolph" and other nicknames related to my name. When I played kickball with the class, I dreaded the teasing and names that they made up because I was so clumsy and uncoordinated. I wasn't an overweight child. I was just tall and nonathletic. The boys would taunt me and say that I ran like a girl. Of course, I was a girl. Back then I was tremendously immature and very sensitive.

These groups of students also bullied me after school. When I walked home, both groups called me names. It also happened when I happened to be outside of my neighborhood. I tried to avoid where I thought these students lived. When I rode the bus, other students would embarrass me or make fun of me.

The bullying impacted my grades, too. Around this time, we began changing classes in math, and I experienced a math teacher who used humor, sarcasm, and embarrassment with students whom he ridiculed when he asked them to work a problem on the board in front of the class. Many of the tough boys would cry, and it made me hysterical. With this intimidating climate, and being bullied from both my classmates and my math teacher, I quickly decided that I hated math and school. I was terrified of math and felt stupid. It had a demoralizing effect on how I felt about myself as a student, even when I took math in college.

I told my teachers, but I don't remember what they did with the information. I told my mother, and she advised me to laugh back at whoever was ridiculing me. She thought they would be mesmerized by what I was laughing at and would leave me alone. This sometimes worked, but as I got older, I developed a harder exterior and finally some toughness. I don't remember how long it took or what changed, but the cruelty that I experienced and the way my classmates treated me seemed to last forever. When it was over, it was like someone had lifted the world off my shoulders. Before that time I not only felt all alone but also felt that I had no one to talk to or confide in. I had no one as a friend at school.

When I moved to junior high school, everything seemed to change. I had a very good year. Then our school transitioned from a junior high to a middle school. In eighth grade, I again had a horrible year. The whole grade had been split into teams, and most of the friends I had made transferred to different schools or were placed on the other teams. I was back with the same group of mean girls who had tormented me and the other girls who weren't in their clique.

I survived and entered high school, where I had many friends who were seniors. I no longer had a problem with bullying in high school because at that stage, I was able to handle my own problems. My senior friends had my back. I toughened up so much that years later when I graduated, a classmate commented on how strong I had become. They reminded me how I put a boy in his place and, subsequently, how no one in our school had a problem with him again.

Case Study: Daughter Was Bullied

Type of Bullying: Taking and stealing food, exclusion
Age of Onset/Gender of Target: Fourth grade, female
How Long Did the Bullying Last? Months
Hot Spots: Cafeteria
Did You Tell? If so, Whom? Parents and teachers

My daughter is nine years old and is in fourth grade. She is an only child and has attended this same school since kindergarten, with most of the same students, except for a few that have moved in and out of the district.

One particular student who was in class would target my daughter. This aggressor was petite and looked like an angel. When I would go to my daughter's class and look at her, I would think that this girl could do no wrong. However, the things my daughter would tell me were shocking. I believed my daughter because, at this time, I had no reason to distrust her.

When I asked my daughter if she ate lunch that day, she said that she had to give her snack to a girl sitting next to her because this student threatened to tell the teacher. I emphatically said that she is doing something wrong by taking my daughter's snack. I then quizzed my daughter about how often this had been happening and if this girl brought any lunch to school.

I remembered an incident that had happened a few months before with this same girl, and it involved food and a vending machine. This girl accused my daughter of stealing a quarter from her to purchase a snack out of the vending machine. I had never had reason to suspect that my daughter would take money from anyone because at home we always had money lying around, and it had never disappeared. If my daughter wanted money, she would ask for it.

However, the school took this girl's word and suspended my daughter from school on a Friday. When I got home, school was closed for the weekend. Monday was a holiday and she had the suspension on Tuesday, so I had to wait until Wednesday to get the story from the school. I was livid because the school made my daughter sign a paper admitting her guilt. She was questioned and disciplined about a serious matter without a parent present.

I asked my daughter what happened, but I could never get a clear picture of what exactly had transpired. It turned out that my daughter had signed the paper because she was coerced to do so—that was what the teacher wanted her to do.

There was also another little girl who was reported to be my daughter's best friend one day, but the next day would tell her that she didn't want to be her friend. She would exclude my daughter from group activities in the classroom or playground and leverage her friends to exclude my daughter as well. My daughter hated going to school and begged me to keep her home. I asked her to report what was happening to the teacher, but the teacher referred to any reporting as "being a tattletale." The teacher, therefore, did not intervene because she saw these incidents, as "girls will be girls" and that girls should be able to work out conflict on their own. The teacher did not understand that my child did not have the skills to stand up for herself against a group of other powerful girls and that this was not conflict, but instead was a power-based behavior called bullying. What are the children supposed to do when an adult does not intervene? I then went to the principal and nothing happened.

POINTS FOR PARENTS

Bullying victimization is not new. It seems that everyone has a story to tell from his or her childhood as an aggressor, victim, or a bystander. These experiences are usually close to the surface because they are so easy to recall, and in the process, adults quickly get in touch with the feelings associated with those memories. Adults who have been victimized are able to recall details, including type of bullying, locations, and—within a few months—the dates and times within a twelve- to fourteen-month period (Rivers 2001). The interesting thing is that their memory is not as clear about the outcomes, such as if they told a teacher and how it was handled.

Looking at the mother's story, it is difficult to determine exactly why the bullying stopped. We can say, however, that when it did stop, she felt strong and she had friends who "had her back." Everyone needs a group of friends that supports one another. She also felt like she had become tough. Perhaps that feeling can be better described as self-assured and confident. It is reasonable to assume, however, that as she got older, she was able to find a group of friends who became her buffer against being targeted by aggressors.

Bystanders are crucial to stopping and preventing bullying behavior. In fact, the role of bystanders is critical to preventing bullying behavior and contributing to prosocial behavior. When bystanders support targets of bullying, their behavior influences the perceptions of the target toward school safety (Gini et al. 2008).

In any case, the fact that so many adults have such vivid recollections of being victimized tells us that even when they are able to gain a group of supportive friends and develop self-confidence, the memories are still painful. In the words of the mother: "I am a stronger person, having survived my mistreatment. Looking back, it seems to me that I had moved through a phase that made me more empathetic. Because I never belonged to a clique in high school, as an adult I learned not only how to relate to types but also how to stand up for myself. I easily identify behavior that is coercive, intimidating, bullying, and abusive. My goal is to minimize any exposures to individuals who bully. To this day, I stay away from conflict, but if I am engaged in it, I can deal with it. What doesn't kill us makes us stronger. When a student is mean and hateful to another student, it doesn't mean that the target is mean and hateful. The perpetrator is battling some demons inside and my advice is 'don't take it personally.'" Many people feel this way, yet research shows that there are long-term effects of bullying victimization that continue into adulthood, including depression and social phobias. The years of childhood joy are lost because of the bullying.

Experiences such as this may influence how the parent viewed her daughter's school experience. Like every parent, she is extremely protective of her child and sees the school as the problem. This may very well be true, but before coming to that conclusion, parents need to be open to hear what the school administration has to say. They must have a meeting with them to fully understand the details.

The daughter's story describes one particular aggressor. The advice she gave the child was to ignore the girl who was bothering her. Although this can be a strategy to handle these issues, when it persisted in this story, there needed to be a more direct intervention on the part of the parent. The parent needed to approach the school to talk about her concerns and to open a dialogue to protect her child.

SUGGESTIONS FOR ACTION

- If you are still having feelings about your own experiences from childhood bullying, it is a good idea to find a trusted counselor. Conversations about those incidents can help you put them into perspective or at least help you to understand your own feelings.
- When the reports are consistently coming home that your child has been victimized, talk to the school immediately. Begin with the classroom teacher and ask open-ended questions about how your child is doing not only academically but also socially.
- Express your concerns to the school counselor if you feel the issue is more widespread or if the teacher does not seem to believe it is an issue.
- Keep your child updated with your conversations with the school, and make it clear that the school is concerned about your child's safety.
- Document and follow up to be certain that the issue is not overlooked.

Case Study: Sibling Bullying

Type of Bullying: Physical, name calling, cursing
Age of Onset/Gender of Target: Elementary grades K-5, males/females
How Long Did the Bullying Last? Four or five months
Hot Spots: Bus
Did You Tell? If So, Whom? Parents complained to the school

A family of five brothers and sisters moved into our town and attended our elementary school. We had never had problems on this particular bus until these five children started riding it. Now, all of a sudden, I was getting bus referrals for a student hitting other students, cursing, and encouraging other students to do the same. Exhausted with the situation, the bus driver asked for an administrator to address the students on the bus so that she could understand why the bus driver was writing up these students.

When I arrived at the bus, the bus driver identified the students creating the problems. I asked for the five students to follow me off the bus and meet me in my office. I then looked around the room and discovered that this group of students who had been reported to hit and curse at other students on the bus were from the same family. I asked the oldest brother why was he hitting and cursing at his brothers and sisters and others on the bus. The oldest brother denied that he had been the aggressor. However, his brothers and sisters chimed right in and insisted otherwise. They said he was the aggressor. One of the siblings said his brother beat them all the time and cursed and threatened them to do what he coerced them to do. I then asked how their mother dealt with the oldest hitting and cursing at them. They said that he never displayed this bullying behavior in front of her.

I made a phone call home, but the mother didn't answer. One of the children replied that she would not be home until 2:30 pm.

214

At 2:30, I called the mom and explained how the older son was treating her children. I stated that if it didn't stop, the children would be not be allowed to ride the bus to and from school. The mother stated that she would talk to him and the other children.

A few days went by, and the bus driver reported no bullying. Then the referrals started again, and the siblings were pushing and shoving all over again. This time it was the older girl hitting the younger girls. Even after having them removed from the bus for a few days, the behavior continued when the children began riding it again. It was amazing to me why and how this continued, but it became clear that the main instigator was the oldest brother. His modus operandi was to use aggressive bullying techniques on his youngest brothers and sisters so that they, in turn, would select other students on the bus to treat in the same way. This older child would laugh at his siblings as they would yell out curse words and hit other students. It appeared to be a game for him to watch his siblings intimidate, threaten, and terrorize other innocent children on the bus.

To be sure I had a record of the incidents and understood the gravity of what had been happening, I viewed the video from the bus. I then pulled every child into my office to view what happened. One of the siblings in first grade used the "F" word more than 45 times. The older brother who was in the back of the bus started laughing. He yelled out, "Do it again, do it again!" Clearly, the bus driver who had never used a seating chart had lost control of the students on the bus. At this time, most of the students were standing in their seats while the bus driver was driving down the road. This first grader then cursed out two different fifth grade girls; one girl defended herself by running to the front of the bus and beating up the first grader, while the other quiet, more reserved girl hit the first grader with her fist six times. The first grader would laugh, which made the older brother burst into more laughter. The oldest brother was clearly encouraging his younger

215

siblings to make fun of, embarrass, and mistreat the other students on the bus. Even though it was humorous to the older brother, it was distressing and humiliating for those who were attacked.

My plan was to sit down with each child to view the video and discuss how each child behaved. The first grader could not look up because he was so ashamed of his behavior. He cried and cried incessantly. His older brother had been suspended from the bus and was not in the room with him. However, when the older students who were suspended from the bus viewed the video, I reminded them that their behavior in the five-minute bus ride home could have caused a horrific accident in which someone could have been hurt, killed, or maimed.

Even though this story seemed to never end, I became a frequent rider on the bus to help supervise the children. One of the last times I rode the bus, I received a call from a parent that evening that some of these children were harassing a kindergartener as they were walking home from the bus stop. They threw down her soft drink and cursed at her. In the end, I suspended the older sibling from riding the school bus for the last half of the school year.

POINTS FOR PARENTS

Sibling bullying is a serious issue and a prevalent part of many children's lives. In fact, some research suggests that 78 percent of siblings report being bullied by a sibling, and 85 percent report bullying their siblings (Skinner and Kowalski 2013). This is significantly higher than the reported rate of bullying among peers. Sibling bullying is "any motoric and/or verbal episode involving one or both of the siblings that included hitting, pushing, kicking, spitting, biting, throwing objects, struggling over toys, name calling, or hostile arguing" (Adams and Kelley 1992). It may be that sibling bullying is so accepted as part of growing up that it does not even command the attention of adults. Bullying is considered a norm between siblings, and adults are not likely to prevent it. When children do not believe that an adult will help them, they are less likely to report it, therefore contributing to its continuation. Furthermore, the child who bullies a sibling is more likely to bully peers (Skinner and Kowalski 2013).

The behavior in this story came to light only after the bullying and aggressive behavior toward others on the bus became seriously disruptive. The principal found that after reporting the incident to the parent, the relief was only temporary. When the main aggressor was removed from the bus, the behavior was transferred to the students who walk. It seems that the intervention of the parent and the removal from the bus had no effect on the behavior.

There are family influences that affect how children behave. Families such as those that are overly permissive are more likely to have children who are aggressive. When there are no clear boundaries and children are allowed to behave without consequences, this encourages a climate in which children do not understand understand limits.

Families that are seriously autocratic and have restrictive rules and severe consequences are also at high risk for cultivating children who are likely to bully others. Ideally, families that are authoritative, i.e., those that have clear rules that are reasonable and consistently enforced, are more likely to raise resilient and empathic children.

SUGGESTIONS FOR ACTION

- Observe and listen to your children. Squabbles between children are a normal part of life, but if you have the sense that it is happening more than you think it should, it may be sibling bullying. Take note of if it happens between the same two children most of the time and if it is between the oldest and the youngest; do you feel there is an inordinate amount of hostility that does not seem to subside?

- Talk to the children on a regular basis, and give them a forum for talking as part of a family. Dinner is a good setting for these conversations.
- If you are concerned, begin by increasing the supervision of your children. In some instances, it may be worthwhile to give them a break by separating them periodically.
- Consistently reinforce expectations of kindness and respect.
- When children fight, use unkind words, or hurt a sibling, there must be a reasonable consequence that supports the family agreement.
- Talk to the school about your concerns. The school counselor may have some suggestions and, if necessary, give you a referral for a family counselor.

A FEW WORDS ABOUT BYSTANDERS

Bystanders are the key to bullying prevention. Bullying is a social climate phenomenon. It occurs in an atmosphere where there is bystander participation. Bystanders can contribute through their actual presence, whether or not they participate. Those who laugh and join in on the bullying become part of the problem and become aggressors themselves. Others who silently witness the bullying can, simply by their presence, exacerbate the problem. Furthermore, the number of people who are present regardless of their role contributes to a climate in which humiliation, meanness, and disrespect are the norm.

Every child should feel respected and accepted by his or her peers. We want all children to be able to speak up and stand up for themselves, but that cannot happen in a hostile atmosphere where bystanders are participating in or ignoring mean behavior. Bystanders set the tone for the climate. Their choices to reject malicious words and actions, simply by not tolerating these unkind words and actions, can literally prevent most instances of bullying from occurring. We know that bystanders witness the majority of bullying behavior. They are the first line of defense, and their disapproval is all it takes to stop bullying. Therefore, we want to teach bystanders that they have a social responsibility to support their peers because it benefits not only the target but also everyone else. They are powerful, and they can make the difference!

Bystander Effect

The term "bystander effect" refers to the phenomenon in which the more people who are present, the less likely people are to help a person in distress. When a situation occurs, observers are more likely to take action if there are few or no other witnesses. Two major factors contribute to the bystander effect. One is that the presence of other people creates a diffusion of responsibility, and there is a need to behave in correct and socially acceptable ways. The other is, when other observers fail to react, individuals may take this as a signal that a response is not needed or not appropriate. Onlookers are less likely to intervene if the situation is ambiguous.

Case Study: The Bystander Effect

Type of Bullying: Emotional, verbal, name calling
Age of Onset/Gender of Target: Fifth grade, male
How Long Did the Bullying Last? Two years
Hot Spots: School bus
Did You Tell? If So, Whom? I did not tell

Bystanders are not immune from impact if they have observed classmates being bullied and have done little or nothing to help. When I was in fifth grade, there was a male classmate, an acquaintance of mine, who lived nearby. He was smaller than his peers, nonathletic, and an introvert. We rode the bus together every day for at least two years. Not having a memory of any other of the details about the bullying of this student on the bus, it still haunts me forty-five years later that I witnessed the merciless bullying of a classmate day in and day out and did nothing about it. Three boys taunted an innocent target who was minding his own business. Today, I feel like a coward for not standing up for him, as I remember he was in tears when he got off the bus. As a girl I felt that I could not hold my own and was at risk for being targeted as well.

I don't recall that the bullying was physical, but it was verbal and just mean and cruel. Even though I was only a witness and did not participate actively in the bullying, I could only imagine how he was treated outside the school bus and during the school day. I didn't know how to react to the situation or what I should have done and thus didn't report it. I presume he told his parents because they would meet him when he rode the bus. I don't think it was reported to any other authority figures.

As a result of the bullying, this student's family transferred him out of school and moved away. I don't know what happened to him, but I often picture him in my mind and wonder how his life progressed and hope that he had friends to support him. Looking back, I feel guilty about not stepping in and wonder why I didn't. I am firmly convinced that we need to educate bystanders more specifically than just telling them to step up. As an observer, I did not have the skills to intervene because I was fearful; I was thankful that it was not happening to me.

I am not sure what motivates a bystander to step up. When I was in fifth grade, I had a deficit of skills in my toolbox. I was a member of a less popular social group who was not powerful and had very little courage to step in. In comparison, students in the popular group did have allies and an extensive support system. They easily had an influence on their peers; clearly, their goal was to do whatever it took to enhance their popularity. Their posse would not have supported standing up for a target. I cried for this target of bullying. I keep wondering if my inability to act caused him lifelong problems. I don't blame the other bystanders because I don't know why they also didn't react or step in. Maybe if I had to do it all over again, I would report it to a caring adult, such as a parent, a teacher, or an administrator.

POINTS FOR PARENTS

Witnessing bullying can have long-term effects, and this is an example of how someone can be haunted by their inaction. Bystanders are not immune from the toxic effects of bullying, nor are they innocent of its occurrence (Vanderbilt and Augustyn 2010). It seems that everyone has a story about bullying, and the majority of the stories are from the perspective of the bystander. This person clearly has not only remembered the incident but also has regret for his or her inaction.

There are different types of motivation for how bystanders respond to bullying incidents when they occur. The question is, what is it that makes a bystander defend, participate in, or ignore the entire incident? Research shows that the students who are likely to be defenders have a strong sense of self-worth and have good coping and problem-solving strategies. They have a strong sense of personal responsibility and feel connected to their community (Pozzoli and Gini 2013). These are the students who are likely to be proactive and help a peer who is in a difficult situation. Furthermore, students who witness bullying have increased feelings of guilt or helplessness for not supporting the victim or confronting the one aggressor (Hoover et al. 1992).

By contrast, the student who distances himself or herself from a bullying situation may recognize the pain but not feel confident or have the skills to help out. This person has a moral conflict because he or she recognizes that the situation is wrong and feels a sense of responsibility but remains passive. Students who are in this place are particularly vulnerable to experiencing the long-term regret that the girl in this story feels.

This information reinforces the importance of dealing with preventing bullying behavior in a systemic way. Since bullying impacts everyone, everyone must be involved in the solution. We have to look at bullying in the social context and deal with the solution ecologically by addressing the individuals, the peer group, and the entire school community (Pozzoli and Gini 2013). Self-confidence as well as problem-solving and coping skills are essential for proactive bystanders. These characteristics need to be fostered in your child. They are the center of the socially conscious response of a student who is willing to stand up for someone else.

SUGGESTIONS FOR ACTION

- At this point, there is nothing that this woman can do about the past incident, except what she is doing—talking about it. If you have had a similar incident, this can be a good springboard for discussion with your child to help him or her understand how to be a proactive bystander.

- When an incident of bullying is discussed beyond the obvious details, ask about the bystanders and what they did or did not do. This is a good time to get into the feelings; ask, "What were you thinking at the time?" "How do you feel about what happened?" "What do you think you would like to have done?" "What do you think you could do if a similar situation arose?" Then talk about options to handle the situation. Ask the child to problem solve with you and brainstorm some alternative ways to intervene.

- Most of all, be sure to let your child know how you feel about the incident and about bystanders who stand up and step up for their friends. It is those values that will help him or her understand social responsibility.

Case Study: Bystanders Making a Difference

Type of Bullying: Physical, verbal, intimidation
Age of Onset/Gender of Target: December of seventh grade, female
How Long Did the Bullying Last? Eighteen months
Hot Spots: Hallways, walking home from school
Did You Tell? If So, Whom? I told no one.

When I was in junior high school, I was quiet and reserved and had a few friends. I was never outgoing, but in seventh grade, I started to be more assertive and vocal in groups. I began getting popular and much happier; however, my family moved during the fall of seventh grade from a metropolitan area to a small town with a population of 6,000 residents. It was hard for me, and I immediately went back into my shell and became that shy and mousy little girl that lacked self-confidence.

The bullying officially started in December, a few months after I enrolled, and lasted until I matriculated from eighth grade to high school. I really do not remember what I did or said to start it off. Maybe I did nothing and just appeared to be an easy target. What I did to make this girl hate me is not clear to me now or even then. She started occasionally bumping into me in the hall and laughing behind my back. It was mild for the first month or two, starting with only her taunting me, but then she had a group of five girls backing her up and doing what she said. She was very well known, somewhat popular, very outgoing, and a tomboy who had lived in the town for her entire life. Because she was aggressive, most other students did what she said for fear that they would be targeted. I didn't report any of the bullying, so I presume she thought she could continue to bully me. The bullying became more frequent; she tripped me, knocked my books out of my arms when I was walking down the hall, slammed my locker, and shoved me into the wall as she walked by. Then I started fearing for my safety.

I would not go to the restroom all day because I was frightened that she would hurt me.

One day in physical education class, she hit me with the ball in volleyball. I thought I would stand up for myself, so I called her a bitch. I was shaking because I had never used the word anytime in my life and didn't even know what it meant. Then things got worse. She would follow me home from school, or she would intimidate me so badly that I would avoid the bus and walk home from school. This made my mom furious, but I never admitted to my mom why I was not riding the bus. I just told her that I was tired of riding the bus.

In class, a popular girl whom I had really never officially met noticed what was happening and came up to me and inquired what I had done to make her dislike me. I think she realized that I was an innocent bystander who was being targeted and had done nothing. I said that I really did not know. She then asked me if I said anything to anyone about her. I said no. This girl then gathered up two of her popular girlfriends and said that they would take care of this and that nothing would happen to me again. Even today, I don't know what they said or did, but the girl who had bullied me never talked to me, touched me, or mistreated me again. She stayed away from me. After college, and 10 years later, this same girl whom I feared tried to befriend me on Facebook after these many years. This caused me so much consternation because all I could think of is why I would want to be friends on Facebook with someone who made my life hell when I was in school. She went on and offered an apology for the way she had acted and said she had no excuse why she acted so mean and aggressively. I replied that I would forgive her but that it didn't mean the same as being friends.

Presently, I am a thirty-nine-year-old administrative assistant working with a large business. I moved from the small town and live in a large western metropolitan city. The aggressor lives in the southern United States and is a single mom.

POINTS FOR PARENTS

This is a powerful story about how one single bystander was able to intervene and stop the bullying behavior. It literally changes the course of the storyteller's school experience. Bystanders witness 80 percent of bullying incidents (Polanin et al. 2012). Adolescent bystanders may separate themselves from a bullied peer to avoid being bullied (Salmivalli 2001). But the fact of the matter is that bystanders are there when bullying occurs—they see it happen, and they have the choice to participate, ignore it, or stop it. They are the vast majority of the student body. Aggressors like an audience, and if the audience disapproves, the aggressors can be discouraged and literally lose the spotlight because they are not getting positive feedback for their mean, hurtful behavior.

We cannot stress enough the importance of the role of the bystander. By focusing on empathy and the skills to support one's peers, we can effectively reduce and even stop bullying behavior. That means teaching kindness, understanding, and empathy through discussion and example. It takes more than just talk—parents need to be the adults we want out children to grow into.

The next thing to think of is courage. It is easy for adults to tell students that they should stand up and speak up for their peers. But we have to consider just what we are asking of a child. It takes courage to stand up to an aggressor, particularly when there are others who are supporting the aggressor. Students who speak up can become a target themselves, or their peers can ostracize them. The retaliation can continue indefinitely in many different ways. Thus, we need to ask students what they could do to intervene in a situation instead of telling them to stand up for their friends. Therefore, we need to help students think of a variety of strategies to help a peer who may be targeted. They can assess the risk and then make a decision that is suitable for the situation.

SUGGESTIONS FOR ACTION

- Talk to your child about the ways to stand up, step up, and speak up.
- Invite the target to leave the situation with you.
- Tell the aggressor to stop and leave the target alone.
- Tell an adult yourself.
- Go with the target to an adult to show support.
- Comfort and talk with the target.
- Talk to your child about courage, and acknowledge how much courage it takes to do the right thing.
- Praise your child for the smallest acts of courage; it sends a message about your values!
- Talk about the responsibility of having friends and social influence. The "popular" girl in this story was the one who was able to make a difference in this girl's life—a great lesson for all of us.

9. Hazing, Bullying, and Intimidation

A FEW WORDS ABOUT HAZING AND BULLYING

This book is about bullying, yet we have included a chapter on hazing. While these are distinctly different, they have some remarkable similarities. When we talk about bullying and hazing in the same breath, we are referring to the culture and climate that allows and even encourages the behavior. Neither bullying nor hazing would occur in an atmosphere where respect, tolerance, acceptance, and peer support are the norm.

Both bullying and hazing are about social and cultural issues. Within both there are many myths and fallacies about the extent and seriousness of these issues. When adults see either of them as "normal" behavior and choose to ignore them, the problems simply escalate. Embedded within both issues is a struggle to identify the line between acceptable and damaging behavior.

With hazing in athletics, even though there are forty-four states that prohibit the behavior, there still is the misconception that it is in "good fun" and will build character and team camaraderie. But we know that many young people have suffered serious injuries and even death from hazing and bullying.

When it comes to bullying, there are very clear messages that imply that since it has been going on for such a long time, it is a normal part of childhood. Some are even worried that unless a student has the opportunity to overcome this difficulty, they will be weak. Furthermore, there is the idea that being bullied helps build character, as students learn to cope with or grow out of it. The sample of stories presented in this book certainly paints a very different picture of the impact of bullying.

These are the cultural issues—the underlying attitudes that open the way for these behaviors to exist and even flourish. When people disapprove and are even outraged, these behaviors are much less likely to continue. Furthermore, the culture influences the way these behaviors are handled. If they are ignored or only given a "wink and a nod," cursory consequences may ensue. This will and does continue to impact not only the students involved but also adults and others. When others witness the misery of those targeted, it makes them feel unsafe, creating a hostile environment.

Both bullying and hazing are about a power imbalance and social identity. Each is about peer abuse and victimization. Hazing is about a hierarchical social structure that requires a form of initiation to belong or stay as part of the group. On the other hand, bullying is about the misuse of power, usually in social settings. This means that in most instances, aggressors misuse their power in order to gain social status.

To simply punish or discipline the offenders will not necessarily stop the problem for either bullying or hazing. It takes leadership, support, and guidance—not only from the adults but also from the students—to make a change in order to prevent reoccurrences and even escalation of the problem. The leadership needs to include a systemic approach to bullying and hazing through education, discussion, agreements, clear rules with consequences, outstanding role models, and community support.

To further clarify, the following are detailed definitions of bullying and hazing:

"Bullying is unwanted, aggressive behavior among school-aged children that involves a real or perceived power imbalance. The behavior is repeated, or has the potential to be repeated, over time. Both kids who are bullied and who bully others may have serious, lasting problems. A way to remember this act is by an acronym 'RIP.' Bullying behavior is Repeated, Intentional, and Power-based" (Carpenter, 2012).

In order to be considered bullying, the behavior must be aggressive and include:

- An imbalance of power. Kids who bully use their power—such as physical strength, access to embarrassing information, or popularity—to control or harm others. Power imbalances can change over time and in different situations, even if they involve the same people.
- Repetition: Bullying behaviors happen more than once or have the potential to happen more than once.

Bullying includes actions such as making threats, spreading rumors, attacking someone physically or verbally, or excluding someone from a group on purpose (Stopbullying.gov).

Hazing, according to Stophazing.org, is "… any activity expected of someone joining a group (or to maintain full status in a group) that humiliates, degrades, or risks emotional and/or physical harm, regardless of the person's willingness to participate. In years past, hazing practices were typically considered harmless pranks or comical antics associated with young men in college fraternities."

These actions are often considered traditional and an integral part of the culture. "These actions are often ritualistic in that they have occurred in past years to those who are now in the position of perpetuating the behavior on the new members. Additionally, these actions may require the target to participate in harmful and/or humiliating practices, and sometimes these actions escalate over time and become more serious, humiliating, and dangerous" (Kevorkian and D'Antona 2010).

In terms of hazing in middle and high school, the website states: "Hazing at any age can be exceedingly harmful. Hazing at the high school level is particularly troubling because the developmental stages of adolescence create a situation in which many students are more vulnerable to peer pressure due to the tremendous need for belonging, making friends, and finding approval in one's peer group. Further, the danger of hazing at the high school level is heightened by the lack of awareness and policy development/ enforcement around this issue. While many colleges and universities in the U.S. have instituted antihazing policies and educational awareness programs related to hazing, very few secondary schools have done the same" (Stophazing.org).

Case Study: Hazing in a Football Town

Type of Bullying: Hazing, physical, exclusion, gossip, rumors, lies
Age of Onset/Gender of Target: Tenth grade, male
How Long Did the Bullying Last? Six months and continued minimally after that point
Hot Spots: Locker room, football field
Did You Tell? If So, Whom? Yes, I told my coach and parents.

I love football. I live in a small rural southern town where my father and I have talked about playing high school football ever since I was a youngster. I have been playing sports since I could walk and throw a football. As you know, in southern towns, football is king.

I was taller than most of my friends and started pushing myself to be even stronger and more physical than most. My father was a big influence and coached me on neighborhood and school teams. In addition, our town was a big supporter of athletics, and everything focused on our high school and, of course, football. Every Friday night most of the town was at the football game in the "ditch."

When I was a sophomore, on my sixteenth birthday, as I was walking to the locker room after practice, several of my team-

mates surrounded me and jumped me. They taped me from my hands to my feet, pulled my pants down, and whipped me with their hands at first and then my sandals. People coming out of the showers exposed themselves near my face. One guy picked up a roll of tape and stuck it in my buttock. When I picked my head up, I was crying, and one of the boys said I was bleeding.

I gathered my things and went to tell the coach that I was quitting football. I told him they took my birthday celebration too far. Without my knowledge, the principal had called my parents. When I arrived home, I walked in through a side entrance, acted like nothing happened, and went directly to the bathroom. Then the phone rang and it was my coach. He asked to speak to me. I briefed my parents on exactly what happened, and my dad asked me to show him what they had done. I then dropped my pants. My parents were shocked when they saw the blood blisters on my buttocks, along with huge welts and lacerations. I felt ashamed and embarrassed that it happened, frustrated with my so-called friends, and disappointed that my coach had not protected me from this atrocity.

When my story got out, our small town became divided. The town was trying to piece together who was to blame. Several players were suspended for a week. Criminal charges were brought against some of my teammates and the popular coach. It was revealed that my coach knew about the hazing incident and did nothing about it. In addition, my parents filed a civil case against my coach and the players.

Some of the community showed its support for my coach by wearing T-shirts. Disgusted with some of the community's reactions, my parents followed up with an ad in the local paper describing what had happened to me and that it was not only wrong but also a crime. Supporters argued that what had happened to me was not right, but they still defended the coach to keep his job because he was a good coach and a good person.

Looking back, we learned that these abusive acts were allowed to happen to other players traditionally on their birthday. Each incident seemed to worsen with the nonverbal consent of the coaching staff. In my opinion, our coach was trying to be our friend instead of a responsible adult who protected us from such cruel and humiliating acts. This abuse, called hazing, was an accepted practice and ritual among the team members.

At first I wanted to keep this incident a secret. However, afterwards I wanted everyone to know that hazing did happen and that it can cause serious physical and psychological damage. Thinking back, two weeks before my incident, a group of boys had another student taped to the bench with his pants down. The coach came in, saw the boys, laughed, smiled, and said that this was a waste of tape.

I know that some in the community were saying that I should have taken this like a man— whatever that meant. They thought that this kind of abusive behavior was acceptable and that boys will be boys. Many friends turned on me. Others ignored me. Some avoided talking to me. It was like politics; some supported your actions and others blamed you for what happened. However, on the positive side, two weeks after the incident, ten senior football players came to my home and asked me to continue to play on the team. After discussing this dilemma with my parents, I chose to continue playing my sophomore, junior, and senior years, and with the same coaching staff.

As you might imagine, the community was horrified that this incident at the local high school was bringing the town constant negative publicity. For three years in a row, a local radio station placed this incident in their top ten stories in our small town. With the attention that hazing has received, it is my hope that in the future, there will be less opportunity to haze and that adults will actively supervise youth—especially those in team sports.

POINTS FOR PARENTS

Unfortunately, this story happens more often than we would like to think. The estimates of the prevalence of hazing in high schools varies greatly. However, a national survey found that 48 percent of high school students reported being subjected to hazing, 43 percent reported being subjected to humiliation, 30 percent said the initiation activities were potentially illegal, and 23 percent involved substance use (Hoover and Pollard 2000). Even though this was some time ago, there is no evidence that these numbers have decreased over time. In fact, on a regular basis, there are news reports of serious events involving hazing. These hazing activities cover a variety of behaviors—from yelling and cursing to physical and sexual abuse.

The experience of the family was not unusual either. Communities quickly polarize when there are allegations of hazing. It is part of the culture to defend the coach and the team. There is confusion about the gravity of hazing. When asked, students say that it is a part of life, and those who complain are whiny and not good friends or worthy of the group. Adults respond in the same way and set the tone for youth by their revulsion of someone who speaks up. They see the report of hazing as ruining the reputation for the rest of the group.

Given the information reported in this story, criminal charges were warranted. This birthday spanking from teammates crossed over the line into both physical and sexual assault, particularly since it had happened before with the coach's knowledge.

SUGGESTIONS FOR ACTION

- Look for the warning signs that your child may be involved in hazing (Girlshealth.gov):
  - When you observe them, the group leaders appear very mean.

— You have heard about dangerous hazing activities from others who have been through it before (this is particularly true in this case, as there was a known tradition of hazing on birthdays).

— You feel a knot in your stomach—trust your instincts!

— You have been warned by teachers or other adults that the group is dangerous.

— You have seen the group make others do things that are against your morals or values.

— You feel afraid to break away from the group.

- In instances such as this, it is important to contact the authorities before you contact the school. At this point, it is a criminal issue, and school staff is implicated, so it is up to law enforcement to interview these parties.

- Consider the emotional impact of the hazing incident on your child and get professional counseling. Beyond the physical harm, there are emotional consequences of hazing, and while one fades over time, the other can have a lasting impact on the victim's emotional well-being.

- In terms of protecting youth, you can look into the school policy on hazing. Ask how students' behavior is monitored and who is responsible to ensure that hazing does not occur.

- Check to see how students and staff are made aware of the policy and the type of education that is offered about hazing.

- Talk to parents of older students to get a sense of the history and the attitude toward hazing.

- As with all of the case studies in this book, we strongly urge talking to your child. Conversation should be an ongoing process of small and large issues. The idea is to keep the lines of communication open.

Case Study: An Intimidating Coach and a Young Aspiring Basketball Player

Type of Bullying: Intimidation, coercion, yelling, spitting, name calling

Age of Onset/Gender of Target: Junior and senior year, male

How Long Did the Bullying Last? Last two years of high school

Hot Spots: Basketball court

Did You Tell? If So, Whom? I shared information with my parents.

I have three children. When my middle son attended high school, he was a leader on the freshman basketball team and the junior varsity squad. During his sophomore year, he was progressing well and was looking forward to moving up to the varsity team; however, there were rumblings of discontent among parents and players regarding the coach.

Prior to his junior year, my son attended summer camp at the school, and the varsity coach was the instructor. He displayed a very demanding, inflexible, and intimidating attitude with the boys on the squad. I tried to understand the situation since I had played basketball in a similar sized high school, which consisted of more than 2,000 students in the student body.

During the summer before school started, my son was at home with his older brother, who was six feet, four inches tall; 200 pounds; and also a basketball player. As we were talking about the summer ending and school starting, out of the blue my younger son surprised us by stating that he was not going to play varsity basketball in the fall. My older son and I were shocked. He described incidents when the coach screamed in the faces of players and threw a chair across the court. My son stated emphatically that he would not play for a coach who coached by intimidating and coercing players and treating them so disrespectfully.

I was disturbed by his decision, knowing that he not only loved the sport but also excelled in it, so after basketball season ended his junior year, I made an appointment with the coach. When the time came, the school held a meeting with my son, the coach, the principal, and the athletic director, but they excluded us, the parents. The three of them convinced my son to come back to the team his senior year and enroll in summer camp.

Summer camp was a somewhat positive experience, even though the coach continued to scream at players. During practice games, he shouted so belligerently that his gum would end up on the court. In addition, the coach's use of mind games would add to the confusion on the squad and was a distraction among the players. The players were hijacked by the volatility of the coach and his impulsive and fear-based coaching techniques.

The preseason games started, and on December 22, my father died. When my son went to practice, he told the coach about the death of his grandfather. Our family then traveled out of state on December 26 to the funeral, causing my son to miss three practices. When he came back to school, he attended three practices before the first game. My son was a starter and the leading scorer. The coach benched my son for three games for missing practice for my father's funeral. At that moment I knew that the coach was using his power and authority to intimidate and coerce not only my son but also other players. There appeared to be no accountability for the coach's actions, and he could hand out punishment with no recourse for his actions and never be questioned by the powers that be. Even when this coach flew into a rage and threw a chair, his behavior was excused because he was a basketball coach.

When the season ended, my son decided on his own that he would not attend the athletic or academic banquet and would not pick up his athletic letter or his academic award. My son gradu-

ated with a 3.7 GPA and was in the advanced academic track for college. He received a full academic scholarship to a university starting his freshman year.

After his graduation, I started a petition about the unethical way this situation was handled by the coach and the school. I met with the superintendent and shared my concerns. He affirmatively supported the coach's decision, along with a teacher who repre-sented the union. Furthermore, an attorney of the teacher's union sent me a cease and desist letter, forbidding me to discuss my son's situation with others.

POINTS FOR PARENTS

This is a story of a coach who uses coercive and abusive techniques to train his team and develop team cohesion. In fact, regardless of whether yon consider his behavior bullying or hazing, research in-dicates that using threats, foul language, and intimidation does not build team cohesiveness (Kowalski ct al. 2010). In fact, just the opposite is true. That type of leadership contributes to a climate of hostility and disrespect. Findings from a recent study show that while many coaches have good intentions, they do not understand that emotionally abusive coaching practices have harmful effects on the athletes (Stirling 2013).

This parent was well within her right to respond to the be-havior of the coach. Clearly, it had an impact on her son and the other athletes as well. The fact that the administration supported the coach is an indicator that the culture is one in which bullying is accepted as part of the athletic experience. Coaches are the ulti-mate role models. It is reasonable to assume that if this is the de-meanor of the coach, others are emulating his behavior (Kowalski et al. 2010).

From that point on, the coach and the administration met with the boy to pressure him to return to the team. Never allow your child to participate in a meeting of this type without a parent or advocate present. Some school districts have policies that require a parent to be notified if their child is involved in any type of a disciplinary action. This gives parents the option to be present at any meetings. In the absence of a policy, when reporting an issue, it is a good idea to tell the school you wish to attend any meetings that involve your child.

SUGGESTIONS FOR ACTION

- When the season begins, check with the coach to see the policy for excused student absences. Situations that do not allow for absences under any circumstances are an indicator of a harsh and restrictive environment. Certainly, being part of a team is a commitment, and that is important for young people to learn. However, there are some circumstances that allow for an absence—after all, even professional teams give a player time off for a death in the family!
- When reporting an issue to the school, make it clear that you want to be a part of any discussions that involve your child. It is your right to be there as an advocate for your child.
- Should your child decide to stay with the team, monitor his or her activities and be aware of his or her mood. If any changes raise concerns, talk to your child to let him or her know you are not only concerned but that you support him or her.

Case Study: Hazing, Bullying, and Football

Type of Bullying: Hazing, intimidation, exclusion
Age of Onset/Gender of Target: High school, college, and NFL
How Long Did the Bullying Last? One or more seasons

I was brought up in a small southern town that was known as a football town back when I was playing in the 1990s. We were usu-

ally ranked in the state each year and were ranked nationally in the top twenty-five. Recalling my high school days, being a football player and being looked up to by my peers, I was a little different from many of my peers. I was brought up on a hog farm in a rural area secluded from civilization and isolated from neighbors.

As far as bullying goes, I never saw anyone being bullied in my presence. However, we had different types of hazing perpetrated by the football team at camp and when traveling to away games. Younger players had to carry pads for the veteran players. On the bus these same players were required to sit up front next to the coaches while the experienced players sat in the back of the bus listening to music on their headphones.

I first started playing football as a high school sophomore. I recognized that the senior class was definitely a different breed. Some players were intimidating and would pick on the younger players, while others were nice guys looking after these youngsters. One senior player who was a classmate of my brother's looked after me and took me under his wing. During my junior year I moved from the bench to being a starter. This junior class exemplified strong leadership and showed respect and support for all the players. There was little bullying or hazing throughout my last two years of high school.

In other campus areas, I did observe a learning-disabled student who was picked on even though he never realized that he was being ridiculed. At lunch, students would gather around and ask him to perform some crazy dance or to jump like Michael Jordan and touch the ceiling. After about a month with four or five students surrounding him and laughing at their escapades, I walked up and asked my classmates politely what they were doing. No one said anything. Then I looked over to the target and asked him if he wanted to walk with me to the weight room. From that day forward, he would meet me in the cafeteria and walk with me to the weight room after lunch. I never saw the others gang up on him again in my presence.

After graduating from high school at seventeen years of age, I received a full scholarship to play football for a private university. Just like high school, I moved up the ranks quickly. I started out being a fourth string linebacker and became a starter during the second game of the season. I beat out one sophomore, two juniors, and a senior after three to four weeks. Many of the players recognized that I was touted to be one of the future leaders on the team.

If hazing does exist in college football, is it fair for coaches to select drills in which players have an unfair advantage over other players because of their experience or size? For example, the first few days after we put on football pads, the coaches matched players one-on-one and had them run at each other at full speed. The players started ten yards apart, and the objective of the drill was to see who would be the last player standing. The coaches purposefully matched me, a seventeen-year-old rookie at 185 pounds, with a senior opponent who was 265 pounds. He was eighty pounds heavier and five inches taller, and I still remember the initial hit like it was yesterday.

Because I was relentless and fought back, I actually never made it to the ground. However, I was clearly dominated by the player's power and size. As the next pair was selected for the knockout drill, a trainer came over to check on me. He had noticed that I had split my chin wide open. The trainer was instructed to stitch me up and place me back on the practice field. I found out later that this drill was a rite of passage and happened each year. The coaches wanted to know how a player could handle a situation in which there was an unfair advantage. It clearly exemplified to players that this knockout drill was an accepted practice by the coaching staff.

I did not get hazed in college, mostly because a senior linebacker respected himself and me too much to create an environ-

ment that used power, intimidation, and coercion. Players expect-ed me to be a future leader for the team when they graduated. Also, in the transition with our new coach, he created an environ-ment in which there was mutual agreement to treat others like we expect to be treated.

When we became juniors, the climate changed with some of the leadership, and the new recruits were coerced by the upper classmen to shave their heads. However, two players were strong-ly opposed to this. After the coaches heard about the controver-sy, they asked the team to not pressure any player who refused to shave his head. Because these two rookie players stood up to the team leadership, they were ostracized for the remainder of the training camp prior to school starting. They were excluded from sitting with the upper classmen during breakfast, lunch, and din-ner. After school started, everything went back to normal.

There was a bullying scenario that involved a fraternity. At campus parties, the football team and fraternity would knock heads. The feud escalated semester after semester. One evening at midnight, as I was walking home, there was a fight between a football player who acted like he owned the fraternity and a gang of fraternity brothers. The incidents were repeated over and over again. The action was intended to do harm to the other side, and the power differential consisted of them ganging up on a single individual.

Another bullying scenario involved a freshman football player whom I call a bully. He picked on family, opposing football play-ers, and regular students. Even though he respected me, he was physically a big man, at six foot four inches and 275 pounds. He was a state wrestling champ and was proportionately very strong. I would laugh at him, but he tried to not bully others around me.

When we took the bus to get to games, this aggressor would board the bus and pick out a weaker student—either a kicker or a new recruit—and sit next to him in the middle of the bus, blocking his path to exit his row. When the bus arrived at the location, he would not budge to let the student leave his seat until everyone was off the bus. He also was found to control a new recruit, forcing him to do whatever he wanted while intimidating him to be his slave. If he wanted to enter a door that was locked, he would tear the door from the hinges. These antics were just a few in which this perpetrator would pick out and humiliate a weaker student. With these and other off-the-field issues, the university revoked his scholarship and released him from the football team.

Similar to high school and college, when I played for the NFL, there were similar issues with intimidation and coercion. However, the climate of the team that I played on was remarkable. We had players who were great people before they started playing for the NFL. They were the leaders of our locker room. As far as bullying goes, I could not give you one example of a bullying incident. I also had the most respect for our head coach and how he treated each player.

With hazing, we had rookies that carried shoulder pads fifty feet from the practice field to the locker rooms. This lasted for two weeks with the new recruits during the training camp. In another scenario, the players ganged up and taped a player to the goal post. Everyone, including the player taped to the goal post, was laughing so hard that we all seemed to enjoy the act. It went a little too far, however, when they left him up there for an hour. To my knowledge, this was not a ritual that had happened before. Lastly, if you made the team (about fifty out of ninety players made the team), there was another rite of passage. Every Saturday I was expected to bring breakfast sandwiches and orange juice for the other linebackers. If you were a first or second draft choice and you received millions on signing day, you were expected to take ten players to a five-star restaurant for dinner. For me, the locker room was a respectful place for the players.

POINTS FOR PARENTS

The takeaway from this story is that bullying and hazing happen at every level. However, the extent of these negative behaviors varies greatly. The words "respect" and "climate" are used in this story to describe how these situations were resolved. This attitude was a contributing factor in the way these issues were resolved. Because of this approach, he was able to stop the problem and, in some instances, protect the target.

He does, however, raise some very important questions about the behavior of the coach. It is up to the parent to examine the coach's practices within the context of the sport and determine if it is reasonable and, of course, safe for their child. For example, while the drill that was described in the story may be acceptable for football, it would be absurd if it were golf. Obviously, the physical expectations are very different according to the sport.

This is advice from the storyteller in his own words: "Parents should take the opportunity to be involved in school and community clubs and sports with their children. They have a responsibility to talk to their children and be present with them. Monitoring what they are doing is critical between the afternoon hours of three and six o'clock. When parents are not around, it is important that other adults are actively supervising them. Participating in extracurricular activities is a protective factor for children."

In order to be able to understand the dynamics of any sport, it is important to understand what actions are suitable and what actions are not. In addition, there is a fine line that distinguishes these actions from acceptable to bullying to abuse and to harassment.

The following are examples of the continuum of destructive actions in sports that escalate into more serious conduct:

Bullying: hitting, kicking, punching, shoving, slapping, or biting; theft of a teammates' sports equipment; exclusion of a peer from the office or locker room.

Abuse: repeated punching, beating, kicking; hitting an athlete with sporting equipment; denying access to needed water, food, or sleep; forced physical exertion beyond the physical capabilities of the athlete; inappropriate sexual contact; sexually oriented comments, jokes, or gestures; demeaning comments and acts of humiliation.

Harassment: physical intimidation; vulgar or lewd sexual comments; degrading or embarrassing jokes to or about an individual; unwelcome, offensive, or hostile facial expressions or body gestures referring to an individual's gender/race/sexual orientation in negative, vulgar, or derogatory terms (Stirling et al. 2011).

SUGGESTIONS FOR ACTION

- Be present for all games and practices when appropriate. Observe the behavior of the coach and the athletes.
- If you are at all comfortable, have a conversation with the coach to get a better understanding of the coach's philosophy. Ask another adult to be present with you.
- Should any of your observations of the interactions with the coach or between the athletes appear to be abusive or harassing, speak with the school administration about your concerns immediately.

Case Study: Hazing in an Inner-City High School

Type of Hazing: Physical, intimidation, threatening, terrorizing others

Age of Onset/Gender of Target: Ninth grade, males and females

How Long Did the Hazing Last? At least through ninth grade

Hot Spots: Cafeteria, outside (Dumpster), locker room, bathrooms

Did You Tell? If So, Whom? I did not tell because I feared retaliation.

When I was in eighth grade, the boys who moved up from middle school to start high school acted frightened. I never knew why until the following year when I went to ninth grade. It was a known fact that hazing was part of their culture.

My high school had a population of about 1,300 students and was part of an inner-city culture. The school was highly competitive in sports and had a mob-like mentality. Also, many students stayed in school to play sports. When I attended football or basketball games, I knew that in order to feel safe, I should go with a large group of students who would protect each other from the intimidation factor.

I never knew what hazing was until I witnessed a young man on his knees who had entered high school with me from middle school pushing a pencil with his nose from one end of the cafeteria to the other. I kept questioning why this student was pushing the pencil. I was told that upperclassmen had told him to. And if he didn't do it, they had threatened to beat him up. Once he was finished pushing the pencil across the floor, he was told to repeat it. After pushing the pencil a second time, he was then taken outside and thrown into a Dumpster. This student broke down and cried, like most of the others who were bullied. This initiation into high school happened to almost every ninth grader the year I went to high school but was only done to the boys. The only other hazing incidents that were rumored were in the boy's locker room. The rumors created a lot of anxiety. The hazing incidents created a fearful and intimidating culture in our school, where the most powerful upperclassmen, ruled the roost.

This hazing continued until a set of parents became upset when they were called because their son was unconscious. When they came to school, they found their son in a Dumpster. After investigating the incident, the parents followed up by filing a lawsuit against the school system for condoning hazing. From that point on, hazing was not allowed.

Up to that time, the freshman did whatever the seniors told them to do. These upperclassmen used coercion and intimidation to their advantage to control the actions of the new freshmen. Teachers and administrators supported the hazing until parents stepped up and complained about it. This ritual had been going on for many years because my older brother, who was five years older, also took part in it.

The girls, on the other hand, dealt with more subtle and covert types of aggression and rituals. For example, pressure was on freshman girls to dress down because if they received too much attention from the boys, the older girls would spread rumors to ruin their reputation. In addition, freshman girls were expected to dumb themselves down on tests and homework assignments. For example, performing one's highest on tests might take attention away from upperclassmen. The popular girls usually chose one girl whom they favored and identified her as the "smart" one. They also orchestrated it so that no other girls would be able to compete with her—or at least that's how it appeared. My teachers would continue to get upset with me because they knew that I was not living up to my potential.

I was fearful of the peer pressure and putting myself in a position that would cause the powerful girls to target me. In school, I walked "like a nervous tick." I was shaking inside, I had migraine headaches, my stomach had butterflies, and I would quiver with trepidation. I was fearful and always concerned about how my friends could protect each other at school, walking home from school and playing in the neighborhood. School was very difficult for me.

POINTS FOR PARENTS

Hazing is not just about what happens in fraternities, sororities, or athletics. It can happen when students transition from one grade level to the next. We have heard many stories of this occurring between middle and high school. Seniors seem to be notorious for hazing freshman when they enter high school. This causes tremendous intimidation, fear, and anxiety for the incoming freshmen.

Fear of retaliation is paramount. That is how these activities can continue without any discouragement from adults. Students do not tell anyone what is going on, and over time they accept the behavior. No one wants to be the "whistle-blower" or the only one who speaks up. The girl in this story talks about an actual physical reaction to her fears. This is not uncommon. Many students tell us that they will not use the bathroom during the school day because they fear being attacked, hurt, or humiliated during those times.

The interesting thing is that the stories of what happens to you when you get to high school become legends that are passed down to middle school students, creating fear. One eighth grader was terrified of the red lockers at the high school. She told us that those were the senior lockers. She said that if a freshman girl walked by, she would be rated by her breast size. It was humiliating but considered "all in good fun," even by the older girls. The difficult thing was that the lockers were in a central part of the high school and were almost unavoidable. These practices are more common than we like to think and become part of the culture and routine, while other antics disappear. Yet the conversation continues to create fear for the targets.

The problem is that many people—both adults and students—see these behaviors as just horsing around or part of building a community. They are passed on year after year as "traditions" and just fun (Hoover and Pollard 2000). Many schools have worked to change these traditions and replace them with more positive experiences. There are better ways of building a community, including social activities that allow students to mix and hang out together, community service that brings students together to work together for a common cause, or partnering an upperclassman with a freshman in a "buddy" program.

SUGGESTIONS FOR ACTION

- Find out from the school how they handle the transition and adjustment of new students. Ask about their specific plan. Most schools have a plan and will share it at a parent evening before the opening of school. If that is not scheduled, contact the school so you can receive details.
- Once you have the information, talk to your child to see if he or she has any concerns. This can be as simple as getting a map of the school to help your child easily find his or her classes.
- Talk to parents of older children and ask about the transition process. If you hear of any "traditions" that are of concern, talk to the school immediately to alert them of the reputation in the community. Also ask how they plan to handle it for the incoming class.
- Continue to talk to your child about his or her experience, and observe your child's behavior once he or she has made the transition. For example, if a child comes home and immediately needs to use the bathroom, it could mean that he or she was

specifically choosing to wait until he or she got home, rather than using the school facility.

- If you have any concerns, contact the school immediately. When schools and parents work together, these "traditions" can be replaced with better, more safe and productive activities.

Case Study: Fallout from a Junior High School Hazing Incident

Type of Bullying: Hazing, harassment, intimidation, emotional

Age of Onset/Gender of Target: Eighth grade, male

How Long Did the Bullying Last? Into ninth grade

Hot Spots: Physical education class, dressing room

Did You Tell? If So, Whom? I told my parents, and together we told the administration.

My husband and I have lived in a small rural southern community for most of our lives. We have three boys, ages fourteen, eleven, and eight. Last February, there was an incident that forever changed our lives. Our son Seth came home very upset and told us there was a lot of "pantsing" going on in our school gym. This term refers to students coming up from behind and pulling a student's pants down. He had first mentioned it in December, but we thought it had died down. Since our family did not condone this type of behavior, it was disturbing to our son that students were being disrespectful to other classmates. Our son continued to share with us that Paul, a popular, attractive, larger, and more developed young man further along in puberty, was the main instigator of the "pantsing." This boy, who was an eighth grader in junior high school with our son, chose to target other boys who were slower to mature. Paul's parents, whom we had known since high school, were friends of ours. Our children also participated in the same church group. Because we had a relationship with the parents, I immediately thought that the best way to handle this circumstance was to inform the mother about the situation so that she could support us as we resolved it. When discussing it, the mother laughed about the "pantsing," which took me off-guard. However, I kept focused on the issue at hand and asked the mother to please not tell her son that I had called. I thought it was better to keep our conversation confidential. The next day at school, Paul and a few of his friends started making fun of Seth and telling everyone that he was a momma's boy and that he needed to cut the umbilical cord and handle things himself. For the next two days, Seth felt overwhelmed with students making disparaging remarks. Then, at a basketball game that same week, another student, Logan, yelled out a remark from the stands: "Hey, Seth, did you enjoy being raped in the locker room?" The crowd who heard it laughed and snickered about the comment. However, it seemed to really affect Seth. A few days later, two students who watched the incident from a distance came to us and told us that more than "pantsing" had occurred. They reported that the three boys had restrained Seth in the locker room; one grabbed his arms, one grabbed his legs, and one pulled his pants down. They then made fun of his genitals. Finally, after confronting Seth with what we had heard, he shared with us the embarrassing details of what happened. We did, however, discover that "pantsing" was primarily a ritual that the basketball team participated in but that Seth had never pulled anyone's pants down. We tried to get a handle on the details and stayed up past midnight, waking up early the next morning and going over exactly what had happened.

The same day, my husband called the father of one of the other boys, Andy, whose parents were also friends of ours, and disclosed to him what we had been told. He told Andy's father that we would be reporting that the three boys had held Seth down, removed his pants, and made fun of his genitals. The father seemed to listen and be understanding. My husband and I then went to the school and met with the principal; he subsequently interviewed Seth individually and later the two onlookers. He concluded that the three boys—Paul, Andy, and Logan—had been involved in hazing and would be expelled from the school immediately. Afterwards, I went to Andy's house to speak with his mother about the incident. We both cried and hugged. As I stated previously, we were friends of Paul's and Andy's families and socialized with them regularly, especially during basketball season and church activities. During these events we had the families over to our home, or we were invited to theirs at least weekly. The boys—Seth, Paul, and Andy— would also have sleepovers on a regular basis. Our relationship with Logan and his parents was not as close; we did not socialize with them, except during basketball. In conclusion, Paul and Andy's parents were understanding of the situation and supported the school in the decision that was rendered. Paul and Andy came over and apologized for their behavior. Then, on the evening that the three students were expelled, my husband received a text from Andy's father stating that he was disappointed in how the school dealt with the incident. He thought we should not have gone to the school and that Seth should have handled it on his own. From that point on, we heard nothing from Andy's family. After a month or more, I contacted the mother and asked if she would meet with me and talk so that we could resolve the matter, but there was no response. However, days later we were taken off as a friend on Andy's Facebook account. Furthermore, I wanted to pursue the comment with the principal about what Logan had yelled out at the basketball game about Seth "being raped in the locker room," asking for this situation to be further investigated. I wanted Logan to know that this behavior was an act of bullying. I knew that if I didn't say or do anything about it, Logan would most likely spread more rumors and gossip. The principal concluded that because he did not see or hear the comment that allegedly was said, he could do nothing about it. What an embarrassment for any child to be publicly humiliated in front of a large group of his peers. It seems the logical reason that Logan embarrassed Seth was to get back at Seth for not inviting him to his birthday party. With Logan's ADHD (attention deficit hyperactive disorder) condition, we knew that his perception was skewed and that he lacked social-emotional skills to make and keep friends. I knew of Logan's condition because his mother, an employee at the junior high school, was a shopping and movie partner of mine. She had shared with me Logan's disappointment that Seth had not invited her son to my son's birthday party. Afterwards, we found out that Logan had twice contemplated suicide and referenced the fact that he was excluded from Seth's birthday party. Rumors became rabid; however, it had been my contention all along that most of the gossip was coming from Logan and his mother. There were rumors that Seth had exaggerated what had happened, that he should have never tattled on his friends, and that he single-handily got the three boys expelled. As we continued to scrutinize social networking sites, we found these and other untruths on Facebook and Instagram. I immediately reported these sites to the school board. Many of these falsehoods were taken down instantly. Then, surprisingly, we found out that Logan had transferred from the junior high school to another school in the district. That was good news, and we thought maybe things would improve. Looking back, we felt that our family had been shunned for standing up and notifying the authorities of the harassment to our son. We had been looked at like we were the aggressors—that we had perpetrated a crime instead of the reverse. The social anxiety that this incident created in our family was unconceivable. I could not go to the grocery store without having a panic attack. The physical stress was overwhelming. My husband and I had lost more than ten percent of our body weight.

After the summer, Andy's parents reached out to us and we picked our friendship up where it had left off. Then, one of Seth's friends, who happened to be a girl, texted him and questioned him about why he told on his friends since they were just boys having fun. "How could you get them expelled?" He replied that she would have done the same thing if a group of girls had exposed her breasts. She responded that she would have never reported it because she would have known that the girls were just having fun. Seth cut ties with her immediately.

To take care of myself, I pursued counseling and was placed on an anti-anxiety medication. I continued to attend counseling regularly and was diagnosed with post-traumatic stress disorder symptoms because of having reoccurring nightmares. I am presently being weaned off of my medication. As for my husband, immediately after the incident, he was throwing up at night and had a bad case of acid reflux. Now, things are settling down and much better.

We did a great job sheltering our younger children from the strife that we had endured. We shared appropriate information with them but did not convey many of our inner thoughts in front of our children. We continued to monitor social networking sites, mostly Facebook and Instagram, to prevent any cyberbullying occurrences. When we did find gossip, rumors, or lies cited, we relayed the information to law enforcement. Looking back at the incident, I wish I had focused more on the coping skills of my son. Instead, I was fixated on the perpetrators and the consequences for their actions. I wish I had focused more on our son instead of trying to fix the environment and make it better. I think I made it worse for him. I am grateful, however, that Seth talked with us and had his grandparents as a support system. Lastly, I relate this incident to having an alarm in our home and our car to prevent burglaries. Why not teach our children to sound an alarm and tell any individual who exploits our body to stop?

POINTS FOR PARENTS

This is yet another story of a behavior that occurred frequently. Some students found it funny, while others turned away. The student who was the aggressor was intimidating in such a way that the others were afraid to report his behavior. He was the same age but larger, more athletic, and more developed. When these parents heard about the "pantsing" from their son, they did not respond other than listen to him.

When the specific incident happened to their son, they chose to talk to the parents of the aggressor. Most professional educators strongly advise against this. Even when you know the family, it can be a very difficult task. In this case, the parent of the aggressor did not see anything wrong with the behavior. Even when both parents agree that the behavior is unacceptable, most parents—on hearing the news—respond defensively. "That is not my child" or "My child would never do that" or "Your child is exaggerating" are just some of the possible responses that can make a difficult situation even worse. This leaves you, as the parent, in a difficult position. It is important to note that both times the parents had a conversation with another parent it ended badly.

It is far better to bring the situation to a neutral party—the school. The administration is in a position to interview all participants and get to the bottom of the issue without allowing any opportunity for blaming. The school also can put mechanisms into place to minimize and even prevent retaliation. We cannot stress enough the importance of working in partnership with the school.

The parents did all the right things in the aftermath. They followed Facebook and Instagram to be certain that there was no retaliation or further discussion of the "pantsing" incident. This is crucial today, as most students communicate electronically. They can reach a larger audience and do so from anywhere.

In addition, they sought professional help for their son and themselves as well. They recognized that there could be serious consequences for their son from this humiliating event. It is entirely possible for the child to experience some sort of emotional reaction such as posttraumatic stress disorder.

The parents returned to the school to discuss the role of the student who shouted out a slanderous remark to embarrass the victim in front of this peers. Bystanders who heard the statement are key to preventing bullying and spreading gossip, rumors, and lies. When there are factions that support covert aggression, they become an important part of why the behavior will continue. These bystanders become part of the problem and have responsibility in the act even though they did not physically participate. We want all bystanders to recognize that they have the power to act in a way that either supports further victimization or ends it. In this story, the aggressor should have had the decency to say nothing rather than humiliate the victim by shouting out an untruth at a basketball game. This behavior was unacceptable, and he should have been called out on his coercive and intimidating antics.

Now the next question to consider is the consequence that involved expelling the aggressors from school. Certainly, it is important for the school to have a code of conduct that includes consequences for negative behavior. However, this cannot be the only method for dealing with these issues. We want students to learn from their actions rather than leave them angry and resentful. Certainly, the consequence can include a teaching component in which the student is required to do something that will allow for restorative practices.

"The principles of restorative justice are based around empowerment, reintegration, restoration, and emotional and social healing (Harris 2003). Empowerment for the offender means, in part, building offender accountability. Offenders have an opportunity to take responsibility for what they have done, to make amends to the victim, and to become reintegrated into the community" (Ahmed et al. 2012). The main focus for the offender(s) is to "repair the harm."

In order to change behavior, it is necessary to be flexible and consider previous bullying instances. Therefore, responding to a bullying incident must be in context to building social relationships and reducing the shame attached to the consequence (Ahmed et al. 2012). Essentially, this means that we want to teach the aggressor that his or her actions have repercussions not only to the victim but also to the community. A consequence that is restorative would make some amends to the victim and teach the aggressor social responsibility.

Restorative practice is a complex issue that will be addressed in the last chapter of this book. However, we are suggesting that it is one of many approaches to dealing with serious issues as discussed in this case study. After all, the goal is to develop empathy and understanding so these behaviors will not continue.

SUGGESTIONS FOR ACTION

- Go to the school immediately before attempting to confront a parent directly when there is an issue that has impacted your child.
- Be prepared with all the relevant details, including who is involved, where it happened, how long it has been happening, who was there, and any information on previous instances.
- Support your child by involving a professional counselor. It may not seem necessary at that point in time, but it is a good idea to establish a relationship with someone should there be any future related problems.
- Be prepared for repercussions from others in the school, but remember that this type of behavior is unacceptable in any setting.

Case Study: Is Indoctrination and Hazing the Same?

Type of Bullying: Embarrassing, not intentionally done to harm but to build character and learn survival skills
Age of Onset/Gender of Target: Individuals not targeted, male
How Long Did the Bullying Last? Indoctrination lasted for first two years
Hot Spots: Hallways, before lunch, dormitory
Did You Tell? If So, Whom? Not reported because it was regular operating procedures

As a member of a service academy and as a combat fighter pilot in the military, I look back and reflect upon what I saw and experienced. It has been forty years since I attended the service academy. My qualifier is I had only positive experiences within the service academy while I was there.

At any service academy, in order to be successful, the new cadets must accept the linear and vertical chain of command and the organizational system of discipline. In the most extreme conditions when individuals were going into combat, it was imperative that individuals take commands without asking questions and getting into a debate. Orders were orders. They needed to be carried out and executed. Thus, there had to be a mind-set change with the populous. The process at the service academies was to strip away what makes a person who they are—their ego and self-identity. Then, the goal is to rebuild the ego with a different set of values and behaviors. When cadets experienced and displayed high levels of emotions, they were still expected to finish each task with a high degree of functioning.

The hope was that training would take over for actions. Thus, the service academy would place individuals under stress, even if it was verbal stress, and expect them to recite trivial information

257

from memory. It was common before a formation or meals each day for a freshman to stand out in the passageway and recite a series of items such as the officers of the day, the menu for the upcoming meal, the movie theaters in the town, the movies that were playing at each of the theaters, and the next sporting event of the rival service academy. We were expected to yell it out quickly while others were in our face shouting at us and asking us more questions. We were embarrassed and humiliated in front of the other cadets while we were being verbally assaulted. The goal was to increase our stress level under arduous conditions.

Another part of indoctrination related to the dormitory. We had to double time or run through the dormitory, and when we came to a junction, we were expected to make a right or left turn with our foot on a metal plate on the floor. Each time we stopped and turned we had to say something that was grungy for our academy, such as "Go Army, Beat Navy!" or "Go Air Force, Beat the Marines!" It had to be loud enough that the other cadets could hear it. If they didn't we were subject to discipline. One punishment was called brace up. We had to suck our chin to the back of our head and run around the dormitory like a fool. Society today might call this abusive. It was definitely embarrassing, yet it served a purpose—and a good purpose for our training.

Additionally, the freshman of the class had to assist the upperclassmen when asked. In the spring and fall, it would be common for the air to be cool in the morning but hot in the afternoon. The dorms were not air-conditioned, and cadets left their windows opened to pull in the night air. In the middle of the night it would get colder, so the windows needed to be closed. Instead of an upperclassman waking up and closing the windows in the middle of the night, one of our jobs was to close the windows of every upperclassman between two and three in the morning without waking them up. It was demeaning, but it was one of our tasks.

Indoctrination seemed to be a catalyst that created a more co-

hesive social bond among the cadets. The four years in the service academy established a bond of intense kinship and camaraderie. At a recent reunion forty years later, I had conversations with other cadets as if I were back in school and time had stood still. I had vivid memories of what we shared and sacrificed and the competitions between us. The environment with the indoctrination served a purpose that bonded us forever.

Society and culture defines lines of gray, and these lines changed from time to time. When I started in the service academy, it was an all-male student body. Women were admitted for the first time when I was a senior in 1976, graduating its first class in 1980. This was a big cultural change for the service academies, and we had to change our modus operandi to accommodate the female cadets. The women who attended this first year were extremely motivated and were stellar examples of women venturing into a man's world.

The values in our culture change from time to time, and behaviors that were appropriate become inappropriate at a different point in time. Thus, we make errors in judgment as we are introduced to different options. Our boundaries fluctuate as our thinking grows and evolves over time.

The three characteristics of bullying apply to indoctrination: repeated to all plebes, intentionally done to embarrass or humiliate them, and power-based (being done by an upperclassman to a lowerclassman). Whether the intentional is with the intent to harm is left to the perception of the target. The intent at the service academy is to learn.

Where do we draw the line? There are examples on the news in which extreme cases resulted in individuals taking their own life. Part of the story shared in the news appeared to draw a cause-and-effect relationship between, for example, suicide and bullying; however, the public is usually not privy to other factors that impacted the situation (e.g., individuals being on medication or having a mental illness). Are there healthy and unhealthy behaviors related to indoctrination, and where does it cross the line?

There were stories at the academy in which behavior crossed the line from indoctrination to hazing with intent to harm, but the incidents were few and far between. With dual genders, however, the incidents appeared to be more numerous in the area of unsolicited sexual advancement, with more and more girls being accepted into a male-dominated establishment. We had training on sexual discrimination regarding the perception of the intent of the giver and receiver, but as you can imagine, it is a slippery slope. This as an example of how we make guesses with the boundaries and then learn from our mistakes. We then learn to make the boundaries more appropriate.

When I first went to the academy in the early 70s, most of my class had preconceived notions regarding homosexuality. The awareness of this issue was different then than it is today. During my four years at the academy, there was a gay ring uncovered and there were several (from eight to ten) individuals within the same company who were discovered and expelled from the academy. This behavior was a violation of the written rules, and there was zero tolerance. It was a big deal, and the academy wanted everyone to know about the incident.

The military training involved with survival and prisoner-at-war camp was an experience from which I learned a great deal. An outside observer may look at prison camp training and call it abusive. There was physical contact for punishment in which I was grabbed by a shirt collar in the back of the neck and slammed against a metal wall. This happened numerous times. My back was black and blue. I was also introduced to waterboarding, which was used to simulate torture. The learning objective was that everyone had a breaking point, and it came about much faster than you thought—no matter how tough that you thought you were. Was waterboarding torture, or was it a highly effective tech-

nique to extract information from someone? When waterboarding was done, there were medical personnel available to monitor the heart rate and blood pressure and to make sure no one would ingest excessive water during the exercise. The tables were inclined where the head was lower than the chest. Even though the individual was strapped down, the water was not able to travel uphill and compromise the condition of the individual. The hardest thing for me was when they asked me to kneel, scrunch down, place your elbows next to your knees, and crawl up like a little ball. The box would be closed, and I was in a very confining space. It was more difficult if the individual was less flexible and/or claustrophobic. I was not sure how long we were expected to stay in the box, but it seemed like an eternity. I was fighting claustrophobia the whole time and thought I would lose the fight. When I did get out, I couldn't walk or stand because the blood had to again circulate in my legs.

There were also demeaning tasks if the class performed poorly. In the middle of the night, without having eaten for two days, our company was expected to use our fingers and carve in a twenty-foot gravel section of a parking area a specific symbol or logo of their choice. The upperclassmen would then walk on top of the design, and our company would start all over again.

In the context that the training was for war, the experience was exceptional and I only had a positive reaction to the practice in and out of the classroom. Ten to twenty-five percent did not make it through the experience; however, most thought it was positive. The goal was for an individual, if caught behind territory lines, to navigate the experience of being a prisoner of war and turn it into a positive learning experience.

Hazing in clubs and fraternities in which individuals are asked to get drunk and wear their pants inside out for no learning purpose is different from my experiences in the academy with indoctrination. I think the differentiation and line can be drawn if there

*is a learning objective—however meaningless or trivial or embar-
rassing from an activity that has a purpose.*

*I can remember it like it was yesterday. When we arrived at
the mock-like prisoner camp, our reality told us that we were not
in America. Intellectually, you know you're in a training environment, but when you open your eyes, it appeared to be reality. After
a while, I found that most of the instructors were smaller than I
was. Instructors were only allowed to hit with an open hand. They
could slap but not punch, so I discovered if I leaned into the instructor when he tried to throw me up against the wall, he could
not get the appropriate leverage to throw me with much force. I
had found a way to beat the system and not be a victim. Furthermore, I don't think this lesson could be learned in an academic
environment. In my opinion, it can only be taught when you have
been worn down from not eating and struggling to stay alive.*

POINTS FOR PARENTS

Indoctrination: At one end of a continuum is indoctrination—a
training process to acclimate an individual to an organization,
which seems highly appropriate and purposeful. On the other end
of the continuum is bullying, which is sometimes referred to as
hazing. However, hazing is inappropriate, has no specific purpose,
and is demeaning and abusive.

While this does not involve young people and school, this story raises some very real questions about indoctrination. There are
some places where these practices are an integral part of training
yet even in these settings, there is a line that moves from acceptable and necessary to harsh, humiliating, and dangerous. This is
true in every arena. It is our responsibility to know the difference
and to respond accordingly.

Certain activities cross all boundaries. There is a line and gray
area in most situations, and we need open communication and
dialogue to talk about things openly and frankly in the spirit of

learning. We need to discuss healthy training and indoctrination procedures and how these boundaries can drift into the areas of hazing and bullying.

SUGGESTIONS FOR ACTION

- Listen for descriptions of activities on a team that include words such as initiation, tradition, or indoctrination, as this can be a red flag indicating hazing activities.
- When there is talk about team building, be certain that all activities are well supervised.
- Know your child's coaches and their reputation. This can be an indicator of their philosophy regarding student behaviors.
- Attend all games and as many of the practices as allowable. Your presence sends a message and shows your vigilance.

10. Toolbox for Parents

HELPFUL INFORMATION FOR PARENTS

What do parents/educators need to know? Should parents be as concerned with behaviors other than bullying?

Fact: the overwhelming majority of school-age students are not involved in bullying. However, with the impact of social media, television, and the Internet—which glamorize and sensationalize news—one would think that at least weekly, there is a suicide of a student or a horrific incident shown on YouTube regarding bullying. This inaccurate information bombards every home, is debated over and over, and portrays that every child is being bullied at school every hour and every day. Parents arm themselves and become hypervigilant to protect their child against being scarred for life. Not only is there concern with students being bullied, but a nominee for the presidency was also proclaimed a bully by the liberal media. Even leaders of countries are said to bully other countries. Furthermore, parents have a goal for schools to provide a caring, learning environment where students feel safe.

Are there signs if a parent suspects that a child is being targeted for bullying? Note: These behaviors may also be signs of other issues that may need intervening.

- Difficulty eating or sleeping (including nightmares)
- Change in personality, behavior, or mood—being sad, angry, anxious, depressed, withdrawn, fearful, lonely, and/or provocative
- Suicidal thoughts or actions

- Reluctance or refusal to go to school
- Torn clothing
- Bruises or unexplained injuries
- Items taken to school that are missing
- Money that is asked to be replaced
- Decline in academic performance or grades
- Self-blaming, feeling helpless, aggressive displays, conflicts with others
- Self-inflicted injury (cutting behavior)
- Complaints of headaches, stomachaches, or pretending to be sick
- Feeling hungry after school from not eating lunch
- Wanting to take a different route to school
- Unable to concentrate

ADVICE FOR PARENTS

- Listen to your child when he or she comes to you and says he or she is being mistreated, bullied, threatened, taunted, called names, gossiped about, etc. Giving a child your undivided attention will speak wonders. By doing so, you will make your child feel comfortable with discussing any future situation. Also, listen to your gut instincts because more times than not, a child may not tell you directly that he or she is being taunted, intimidated, coerced, or bullied. Start observing.
- Parents should ask administrators how often they examine the bullying hot spots, such as the lunchroom, hallways, playground, recess, locker room, etc., as part of a continual process of developing a climate that promotes students feeling safe and secure.
- Parents should expect schools to continuously work toward developing an inclusive school climate where diversity is welcomed, tolerance is part of the culture, and students feel appreciated.

265

- Parents should listen to their gut instinct. If you are suspicious that your child is being bullied, follow up with the school immediately, and log each communication and incident.
- Be aware of any change in your child's behavior, and share your concerns with the school.
- If your child is asking for help, contact the school to make sure that he or she feels safe.
- When your child is being bullied, ask him or her to ask for help from an adult at school and an adult at home. If he or she doesn't get help, ask your child to go to a different adult at school until help is rendered.
- Parents should be aware of the signs that their child might be the target of bullying or the perpetrator. Work as a team and be open-minded. Be your child's advocate.
- Parents should realize that schools have a responsibility to protect children from harm. The ultimate role falls to employees, who act on behalf of the school to actively supervise and reasonably protect children's health, safety, and well-being. The goal of the school is to minimize the risk and frequency of bullying and to curtail any catastrophic incident. However, we must acknowledge that bullying is on a continuum; it is our goal to minimize risk, and it is impossible to negate all bullying behavior.
- When there has been a bullying incident, parents should ask the school to describe what reasonable staff behavior looks like when children are being protected from harm. In addition, ask what a reasonable staff member might do in a similar situation to keep a child safe.
- Parents should insist that the school have both a proactive and reactive plan. Ask how often the school performs a safety check for bullying hot spots and checks on equipment that blocks children from being actively supervised. Find out what the supervisory requirements based on children's age and number

are and what the specific staff responsibilities and procedures are. A special needs class may require additional resources to ensure child safety. Check if there are accountability measures and if protocol is being followed.

- When children are at school, the staff has a responsibility to care for and protect every child from harm. The staff has a duty to act in a way that minimizes risk and maintains the health, safety, and well-being of all children under the school's supervision.

MAJOR FOCUS FOR PARENTS: ASK, DON'T TELL!

Parenting in general—whether it is about our reactions to bullying, hazing, harassment, or intimidation—is challenging and rewarding at the same time. How we confront, react, and respond to difficult situations is paramount to what type of relationship and connection we will foster with our children.

Most individuals—adults and children alike—do not like to be told what to do. Instead, it is clear that if we ask the right questions at the right time and in the right way, individuals are more likely to problem solve and figure out a better way to handle a situation.

The following questions are thought-provoking, with the goal of stimulating a higher level of thinking in the brain. Before choosing the appropriate question, take into consideration where the individual is in his or her developmental growth. This process is all about self-regulation—being able to identify, control, and regulate our emotions.

Choosing which question to begin and follow up with will differ each time a parent or school staff intervenes with a child. The goal is to ask the question in a nonthreatening, noncoercive manner and with a pleasant tone of voice, using appropriate eye contact. Then, listen to the child's response and afterwards summarize some of the major points of what was heard. Your goal is to listen to what your instincts are telling you and read the child's body language. Hear what the child is not saying. The person doing the questioning should not be the same person who instills the discipline. However, if you are a single parent, your objective is to establish agreements early on about how you want your child to act and not to belabor consequences because they have already been established. During this discussion, collect specifics and discuss how differently the child can handle the incident in the future or what he or she needs from the parent, school staff, and peers.

The following questions have been adapted from the applied and perceptual control theory. We have developed these questions because they best exemplify how to have a meaningful dialogue with students. When using these questions, it may not be necessary to go in sequence or to ask all the questions. Depending on the responses, you may want to build on a specific question and follow up in that direction. These questions are meant to be a lead-in to getting at the motivations and feelings behind actions. If you receive a response that is challenging (e.g., "I don't know" or "I don't care"), remember that your goal is to be nonthreatening and noncoersive. These are questions that are thought-provoking and may take time for the student to respond to.

Here are some questions for students who have been bullied.

  What do you like best about school?
  How do you want to be treated?
  What can I do to help you feel safe at school?
  Where/when do you feel the safest? Where/when do you feel
    the most unsafe?
  What do you like best about yourself?
  How would we know that things are getting better?
  What one thing could parents, staff, and students do to make
    things better for you at home and at school?

Here are some questions for students who bully.

What principle(s) do you think it is most important to live by?

How do you want to be remembered at school?

What are your goals about schooling?

What do you believe about mistakes?

What do you do when you make a mistake?

How important is it to "repair harm" or make amends? What does that look like?

How is it best for you to "repair harm"?

How is this plan helping you to get what you wanted?

Describe the kind of person you want to become.

How does what you are doing right now fit with who you said you want to become?

Name one way you upheld our agreement?

What could you do to make things better?

How did you do on following your agreement at school today? (Be specific.)

How do you want to act when you see someone you think is being taunted?

What can I do to get you to work together to make it right?

I could fix this or you could fix it. What do you want to do?

Let me know when you want to make amends, and I'll help you come up with a solution.

What do you want me to be when you are not who you said you want to be?

What type of person do you aspire to be?

Some questions that could be shared with students who have been bullied, the perpetrators themselves, and bystanders.

What strengths/gifts do you bring to the table?

What would your parents/teachers say about your successes?

What would you like to give yourself credit for today?

How do you want me to act when you are not holding up your agreement with yourself or others?

Tell me what makes you successful.

What is different about those times where you are successful?

What is a motto you want to live by?

What is your agreement with yourself? With your class? With your school?

Who is the person you said you really wanted to be at home and at school?

How is what you are doing helping you to get what we agreed to?

What goal(s) do you want to set during this year?

Who might be able to help you?

What is your next step toward doing better?

How are you going to evaluate how your plan is working?

INSIDE VIEW FOR A COUNSELOR WHO USES PERCEPTUAL CONTROL THEORY: WHAT IT "LOOKS LIKE" WHEN ADDRESSING BULLYING BEHAVIOR

When I deal with students who use bullying behavior, I keep the following three practical points in mind:

First, ask questions but do not label the behavior. The ultimate goal is to get your child to evaluate himself or herself and address how he or she played a part in the incident. For example, if a child is bullying another child, the first thing the parent might do is address the aggressor and state that his or her behavior is mean and unacceptable, and to not do that again. That is telling someone what to do, and there is no thinking in the process. When addressing the perpetrator, don't label the behavior as mean. When the child labels the behavior, he or she is more likely to own it. Ask, "What are you doing? What do you want from what you are doing?" The child may respond that he or she wants a toy or to be in charge. Then ask, "How do you want to be in charge?" and brainstorm different ways to be in charge without using aggression and coercion.

The suggested approach is to focus more on the target at whom the coercion is directed. Ask, "What do you think the person wants? Why do you think he or she is doing that?" The conclusion is that the aggressor is getting something that he or she wants. Parents need to empower the target so that he or she does not have to engage in the encounter, thereby developing a pattern of behavior such as giving away a toy, crying, or screaming back. Again, stay away from labeling the child's behavior. Let the child label the behavior. This gives the child power and more responsibility for how he or she will respond in the future. When the child does not yell back or sulk, the child develops power. Thus, the goal is for the child to not give power away when responding to an aggressor's attacks.

Second, remember—what you do is what you teach. If a parent is frustrated, how we display dealing with frustration at that moment may be modeled by a child when he or she deals with peers. When a parent uses bullying behavior or steps in as a bystander, the child may react the same way that he or she has seen behavior modeled. This is how youth gain the possibilities and experiences of how to act and what to do.

Third, do not teach your children to "bully the bully." Parents should not teach their children to use bullying, aggressive behavior, or coercive language with a perpetrator. This shows that the way we deal with bullying is to bully right back. To use an analogy, the rumor that starts off small quickly and exponentially increases in size, and we want to decrease the exposure for injury.

What can parents do to be proactive and to prevent bullying from becoming a threat?

When communicating with your child, be observant and listen to what your instincts are telling you. When gathering the facts, be patient and supportive and start a written log. Help your child describe specifically what happened. Write down when and where the incident occurred (date, time of day, hot spot), what transpired, who was involved, if any witnesses were there, and any reaction by the target/victim. It is important to note that some children (called provocative) who report being bullied also play a part in the bullying. Since it is difficult to detect who initiated the bullying, address both parties individually. Develop an agreement from this point on—if one has not been developed—that bullying behavior will not be tolerated. Be specific. When or if the agreement is broken, the expectation from this point on is for the target to walk away and immediately report the incident to an adult. It should be made clear that the aggressor will have consequences that have been determined ahead of time.

Avoid asking too many questions; instead, use open-ended, noncoercive statements. Select a time when you are alone with your child and when you are both relaxed and not distracted. Engage your child by asking him or her about an observation of yours regarding school. It could be about your child or about friends. Remember, use active listening to summarize what your child said and make a conscious effort to reflect on what you heard and to understand what your child said and felt. Try summarizing and repeating back exactly what you were told.

Brainstorm ideas with your child on how bullying, intimidation, and coercion can be prevented from reoccurring from that point on, at all identified hot spots. Ask your child to take the information and share it with the school or other place of incident. Make it clear that you will follow up with a phone call. Ask your child to keep a confidential log and share it with a trusted adult at school and at home. If there are other incidents, schedule a follow-up meeting immediately, and ask for your safety plan to be modified.

WHAT PARENTS CAN DO IF THEIR CHILD IS DISTRESSED OVER BULLYING

Parents with children of all ages—from toddlers to preschoolers to elementary ages to preteens to teenagers and even young adults—are seeking more effective ways to communicate with their child. One goal of this book is to help parents have the persistence and fortitude to seek help for and support their child as he or she passes through each developmental stage. For this skill set to be developed and strengthened, parents need continuous feedback as they guide and empower their child through the process. This change does not come about in a day, nor is it the responsibility of the parent to remedy or fix the situation. However, it may be the parent's obligation to advocate for their child and ask appropriate questions, listen intently, and support their child to make a decision, thereby teaching the child to problem solve and learn by his/her mistakes.

Be observant. Go with your gut instincts. Ask your child to identify a time to talk.

If you observe a behavior change or if your child seems moody, check it out by saying:

- "I'm not sure how you are feeling, but if and when you want to talk, let me know. I will be here," or
- "You seem anxious and frazzled. I felt the same way recently. When you are ready to talk, I'll be there."

Take every opportunity to talk with your child one-on-one.

Children talk more when they are engaged in another activity. For example, when you're in the car driving to an appointment or when you're having lunch, ask an open-ended question, such as:

- "How did your day go today? What was the best part of your day?" or
- "I noticed yesterday when I picked you up that you were laughing and joking, but today you seem more distant. If you would like to talk, we can go and get some ice cream".

If you're not sure if your child is ready to talk, say the following:

"When you're ready, let me know and I'll be there."

If your child says that he or she doesn't know if he or she wants to talk, ask:

"Do you want to know"?

Listen and help your child to identify his or her feelings. Ask clarifying statements, such as:

- "Can you tell me more about what happened earlier?" or
- "How did you feel about what happened to your friend?" or
- "When you said you felt good about what happened, can you use a different word that describes your feelings, like happy, scared, sad, etc.?"

After your child has been targeted, ask him or her to write up what happened and log any future incidents.

It is essential to record what happened in as much detail as possible. If your child is too young, record it for your child or ask him or her to draw what happened. A written description of what, when, and where the bullying happened; the names of the aggressors, additional targets, and bystanders; and how your child responded to the incident should be included. This document then becomes a legal reference.

Share the log with an adult.

When you feel you have enough facts to justify your intervening, make an appointment with either the adult who was in charge at the time of the incident, the adult's supervisor (e.g., principal), or both. Request that your child be present, and ask for someone to take notes creating action items (i.e., when the event occurred and who is responsible) so that this information can become part of your child's file.

When sharing the log, do not identify the behavior as bullying. Instead, identify and describe the specific observable behaviors. For example, "Sally hit James in the head with a ball. Then James got his two best friends and pushed Sally against the wall." Identify clearly what you, the parent, want to see happen—not as a consequence for the perpetrator, but to support your child. Use language such as "My goal is to offer a safe learning environment for all children."

The goal for this meeting is to reduce any future incidents or retaliation by jointly developing a safety plan for your child at each hot spot. Ask about how the plan will use cameras and adults to actively supervise the hot spot(s) in question, and then brainstorm ideas on how the target can reduce any risk of these incidents reoccurring (e.g., avoiding the area or walking in the area with friends).

While the target is not at fault for being bullied, he or she may inadvertently escalate the situation. Reactions including, but not limited to, nonverbal negative actions, pushing, and name calling should be replaced by a different response that is not provocative. Ask the target to role-play what he or she will say.

Before the meeting ends, ask to schedule a follow-up meeting to share any feedback and modify or make adjustments if the plan is not working. In addition, you and your child should continue to log any future incidences. It is important to note that no one individual has control over another individual. The change has to be inside of the child.

HOW PARENTS WORK WITH SCHOOLS THAT USE ZERO TOLERANCE

Zero tolerance is a policy that is found in many school systems. It became popular when students were involved in safety issues and schools wanted to reduce students bringing weapons and drugs to schools. When students started bringing guns to school or were found to possess drugs or drug paraphernalia, law enforcement—in conjunction with schools—enacted zero tolerance policies. This policy imposes automatic punishment for infractions of a stated rule with the intention of eliminating undesirable conduct. For example, in many school systems, if a student is found with a gun, knife, or explosive, the student is expelled with no questions asked. If a student is found selling a drug on campus, the consequences are the same. In the area of bullying, the policy is used if a child is involved in a fight or a bullying incident.

Zero tolerance is used against both parties if both were fighting or if both were involved in bullying—even if retaliation sparked the incident. There are numerous situations when one child is provoked and taunted for weeks, months, or years by a group of perpetrators and the victim finally has had enough and stands up and physically attacks one of the aggressors. The school may react to punish the victim because he or she seemed to be the aggressor, or the school elects to punish both parties equally. After a thorough investigation schools do not alter their consequences but instead use the zero tolerance policy even though it has been proved to be ineffective in reducing future fighting or bullying incidents.

It is suggested that if parents can create an atmosphere where a child will share if they are being bullied early on, the parents and target should immediately call a meeting with a counselor and administrator to share the specifics of what has been occurring. Then, as a team, the goal is to develop a safety plan to minimize any future bullying. However, part of the discussion should be about how future incidents will be handled. If the target does defend himself or herself or knows that an altercation is going to happen, will the school be understanding of the situation and work with the parents and target to not only keep him or her safe but to prevent their child from being suspended or expelled?

RESTORATIVE PRACTICES AND CHANGING BEHAVIOR

Many schools use a punishment-based approach when dealing with incidents in which rules are broken or individuals are hurt. They discipline the perpetrator with either in-school suspension or out-of-school suspension. They concentrate their efforts on asking who did it, identifying what rules were broken, and delivering punishment. These efforts usually do not prevent future occurrences, nor do they change behavior. What makes the situation even more problematic is when schools use the zero tolerance policy, thereby giving equal punishment to the perpetrator and the victim when the victim defends himself or herself after months of being tormented.

Restorative practices are all about increasing individual accountability and repairing harm. Individuals who participate must agree to be present, to openly talk about what happened, and to take responsibility for their actions. Instead of being suspended for fighting, stealing, talking back, or other disruptive behavior, students are being asked to listen to each other, write letters of apology, work out solutions with the help of parents and educators, and/or engage in community service. All of these practices fall under the umbrella of "restorative practices"—asking offenders to make amends before resorting to punishment. Punishment does not usually work to change behavior.

One counselor told us: "As a young child growing up, I took a boat paddle from a friend's home that I was visiting with my parents. When my parents discovered what I had done, they drove me over to my friend's home, and I had to return the paddle and explain to the parents that I had taken the paddle. I was then expected to apologize before I left. As you can tell, the memory of this incident has stuck with me fifty years later."

Restorative practices examine the harm to all individuals and the community alike, what needs to be done to repair the harm, who is responsible for this repair, and what needs to occur to prevent similar harm in the future.

Questions asked to the offender include: What happened? What were you trying to accomplish? At the time, why did you think this was okay? Was anyone else supporting you in your thinking that this was okay? If so, who and how? What challenges are you facing that contributed to what you did? How do you think the other student felt? Now what are your thoughts about what you did? How would you feel if someone treated you like you treated this other student? What could you do now to help make things right?

In the accountability phase, the offender acknowledges what he or she did wrong, takes action to remedy the harm to those who were harmed, and may deliver a sincere apology and/or have an in-person meeting and commit to avoid engaging in future hurtful acts.

WHEN THE SCHOOL'S APPROACH IS NOT EFFECTIVE

There are some schools that do not know how to effectively handle bullying behavior. Instead of employing best practices, they are still using mediation, zero tolerance, or some other form of prevention that is neither research-based nor appropriate and effective. This makes it difficult for the parent to deal with the school when their child is being bullied. Parents have told us that it is better not to involve the school if they know that the school will, as a matter of practice, put the aggressor and the target together to mediate the problem or even to hold both parties accountable as part of zero tolerance.

It makes sense for the parent to avoid the school because if, for example, the school makes a victim and an aggressor work out the problem themselves, it does nothing but revictimize the target. Bullying is about victimization—it is not a conflict, and it requires an adult to help resolve the issue. Bullying is a very complex issue, and there is no one way to deal with it when it occurs. But at the very least, there needs to be some plan to protect the target from retaliation—support for both students. The target needs to feel safe, and the aggressor needs redirection and supervision.

It is important to have a conversation with the school to find out not only how they handle bullying instances but also what they are doing for bullying prevention. In most school districts, you can get that information right from the school website. You can then compare that information with what the school describes as their policies and procedures for handling bullying behavior. The optimal solution is to partner with the school to develop a plan to support your child. However, if you find a discrepancy in the district intervention policy and the actual way bullying is being handled, or if you feel uncomfortable with the practices, there are a few things that we have seen parents do to protect their child from being targeted by their peers.

Work to give your child some outside social experiences. This can include clubs, scouting and sport teams, youth church groups, or hanging out with cousins or friends outside of school. Give your child an opportunity to develop a special skill. This can be anything from learning to play a musical instrument to participating in martial arts classes. The goal is to give the child an area where he or she can shine and develop positive relationships. It can also help him or her develop self-confidence and internal and external assets.

Watch your child's behavior closely and keep those lines of communication open. Listen carefully for any stories of mean or hurtful incidents. Keep a log of every inappropriate incident that you see or hear.

Finally, approach the school with your information. If the response from the school is that they are planning to bring the bully and aggressor together to investigate or to help the students resolve the issue, you have the right to refuse to have your child participate. You can say that you are concerned about the continuation of the behavior and future retaliation, and that your preference is to have the students interviewed separately. From that point on, you can be directive about your expectations for how the school plans to prevent future problems. This can be through closer supervision in hot spots, a person (or persons) on staff who will check in regularly with your child to see how he or she is doing, or having a plan to connect your child with another student as a school or bus "buddy." If your child has special needs and has an Individual Education Plan (IEP), these measures can be included in the plan.

THE OTHER SIDE OF THE COIN: STUDENTS WHO MISREPORT, MISREPRESENT, AND MISPERCEIVE WHAT IS ACTUALLY HAPPENING

From a school counselor's perspective

In most cases, when children report bullying, it is reported accurately. We don't want to report this concern with extreme pessimism. These are less extreme cases. However, even though we are talking about a handful of cases, it seems that this group has grown exponentially for a period of time.

Recently, and more often than not, there is a significant increase in cases where a student will go home and relay to his or her parents an incident that is skewed by the student's perception. The parents accept the student's story of the incident without any consideration of the fact that some of the information may not be accurate. Furthermore, the parents make judgments, decisions, and a plan of action based on the child's reality without consulting the school on what really happened. The issue is that the student's misperception more likely than not will be taken at face value. Thus, a number of future interactions between the parent and the school are based on these strings of misperceptions. Trust becomes nonexistent, and the parent believes that he or she has all the truth about what actually happened.

Two examples that exemplify this phenomena are the following:

At recess, two students were playing with some dominos, and a third student came over in an attempt to join in. The two students were not interested in his style of play and continued to play without including him. An adult came over to intervene in the encounter. The adult decided to divide the dominos equally between the three students. Minutes later, the adult was asked to intercede again, and it was discovered that the student who felt excluded the first time had confiscated more than his share of dominos. The next day, the father of the student who was left out called and reported that his son was so angry because he had been bullied by two other students and excluded from playing dominos.

Another example also occurred during recess. One female student reported being physically assaulted in a way that seemed humanly impossible. As a reaction, I decided to oversee the playground and actively supervise the area so that I could see with my own eyes any incidents of physical maltreatment. After supervising the playground, the victim in question reported that she had been knocked to the ground and kicked in the stomach three times during the walking club, a walking-talking event. The mother came to school extremely upset, reporting that her daughter was assaulted by a student. During the conference, the daughter admitted that this event had not happened. The mother concluded that she wanted this girl that her daughter was fearful of to be placed in a different class. No discussion ever ensued that her daughter had made up the entire incident.

We have discovered that some students go home and share their misperceptions or misinterpretations of an incident or decide to convey a purposeful misinterpretation of an incident. When this happens, the student may feel internally reinforced that he or she single-handedly can control the parent's defensive reaction with the teachers in a negative way. This manipulative behavior can develop into a pattern of purposefully misleading the parent to accept what the student says at face value.

This wave of parental response of protecting the child comes out of grave concern and societal awareness of the presence of bullying. The pendulum seems to be swinging past the center in the direction of parents believing that everything a child says is actually taking place. In the past, anything a child said was taken with a grain of salt. Now, with heightened awareness, it seems that too much emphasis is focused on what the child reports and that the school is negligent in whatever actions they take. All trust is in the child, and none is in the school. The thought that "my child would never do that" or "my child does not lie" swings too far in the other direction.

Another occurrence is children ganging up and getting retribution against a perpetrator by reporting falsehoods. These children want to get back at the aggressor because of how he or she once treated them. This muddies the investigation process because, for the first time, the students who were trustworthy are misrepresenting on purpose and deliberately reporting falsehoods about the perpetrator. Their goal is retaliation.

The goal of the parent is twofold: to achieve a healthy balance between believing everything a child says at face value, asking appropriate questions to decipher if a child has a pattern of misperceiving or grossly misrepresenting what occurred, and questioning the accuracy of what is reported, and to work collaboratively with the school to hold every student accountable for his or her actions while protecting the positive learning environment in the school.

POINTS FOR PARENTS

There are schools all over the country with dedicated staff and administrators who are working diligently to make schools safe for their students. But there are those who either do not know how to handle bullying problems or who choose not to because of personal beliefs about the definition of bullying.

Furthermore, there are some instances in which the school— after an exhaustive investigation— determines that bullying is not the problem. We know that much of bullying is a perceptual issue. Perception can skew the facts. In essence, there is always the possibility that a student's perception is skewed, that the student is reading messages that are not there, or that the student has been so injured by the bullying experiences that he or she cannot distinguish between bullying and other benign behaviors.

We mention this with great trepidation because, too often, the target of bullying is labeled as a "whiner," and the bullying behavior is dismissed. In some cases—such as in the scenario mentioned above—in which there is an incident of assault or when it is repeated accompanied by other forms of bullying, the impact on the victim can be severe. We have to acknowledge that there are some cases in which the perception of the target is not accurate because of these experiences. Parents need to be open-minded and weigh all the possibilities when evaluating a situation.

This leads to two ways to handle a situation once you have established that the child is part of the issue. The first is to get counseling for the student. Clearly, there are some serious issues that need to be discussed in counseling. Secondly, even though there may be a tendency on the part of the target to misinterpret and exaggerate what happened, all reports of bullying must be taken seriously. Since perception is an important component of bullying behavior, it is important that the message for everyone is that bullying is a serious matter that will be handled accordingly. In addition, there need to be discussions with all students about being respectful and understanding of others who may have a difficult time handling actions the students consider playful or teasing but are hurtful for someone else.

THE IMPORTANCE OF INCLUSIVITY!

When bullying occurs, an individual usually feels fearful. This happens when he or she is singled out and cannot defend himself or herself against the perpetrator(s). A word that counters the fear of bullying is "inclusive." Treating individuals with acceptance and respect demonstrates "inclusivity." In order for schools to build a positive and nurturing learning environment, it is necessary for students to learn to be inclusive.

To reinforce inclusive behavior, it would be extremely helpful if parents demonstrated inclusivity in their day-to-day lives and with family members by discussing what it looks like and how family members should model it. Using teachable moments are great ways to strengthen how siblings model inclusive behaviors.

We have all overheard those conversations in a car, at a sporting event, or during a playdate that are unkind or exclusionary. These exclusionary remarks and behaviors may sound like "I don't like you," "You're not my friend," "You can't sit at our table," "You're not invited to my birthday party," "This seat is saved," or "You can't play with us." These remarks are hurtful and should be declared as inappropriate and off-limits when you are teaching your children about being inclusive.

At the first opportunity, have a conversation with your child and talk about your concerns. It is not that your child is making a choice about whom he or she is with—it is about how it is done. For example, it is okay to choose whom you want to attend a birthday party, but it is not okay to taunt others about the fact that they have not been invited. This exclusionary behavior may not itself be bullying; remember, bullying is RIP (repeated, intentional, and power-based). However, it is hurtful and does not foster respect or acceptance.

Empathy is an important component of being inclusive. A student who is truly empathic knows what it is like to stand in someone's shoes. For example, this individual might be the first to observe a classmate on the playground who feels alone, because he or she knows how it feels to be alone. When we observe a student being inclusive, it is important to praise the child for doing the right thing. If others in the group are unaware that a student(s) is being excluded, brainstorm some ways that the child who was left out could be given the opportunity to participate.

Parents can also demonstrate inclusivity in dozens of ways every day. It does not take much to do so. For example, opening a door for an individual or being the first to say hello is an inclusive act. Being the first to introduce a friend to a stranger, put your hand out to shake someone else's hand, or call the person by his or her name is not only a kind and respectful act but is also a demonstration of being inclusive. These simple courtesies can go a long way to teach a child about kindness, respect, and inclusion.

In summary, children are watching their parents' and friends' every move. They notice when parents and friends are abrupt, insincere, disrespectful, and partial to others. Thus, we all have a responsibility to treat each other with an inclusive generosity, even though some may demonstrate exclusive behavior in return. We cannot control how others behave, but we can control how we treat others and what we say to family members and friends who do not live up to their agreement and our expectations about being inclusive.

It is most important to remember that bullying is a social climate issue. The solution is embedded in how all of us—not just children—treat each other. Our focus should be on understanding and cultivating quality relationships. We want our children to know what a real friend is and how to differentiate that from an acquaintance. We want them to understand how to cultivate those relationships with understanding and respect. If within the school and community children are given the opportunity to develop social competencies and leadership skills, the need for bullying intervention will be eliminated. In the end, all children will not only feel safe and connected to school but will also perform better academically.

References

Chapter 2. Relational Aggression/Bullying

Crick, N. R., and Grotpeter, J. K. (1995). "Relational Aggression, Gender, and Social-Psychological Adjustment." *Child Development* 66(3), 710–722.

Espelage, D. L. (2002). "Bullying in Early Adolescence: The Role of the Peer Group." *ERIC Digest*.

Guerra, N. G., Williams, K. R., and Sadek, S. (2011). "Understanding Bullying and Victimization During Childhood and Adolescence: A Mixed Methods Study." *Child Development* 82(1), 295–310.

Popp, A. M., and Peguero, A. A. (2012). "Social Bonds and the Role of School-Based Victimization." *Journal of Interpersonal Violence* 27(17), 3366–3388 (originally published online May 18, 2012; DOI: 10.1177/0886260512445386).

Shemesh, E., Annunziato, R. A., Ambrose, M. A., Ravid, N. L., Mullarkey, C., Rubes, M., Chuang, K., Sicherer, M., and Sicherer, S. H. (2013). "The Effect of Parents' Knowledge About the Child Being Bullied on the Parents' and the Child's QoL." *Pediatrics* 131; e10 (originally published online December 24, 2012; DOI: 10.1542/peds.2012-1180).

Waasdorp, T. E., Pas, E. T., O'Brennan, L. M., and Bradshaw, C. P. (2011). "A Multilevel Perspective on the Climate of Bullying: Discrepancies Among Students, School Staff, and Parents." *Journal of School Violence* 10(2), 115–132.

Chapter 3. Cyberbullying

Byrne, S., Katz, S. J., Lee, T., Linz, D., and McIlrath, M. (2014). "Peers, Predators, and Porn: Predicting Parental Underestimation of Children's Risky Online Experiences." *Journal of Computer-Mediated Communication* 19(2), 215–231.

Carpenter, M. R., Roy, S. A. W., and Smith, G. M. (2012). *Setting the Tone: A Connected School Approach to Creating Bully-Free Classrooms*. New View Publications, Chapel Hill, NC, p. 33.

D'Antona, R., Kevorkian, M., and Russom, A. (2010). "Sexting, Texting, Cyberbullying and Keeping Youth Safe Online." *Journal of Social Sciences* 6(4), 521.

Juvonen, J., and Gross, E. F. (2008). "Extending the School Grounds?—Bullying Experiences in Cyberspace." *Journal of School Health* 78(9), 496–505.

Kwan, G. C. E., and Skoric, M. M. (2013). "Facebook Bullying: An Extension of Battles in School." *Computers in Human Behavior* 29(1), 16–25.

Livingstone, S., Haddon, L., Görzig, A., and Ólafsson, K. (2011). "Risks and Safety on the Internet: The Perspective of European Children: Full Findings and Policy Implications from the EU Kids Online Survey of 9-16 Year Olds and Their Parents in 25 Countries." *EU Kids Online*, Deliverable D4. EU Kids Online Network, London, UK.

Nock, M. K. (2010). Self-injury. *Annual Review of Clinical Psychology,* 6, 339–363.

Norton Online Family Report (2010). "Global Insights into Family Life Online." Retrieved from http://us.norton.com/content/en/us/home_homeoffice/media/pdf/nofr/Norton_Family-Report-USA_June9.pdf

Tokunaga, R. S. (2010). "Following You Home from School: A Critical Review and Synthesis of Research on Cyberbullying Victimization." *Computers in Human Behavior* 26(3), 277–287.

Zimmer-Gembeck, M. J., Pronk, R. E., Goodwin, B., Mastro, S., and Crick, N. R. (2013). "Connected and Isolated Victims of Relational Aggression: Associations with Peer Group Status and Differences Between Girls and Boys." *Sex Roles* 68(5-6), 363–377.

Chapter 4. Physical Bullying

Baldry, A. C. (2003). "Bullying in Schools and Exposure to Domestic Violence." *Child Abuse & Neglect* 27(7), 713–732.

Bender, D., and Lösel, F. (2011). "Bullying at School as a Predictor of Delinquency, Violence and Other Anti-Social Behaviour in Adulthood." *Criminal Behaviour and Mental Health* 21(2), 99–106.

Brown, J. R., Aalsma, M. C., and Ott, M. A. (2013). "The Experiences of Parents Who Report Youth Bullying Victimization to School Officials." *Journal of Interpersonal Violence* 28(3), 494–518.

Crapanzano, A. M., Frick, P. J., and Terranova, A. M. (2010). "Patterns of Physical and Relational Aggression in a School-Based Sample of Boys and Girls." *Journal of Abnormal Child Psychology* 38(4), 433–445.

288

Dishion, T. J., and Tipsord, J. M. (2011). "Peer Contagion in Child and Adolescent Social and Emotional Development." *Annual Review of Psychology* 62, 189.

Giesbrecht, G. F., Leadbeater, B. J., and Macdonald, S. W. S. (2011). "Child and Context Characteristics in Trajectories of Physical and Relational Victimization Among Early Elementary School Children." *Development and Psychopathology* 23(1), 239–252. DOI: http://dx.doi.org/10.1017/S0954579410000763.

Gladden, R. M., Vivolo-Kantor, A. M., Hamburger, M., and Lumpkin, C. (2014). "Bullying Surveillance Among Youths: Uniform Definitions for Public Health and Recommended Data Elements, Version 1.0." Centers for Disease Control and Prevention, Atlanta, Georgia, and the United States Department of Education, Washington, D.C.

Lodge, J., and Feldman, S. S. (2007). "Avoidant Coping as a Mediator Between Appearance-Related Victimization and Self-Esteem in Young Australian Adolescents." *British Journal of Developmental Psychology* 25(4), 633–642.

Marks, P. E., Cillessen, A. H., and Crick, N. R. (2012). "Popularity Contagion Among Adolescents." *Social Development* 21(3), 501–521.

Olweus, D. (1994). "Bullying at School: Basic Facts and Effects of a School-Based Intervention Program." *Journal of Child Psychology and Psychiatry* 35(7), 1171–1190.

Padilla-Walker, L. M., Carlo, G., Christensen, K. J., and Yorgason, J. B. (2012). "Bidirectional Relations Between Authoritative Parenting and Adolescents' Prosocial Behaviors." *Journal of Research on Adolescence* 22(3), 400–408.

Salmivalli, C., Voeten, M., and Poskiparta, E. (2011). "Bystanders Matter: Associations Between Reinforcing, Defending, and the Frequency of Bullying Behavior in Classrooms." *Journal of Clinical Child & Adolescent Psychology* 40(5), 668–676.

Sawyer, J. L., Mishna, F., Pepler, D., and Wiener, J. (2011). "The Missing Voice: Parents' Perspectives of Bullying." *Children and Youth Services Review* 33(10), 1795–1803.

Storch, E. A., Masia-Warner, C., Crisp, H., and Stein, R. G. (2005). "Peer victimization and Social anxiety in adolescence: a prospective study." *Aggressive Behavior* 31, 437–452.

United Nations (1998). "UN Convention on the Rights of the Child." Retrieved November 22, 2008, from *http://www.unicef.org/crc/*.

Chapter 5. Kids Who Appear Different

Eliot, M., Cornell, D., Gregory, A., and Fan, X. (2010). "Supportive School Climate and Student Willingness to Seek Help for Bullying and Threats of Violence." *Journal of School Psychology* 48(6), 533–553.

Limber, S. P., Olweus, D., and Wang, W. (2012). "What We Are Learning About Bullying: Trends in Bullying Over 5 Years." Paper presented at the meeting of the International Bullying Prevention Association, Kansas City, MO.

Peterson, R. L., and Schoonover, B. (2008). "Fact Sheet #3: Zero Tolerance Policies in Schools." Retrieved on September 25, 2008.

Reynolds, C. R., Skiba, R. J., Graham, S., Sheras, P., Conoley, J. C., and Garcia-Vazquez, E. (2008). "Are Zero Tolerance Policies Effective in the Schools?: An Evidentiary Review and Recommendations." *The American Psychologist* 63(9), 852–862.

Rosenberg, M. S. (2012). "Violence Prevention and Students with Disabilities: Thinking Functionally and Providing Evidence Based Supports and Accommodations." *Behavioral Disorders* 37(3), 206-209.

Samson, A. C., Huber, O., and Ruch, W. (2011). "Teasing, Ridiculing, and the Relation to the Fear of Being Laughed At in Individuals with Asperger's Syndrome." *Journal of Autism and Developmental Disorders* 41(4), 475–483.

Sofronoff, K., Dark, E., and Stone, V. (2011). "Social Vulnerability and Bullying in Children with Asperger Syndrome." *Autism* 15(3), 355–372.

Twemlow, S. D., and Sacco, F. C. (2013). "Bullying Is Everywhere: Ten Universal Truths About Bullying as a Social Process in Schools & Communities." *Psychoanalytic Inquiry: A Topical Journal for Mental Health Professionals* 33(2), 73–89, DOI: 10.1080/07351690.2013.759484.

U.S. Department of Education (2000). "Prohibited Disability Harassment: Reminder of Responsibilities Under Section 504 of the Rehabilitation Act of 1973 and Title II of the Americans with Disabilities Act." Retrieved August 10, 2005, from *www.ed.gov/about/offices/list/ocr/docs/disabharassltr.html.*.

Chapter 6. Kids Who Have Weight Issues

Baker, J. L., Olsen, L. W., and Sørensen, T. I. (2007). "Childhood Body-Mass Index and the Risk of Coronary Heart Disease in Adulthood." *New England Journal of Medicine* 357(23), 2329–2337.

Farhat, T., Iannotti, R. J., and Simons-Morton, B. G. (2010). "Overweight, Obesity, Youth, and Health-Risk Behaviors." *American Journal of Preventive Medicine* 38(3), 258–267.

Gray, W. N., Janicke, D. M., Ingerski, L. M., and Silverstein, J. H. (2008). "The Impact of Peer Victimization, Parent Distress and Child Depression on Barrier Formation and Physical Activity in Overweight Youth." *Journal of Developmental & Behavioral Pediatrics* 29(1), 26–33.

Kukaswadia, A., Craig, W., Janssen, I., and Pickett, W. (2011). "Obesity as a Determinant of Two Forms of Bullying in Ontario Youth: A Short Report." *Obesity Facts* 4(6), 469–472.

Tenenbaum, L. S., Varjas, K., Meyers, J., and Parris, L. (2011). "Coping Strategies and Perceived Effectiveness in Fourth Through Eighth Grade Victims of Bullying." *School Psychology International* 32(3), 263–287.

Chapter 7. Bullying, Harassment, and Protected Groups

Blumenthal, H., Leen-Feldner, E. W., Badour, C. L., and Babson, K. A. (2011). "Anxiety, Psychopathology and Alcohol Use Among Adolescents: A Critical Review of the Empirical Literature and Recommendations for Future Research." *Journal of Experimental Psychopathology* 2(3), 318.

Cartwright-Hatton, S., McNicol, K., and Doubleday, E. (2006). "Anxiety in a Neglected Population: Prevalence of Anxiety Disorders in Pre-Adolescent Children." *Clinical Psychology Review* 26(7), 817–833.

Fisher, H. L., Moffitt, T. E., Houts, R. M., Belsky, D. W., Arseneault, L., and Caspi, A. (2012). "Bullying Victimisation and Risk of Self Harm in Early Adolescence: Longitudinal Cohort Study." *BMJ: British Medical Journal,* 344.

Kennedy, M. M. (2010). "Attribution Error and the Quest for Teacher Quality." *Educational Researcher* 39(8), 591–598.

Leiner, M., Dwivedi, A. K., Villanos, M. T., Singh, N., Blunk, D., and Peinado, J. (2014). "Psychosocial Profile of Bullies, Victims, and Bully-Victims: A Cross-Sectional Study." *Frontiers in Pediatrics* 2.

Milburn, W., and Palladino, J. (2012). "Preservice Teachers' Knowledge, Skills, and Dispositions of LGBTQ Bullying Intervention." Online submission.

Poteat, V. P., and DiGiovanni, C. D. (2010). "When Biased Language Use Is Associated with Bullying and Dominance Behavior: The Moderating Effect of Prejudice." *Journal of Youth and Adolescence* 39(10), 1123–1133.

Poteat, V. P., DiGiovanni, C. D., and Scheer, J. R. (2013). "Predicting Homophobic Behavior Among Heterosexual Youth: Domain General and Sexual Orientation-Specific Factors at the Individual and Contextual Level." *Journal of Youth and Adolescence* 42(3), 351–362.

Poteat, V. P., and Rivers, I. (2010). "The Use of Homophobic Language Across Bullying Roles During Adolescence." *Journal of Applied Developmental Psychology* 31(2), 166–172.

Thornberg, R., and Jungert, T. (2013). "School Bullying and the Mechanisms of Moral Disengagement." *Aggressive Behavior*.

Chapter 8. Different Perspectives

Adams, C. D., and Kelley, M. L. (1992). "Managing Sibling Aggression: Overcorrection as an Alternative to Time-out." *Behavior Therapy* 23, 707–717.

Gini, G., Pozzoli, T., Borghi, F., and Franzoni, L. (2008). "The Role of Bystanders in Students' Perception of Bullying and Sense of Safety." *Journal of School Psychology* 46(6), 617–638.

Hoover, J. H., Oliver, R., and Hazler, R. J. (1992). "Bullying: Perceptions of Adolescent Victims in Midwestern USA." *School Psychology International* 13, 5–16.

Perren, S., Gutzwiller-Helfenfinger, E., Malti, T., and Hymel, S. (2012). "Moral Reasoning and Emotion Attributions of Adolescent Bullies, Victims, and Bully-Victims." *British Journal of Developmental Psychology* 30(4), 511–530.

Polanin, J. R., Espelage, D. L., and Pigott, T. D. (2012). "A Meta-Analysis of School-Based Bullying Prevention Programs' Effects on Bystander Intervention Behavior." *School Psychology Review* 41(1).

Pozzoli, T., and Gini, G. (2013). "Why Do Bystanders of Bullying Help or Not? A Multidimensional Model." *The Journal of Early Adolescence* 33(3), 315–340.

Remillard, A. M., and Lamb, S. (2005). "Adolescent Girls' Coping with Relational Aggression." *Sex Roles* 53(3-4), 221–229. DOI:http://dx.doi.org/10.1007/s11199-005-5680-8.

Rivers, I. (2001). "Retrospective Reports of School Bullying: Stability of Recall and Its Implications for Research." *British Journal of Developmental Psychology* 19(1), 129–141.

Rothon, C., Head, J., Klineberg, E., and Stansfeld, S. (2011). "Can Social Support Protect Bullied Adolescents from Adverse Outcomes? A Prospective Study on the Effects of Bullying on the Educational Achievement and Mental Health of Adolescents at Secondary Schools in East London." *Journal of Adolescence* 34(3), 579–588.

Salmivalli, C. (2001). "Group View on Victimization: Empirical Findings and Their Implications." In J. Juvonen, & S. Graham (Eds.) *Peer Harassment in School: The Plight of the Vulnerable and Victimized* (pp. 398–419). New York, NY: Guilford Press.

Skinner, J. A., and Kowalski, R. M. (2013). "Profiles of Sibling Bullying." *Journal of Interpersonal Violence* 28(8), 1726–1736.

Ttofi, M. M., Farrington, D. P., and Lösel, F. (2012). "School Bullying as a Predictor of Violence Later in Life: A Systematic Review and Meta-Analysis of Prospective Longitudinal Studies." *Aggression and Violent Behavior* 17(5), 405–418.

Vanderbilt, D., and Augustyn, M. (2010). "The Effects of Bullying." *Paediatrics and Child Health* 20(7), 315–320.

Chapter 9. Hazing, Bullying, and Intimidation

Ahmed, E., and Braithwaite, V. (2012). "Learning to Manage Shame in School Bullying: Lessons for Restorative Justice Interventions." *Critical Criminology* 20(1), 79–97.

Carpenter, M. R., Roy, S. A. W., and Smith, G. M. (2012). *Setting the Tone: A Connected School Approach to Creating Bully-Free Classrooms*. New View Publications, Chapel Hill, NC, p. 33.

Girlshealth.gov. "Warning Signs of Hazing." *http://www.girlshealth.gov/bullying/hazing/*. Last visited 3/5/14.

Harris, N. (2003). "Evaluating the Practice of Restorative Justice: The Case of Family Group Conferencing." In L. Walgrave (Ed.), *Repositioning restorative justice: Restorative Justice, Criminal Justice and Social Context*. Cullompton: Willan Publishing.

Hoover, N. C., and Pollard, N. J. (2000). "Initiation Rites in American High Schools: A National Survey." Final Report.

Kevorkian, M., and D'Antona, R. (2010). *Tackling Bullying in Athletics: Best Practices for Modeling Appropriate Behavior*. R&L Education.

Kowalski, C., and Waldron, J. (2010). "Looking the Other Way: Athletes' Perceptions of Coaches' Responses to Hazing." *International Journal of Sports Science and Coaching* 5(1), 87–100.

Stirling, A. E. (2013). "Understanding the Use of Emotionally Abusive Coaching Practices." *International Journal of Sports Science and Coaching* 8(4), 625–640.

Stirling, A. E., Bridges, E. J., Cruz, E. L., and Mountjoy, M. L. (2011). "Canadian Academy of Sport and Exercise Medicine Position Paper: Abuse, Harassment, and Bullying in Sport." *Clinical Journal of Sport Medicine* 21(5), 385–391.

Stopbullying.gov, "Definition of Bullying." *http://www.stopbullying.gov/what-is-bullying/definition/index.html*. Last visited 3/5/14.

Stophazing.org, "Definition of Hazing." *http://www.stophazing.org/high_school_hazing/index.htm*. Last visited 3/5/14.